# Teaching Early Modern English Literature from the Archives

**Modern Language Association of America
Options for Teaching**

For a complete listing of titles,
see the last pages of this book.

# Teaching Early Modern English Literature from the Archives

Edited by
**Heidi Brayman Hackel**
**and Ian Frederick Moulton**

The Modern Language Association of America
New York                                                2015

MLA and the MODERN LANGUAGE ASSOCIATION are trademarks owned by the Modern Language Association of America. For information about obtaining permission to reprint material from MLA book publications, send your request by mail (see address below) or e-mail (permissions@mla.org).

Library of Congress Cataloging-in-Publication Data

Teaching early modern English literature from the archives /
edited by Heidi Brayman Hackel, Ian Frederick Moulton.
    pages cm. — (Options for teaching, ISSN 1079-2562 ; 36)
  Includes bibliographical references and index.
  ISBN 978-1-60329-155-2 (cloth : alk. paper) —
  ISBN 978-1-60329-156-9 (pbk. : alk. paper) —
  ISBN 978-1-60329-157-6 (EPUB) —
  ISBN 978-1-60329-158-3 (Kindle)
  1. English Literature — Early modern, 1500–1700 — Study and teaching (Higher) 2. Archives — Study and teaching.   I. Brayman Hackel, Heidi, editor.
  II. Moulton, Ian Frederick, 1964– editor.
  PR421.T4   2014
  820.9'003 — dc23     2014020777

Options for Teaching 36
ISSN 1079-2562

Cover illustration of the paperback and electronic editions: Lu Xinjian, *Invisible Poem / Shakespeare Sonnet CXXVIII*, 2012, acrylic on canvas.

Published by The Modern Language Association of America
26 Broadway, New York, NY 10004-1789
www.mla.org

*To the memory of Douglas A. Brooks*
*(1956–2009)*

# Contents

# Acknowledgments

The editors share several teachers—Margaret W. Ferguson, Jean E. Howard, David Scott Kastan, Anne Lake Prescott—and would like to thank them and the many other teachers, curators, and fellow scholars who introduced us to the archives in a time before *EEBO* and *ESTC*. We would also like to thank Lauren Shohet, who helped us hatch the plan for this book, and all the contributors for their commitment to this volume. At the MLA, Joseph Gibaldi, Margit Longbrake, and Angela Gibson oversaw the development and production of the volume; we are grateful to the Publications Committee, the MLA book publications staff, and our many anonymous consultant readers for guidance and support. To our families—Steve, Anna, and Gabriel; Wendy and Sophia—our love. We dedicate this book to our friend and colleague Douglas Brooks, who loved teaching, archives, collaboration, and friendship.

**Heidi Brayman Hackel and Ian Frederick Moulton**

# Introduction

*Teaching Early Modern English Literature from the Archives* focuses on the use of archival and primary source materials—especially those accessible electronically—in early modern English literature courses. It outlines practical methods for incorporating digital and traditional archival resources into the undergraduate and graduate curriculum, addresses theoretical issues that arise from the use of online archives, and identifies a range of archives, both physical and virtual, useful in the teaching of early modern literature.

In the past, few students, especially those at the undergraduate level, had access to printed books or manuscripts from the early modern period. Undergraduate teaching relies almost entirely on modern, edited, and annotated versions of early modern texts. With their modernized spelling and typography, as well as their copious notes explicating archaic words and unfamiliar cultural references, such texts fulfill a vital function. Nonetheless, there are clear advantages to introducing undergraduates to materials from the early modern period. In the past, it was difficult for most undergraduates to access early modern books, either because they lived and studied too far from the collections that housed the books or because many such collections understandably restricted reading privileges

1

to advanced graduate students and professional scholars. But digitization and the Internet are in the process of fundamentally changing what access to early modern texts means. Various online databases now provide access to the original and early editions of works by Shakespeare, Spenser, Milton, Donne, and every other major English writer of the period. Some of these are transcriptions; some are digital copies of microfilm; some are color photographs of the pages from the volumes. More important, the Internet makes thousands of noncanonical texts available for classroom use: ballads, sermons, medical texts, primers, chronicle histories, self-help manuals, political documents, romances, and more. The availability of these texts for online use in the classroom is revolutionizing the teaching of early modern literature.

This volume attempts to provide a snapshot of this revolution by bringing together essays by scholars, teachers, Web site designers, and research librarians on the many ways that early modern source materials can now be productively integrated into undergraduate literature classrooms and graduate seminars. We hope that the volume will be useful to teachers who now have access to this wealth of material but little experience in how to integrate these new resources into their teaching practice and their training of graduate students.

But this volume cannot be simply about online resources, for traditional and electronic archives are very much in conversation with each other. The ubiquity of online texts is allowing a generation of students and scholars to develop an unprecedented familiarity with archival materials. While digital facsimiles and transcriptions are not the same as actual books and manuscripts, the experience of reading and exploring early modern books and manuscripts online cannot help encouraging more scholars and advanced students—once equipped with a set of skills and alert to the possibilities of archival research—to venture into traditional archives. Further, electronic resources are changing scholars' relation to physical documents and altering the research and reading methods they use at major archives. A mere fifteen years ago, a scholar might have principally devoted time in a distant archive to transcribing a few manuscripts and passages from printed books. That same scholar today, after traveling to the Folger, the Huntington, or the London Metropolitan archives, might well examine these material objects and then capture the same passages with a digital camera for later scholarly reference and, we would hope, possible future use in the classroom, thus freeing up time for further exploration in the archives.

Online archives make available digitized versions of physical documents, but many of the skills necessary to read and analyze those documents have traditionally been developed in actual archives. More critically still, some research relies entirely on the material objects themselves, and any full, responsible use of online archives depends on a familiarity, preferably a deep one, with the material qualities of early modern books and manuscripts. As several of our contributors demonstrate (Tribble; Herman; Rubright), digital images omit or distort essential aspects of their originals: weight and heft, relative scale, color. Even something as seemingly ephemeral and evocative as smell might have a story to tell, albeit one easily forgotten with digitization. In an essay on dust and the dematerialization of archives, William Sherman relays a historian's anecdote from a dusty archive:

> I longed for a digital system that would hold the information from the letters and leave paper and dust behind. One afternoon, another historian came to work on a similar box. He read barely a word. Instead, he picked out bundles of letters and, in a move that sent my sinuses into shock, ran each letter beneath his nose and took a deep breath, at times almost inhaling the letter itself but always getting a good dose of dust. Sometimes, after a particularly profound sniff, he would open the letter, glance at it briefly, make a note and move on. Choking behind my mask, I asked him what he was doing. He was, he told me, a medical historian. . . . He was documenting outbreaks of cholera. When that disease occurred in a town in the eighteenth century, all letters from that town were disinfected with vinegar to prevent the disease from spreading. By sniffing for the faint traces of vinegar that survived 250 years and noting the date and source of the letters, he was able to chart the progress of cholera outbreaks. (Brown and Duguid 173–74, qtd. in Sherman, "Digging" 257)

Even as digitization revolutionizes scholarly access and brings some aspects of early modern texts into sharper view (through zoom features, for example), digitization also removes critical evidence—sometimes evidence we don't even know to look for, though it may be right under our noses.

The most comprehensive of the online archives in our field, *Early English Books Online* (*EEBO*), poses a further problem: *EEBO* typically provides digital images of a single copy for each edition in its database, based on decades-old microfilm images that routinely omitted bindings and flyleaves and often obscured readers' marginalia. Without explicit reminders from instructors and, ideally, counterexamples of material books, students introduced to these virtual books miss a valuable lesson about copy-specific differences and readers' use (Sherman, *Used Books* 216n1). To begin to redress these and other omissions, therefore, we must do what we can to put early modern books into our students' hands. This volume, accordingly, includes substantial discussions of ways to integrate traditional archival materials into both undergraduate instruction and graduate training.

Though teachers of other periods of English literature and of other national literatures may find the theoretical approaches and pedagogical strategies in our volume useful, this collection deals primarily with the period from 1473 to 1700. This time frame corresponds to the periodization of the standard finding aids for early modern manuscripts and printed books as well as to the constraints of the major electronic resources. While the emphasis of the volume is on English literature and culture, individual contributors describe comparative approaches involving Latin, French, Spanish, German, and early American texts and resources. Other essays move beyond literature to incorporate visual materials, ballads, domestic treatises, atlases, music, and historical documents into the teaching of literature.

One of the major changes prompted by recent technological developments is the shifting definition of the term *archive*. Traditionally, archives are distinct from libraries in that they hold individual, unpublished, and unique documents. They are also usually affiliated with either a governing body or a corporate entity. The word *archive* is an early modern coinage, around 1645, denoting "a place in which public records or other important historic documents are kept." The term comes to English from French and Italian, ultimately deriving from the Greek *arche* (αρχη), a word meaning "government" or "rule" but also connoting origins and beginnings.[1]

In current general usage, however, *archive* has come to have the much vaguer meaning of "a collection of useful or valuable documents." This change has come in part from the use of the verb *archive* in computing to mean "to save or keep; i.e. to make a copy of." Or, as the *Oxford English Dictionary* puts it, "in *Computing*, to transfer to a store containing infrequently used files, or to a lower level in the hierarchy of memories, esp. from disc to tape." This looser usage is evident in the names of many collections of online documents, including *The Internet Archive*, a not-for-profit digital library of Internet sites and other cultural artifacts in digital form; NASA's daily archive of photographs from space; and the *English Broadside Ballad Archive*. Whether such sites are affiliated with government or corporate entities, it is hard to argue that the materials they contain are in any way unique or individual. The collections exist, in fact, to make, circulate, and preserve copies of the texts and images they contain. Though it seems new, this more fluid sense of *archive* finds resonance in the notion recovered by Jennifer Summit of an early modern library as both a place and a function (234–37).

For our purposes, we define "teaching from the archives" as any pedagogical use, in or out of the classroom, centered on early modern printed texts and manuscripts or their facsimiles, as opposed to modern, edited texts. "Teaching from the archives" carries with it an acknowledgment of the historical conditions of production, reception, circulation, and preservation of texts. Further, to teach from the archives is to introduce into the classroom the awareness that literary texts are artifacts and that they survive by design and by chance as part of larger collections of texts and materials. In her essay in this volume, Laura McGrane wants her students to grasp that an archive is "always an action, an argument, a statement, and an endeavor shaped both by the archivist and by the reader and that the very shape, media form, and order of an archive become part of its content." In that spirit, this volume looks not only back to artifacts and survivors but also forward to emerging archives and new ways of collecting, organizing, and creating knowledge. Our contributors argue for the expansion of the category of archive to include virtual theatrical spaces (Rowe), word-cloud generators (Howard, Keeran, and Bowers), and word frequency software (Ehrlich), and they describe the digital archives their students have helped envision and build (Jenstad; McGrane).

Like all volumes in the MLA series Options for Teaching, this one addresses professional, scholarly, and pedagogical issues, balancing traditional and innovative approaches and drawing on the experiences of faculty members at a range of institutions. The main professional issue involved in teaching archival materials is that of access. Access to traditional archives is limited by geographic location and by the fact that undergraduates and even beginning graduate students are not eligible for reading privileges at many major research centers. Access to online archives is also limited, by the cost of subscribing to a database or by the unavailability of classroom technology. Contributors consider the economics of subscription to be a departmental concern (e.g., McGrane) and describe their own solutions to teaching far away from the archives at institutions without subscriptions to the most expensive databases (e.g., Laroche; Eckhardt). But the asymmetries of access pose ethical questions for the profession at large: Will increased access to online archives at wealthy institutions contribute to a digital divide? Do scholars privileged with access have a responsibility to push for universal access? How might we work collectively?[2]

Getting access to archival materials is, of course, only the beginning. One must also know how to navigate the vast amounts of material available both in traditional archives and online. Our volume describes ways to find both manuscript and print resources online, and individual essays deal with theoretical issues raised by online archives: Can electronic archives stand in for physical archives? How do online reproductions of texts differ from their material originals? What is included in online databases and what is not? How do these inclusions and omissions shape research questions and answers?

## Introducing Archives

In the volume's first section, "Introducing Archives," seven essays address the larger issues involved in incorporating primary source material into undergraduate classrooms. Sarah Werner draws on her experience running the Folger Shakespeare Library's undergraduate program to discuss what is involved in bringing undergraduates into archives. Bringing students into contact with early modern books leads them to consider how the material forms of texts provide crucial information about their production and reception. In the process, students not only gain a better understanding of how and what the texts mean, they also learn research and interpretive skills that they can bring to bear on other classes and research projects. Heather Wolfe's "Manuscripts and Paleography for Undergraduates" outlines ways to introduce students to the joys and challenges of deciphering seventeenth-century handwriting—a process that has been transformed by the existence of several excellent online tutorials in which students can practice reading texts in a variety of early modern hands.

Because most teachers and students obviously do not have the resources of the Folger Shakespeare Library at their disposal, the other essays in this section deal with the classroom use of digital copies and facsimiles of early modern books. The first pair addresses the problems that arise when early modern books and manuscripts are digitized. They survey several major online collections of archival, rare, and primary source materials for early modern studies that are now widely available on the Internet. In "Images, Texts, and Records: Electronic Teaching in a Confusing

Landscape," Shawn Martin discusses the benefits and limitations of the major textual databases in early modern studies. Evelyn Tribble's essay, "The Work of the Book in an Age of Digital Reproduction," argues that the proliferation of digital texts and images makes it more important than ever that students and scholars have experience with material books.

In "The Death of the Editor and Printer: Teaching Early Modern Publishing Practices to Internet-Raised Undergraduates," Arnold Sanders considers how the reading habits of online readers, particularly of those belonging to a generation coming of age in the electronic era, differ from the strategies of readers of printed books. In "The Translingual Archive," Patrick M. Erben critiques the monolingual bias of online databases. Although early modern literary culture was characterized by its multilingual nature, most online resources are organized by language. Erben demonstrates that students who are trying to understand the formation of English literature and culture in the early modern period should consider the influences of German, Italian, Dutch, French, Spanish, Portuguese, and other European literatures.

Finally, Katherine Rowe expands the notion of an archive by demonstrating that new media make possible the collecting and centralizing of the experience of built space. Her "Virtual Theater History: Interpreting the Space of Play in a Shakespeare Class" explores how that most canonical of courses, the undergraduate Shakespeare lecture, may be enriched by leading students into *Second Life* virtual theatrical spaces.

## Building Archives

The next section, "Building Archives," features essays by creators of online resources for early modern literary studies who describe the sites they have developed and suggest applications for classroom teaching. In "Teaching the Metadata: Playbook History in the Undergraduate Classroom," Zachary Lesser writes about the *Database of Early English Playbooks* (*DEEP*), an analytic database of playbooks published before 1660 that allows scholars and students to search books by genre, printer, playing company, theater, or author. In "Engendering the Early Modern Archive," Sheila Cavanagh, Gitanjali Shahani, and Irene Middleton discuss the *Emory Women Writers Resource Project*, a database of three hundred female-authored or female-centered texts that expands the body of electronic materials related to women's writing and has given many Emory University students direct experience in the process of creating a digital archive. In "The *English*

*Broadside Ballad Archive*: From Theory to Practice," Patricia Fumerton, Simone Chess, Tassie Gniady, and Kris McAbee discuss the theoretical, technical, presentational, and pedagogical issues involved in the construction and implementation of the *English Broadside Ballad Archive*, a database containing texts and facsimiles of sixteenth- and seventeenth-century English ballads. Janelle Jenstad's "Restoring Place to the Digital Archive: *The Map of Early Modern London*" chronicles her efforts to resist digitization's detachment of archival materials from the archives themselves. Like the reconstructions of the Globe Theater described in Rowe's essay, Jenstad's *Map of Early Modern London* makes spatial experience available virtually. All four essays not only outline the design and function of these resources but also suggest classroom uses for these materials, all of which are freely accessible online.

## Teaching Texts

"Teaching Texts" offers nuts-and-bolts approaches to teaching specific early modern texts. This section covers canonical and noncanonical texts and offers essays that will both support the most commonly taught courses — Shakespeare, the survey of British literature — and inspire teachers of more specialized, narrowly focused courses. The section, moving from undergraduate to graduate teaching, presents strategies for using subscription databases and for improvising at institutions that do not provide them. Jeremy Ehrlich's "'Magic in the Web'" provides a practical overview of online resources for undergraduate Shakespeare courses, ranging from online versions of existing tools that lower the barrier for students to engage with primary sources to experimental sites like *TextArc* (or those presented in Rowe's essay) whose full pedagogical potential is still being discovered. Rebecca Laroche's "Early Modern Women in the Archives" identifies the online resources that have helped define the field of early modern women writers and maps out a lesson plan for introducing students to Isabella Whitney and, through her example, to the persona of the female poet. Laroche's essay also shows how an archive-savvy scholar can translate the excitement of traditional archival discoveries to the undergraduate classroom, even one not equipped with the latest and most expensive electronic resources.

The next two essays propose solutions for instructors who are teaching far away from the archives. In "Opening Up *The Roaring Girl* and the Woman Question with *EEBO*," Peter C. Herman shifts attention to the teaching of a single play, contextualizing it in the world of early modern publishing and placing his pedagogy in larger critical and theoretical sea changes in the field. While acknowledging the drawbacks of teaching with *EEBO*, he describes its effectiveness for introducing undergraduates to nonliterary texts, contemporary polemics, and printing history. In "Teaching Verse Miscellanies," Joshua Eckhardt describes the survey of early modern English poetry that emerged from his scholarly engagement with manuscript verse collections and that relied on his resourcefulness, at an institution without a subscription to *EEBO*, in introducing his undergraduates and terminal master's students to verse miscellanies as a superior alternative to modern anthologies. As Eckhardt acknowledges, the miscellanies for his courses have been "doubly remediated," and yet in its attention to anonymous and understudied texts and to the production and dissemination of texts, and even its requirement that students share a single book at the university library, his seminars in many ways provide an archival experience for his students.

Remediation is central to the collaborative courses described by W. Scott Howard, Peggy Keeran, and Jennifer Bowers. Pairing *Richard II* and *Eikon Basilike*, their "Archives on Trial" presents a series of exercises that reveal the complexity of early modern print and visual cultures through multiple editions, contemporary political tracts and ballads, and iconographic portraits. A culminating assignment requires students to create, edit, and publish word-cloud collages of key moments in *Richard II*.

Finally, Angelica Duran insists on the complementarity of what she calls legwork and fingerwork in "Not *Either-or* but Rather *Both-and*: Using Both Material and Electronic Resources." Working with her university's special collections and a range of electronic resources, she devises a series of assignments to introduce her graduate students to the basic skills, tools, and intellectual flexibility necessary for rewarding archival research. Like Erben, she demonstrates the limits of monolingual research, and in her lesson about Milton's currency across disciplines she anticipates the interdisciplinarity of the next section.

## Beyond Literature and Finding Archives

"Beyond Literature" explores a range of ways to supplement the teaching of literature by introducing students to visual, typographic, cartographic, acoustic, and historical sources. Joseph M. Ortiz's "Teaching the Early Modern Music Archive" surveys traditional and online resources for integrating archival musical materials into Shakespeare and Renaissance literature courses. Developing students' historical and theoretical sensitivity to how music was represented and understood, Ortiz encourages students to explore both the incongruity and complementarity of language and music.

The next three essays deal with incorporating visual materials into student-centered pedagogies for undergraduates. In "Typefaces and Title Pages," Phillip John Usher uses the visual layout of early modern books to introduce students to the excitement of archival materials. Taking his primary examples from Rabelais and Montaigne, he demonstrates how his approach supplies an entry into difficult early modern texts in any national language. Erin Kelly's "Online Emblems in the Classroom" advocates using emblems to introduce undergraduates to early modern habits of thought and systems of value. An unexpected benefit that Kelly discovers about her approach and its reliance on free databases is its application to K–12 education, which increasingly stresses multiple literacies and visual learning. Students who will be teachers, having taken her Shakespeare course and studied emblems in it, can envision introducing high school students to archival materials. In "Charting New Worlds," Marjorie Rubright guides her students to explore the epistemologies of race circulating in and across early modern plays and atlases. Combining online resources with instruction in her university's special collections, she insists on the feedback loop between electronic and traditional sources.

Laura McGrane's "News and Material Culture" offers exercises in popular print that provide her liberal arts college students with the tools of the trade for future archival work. To help them realize that archives make arguments, McGrane asks them to become amateur archivists and build digital archives of their own on the basis of her course materials. Georgianna Ziegler, head of reference at the Folger Shakespeare Library, provides a detailed survey of historical resources for students of early English literature.

The volume's final section, "Finding Archives Online," provides an annotated list of major databases and useful Web sites for the study of early modern literature, including Web sites for the major libraries and traditional archives used in research of the early modern period.

### Notes

1. John Florio's Italian-English dictionary, published in 1611, defines the Italian term *archivo* as "a treasury of monuments, characters or rowles, a place where records or evidences be kept. Also the chancery of exchequer office, or the office of the master of the rowles. Also the Arches or Spirituall court."

2. Exemplars of broadening access, the Renaissance Society of America in November 2013 began including access to *EEBO* as a benefit of membership, and as of July 2013 the Huntington Library has provided remote access to *EEBO* and other major electronic resources to anyone with a current reader's card. Further, the *Text Creation Partnership*, a project administered at the University of Michigan Library and supported by roughly 150 partner libraries, has been encoding *EEBO* texts since 1999 and providing access to searchable full-text transcriptions for its member institutions. On 1 January 2015, *TCP* will make publicly available the 25,000 *EEBO* texts encoded during phase 1 of its project (which was completed in 2009 and covered by an "exclusivity period" in the interim). *ECCO-TCP* and *Evans-TCP* are already publicly available. *EEBO-TCP* phase 2, with a goal of encoding another 44,000 texts, is under way.

## Works Cited

"Archive." *The Oxford English Dictionary*. 2nd ed. 1989. Print.

Brown, John Seely, and Paul Duguid. *The Social Life of Information*. Cambridge: Harvard Business School, 2000. Print.

Florio, John. *Queen Anna's New World of Words*. London, 1611. *EEBO*. Web. 10 Aug. 2010.

Sherman, William. "Digging the Dust: Renaissance Archivology." *The Forms of Renaissance Thought: New Essays in Literature and Culture*. Ed. Leonard Barkan, Bradin Cormack, and Sean Keilen. New York: Palgrave-Macmillan, 2009. 246–60. Print.

———. *Used Books: Marking Readers in Renaissance England*. Philadelphia: U of Pennsylvania P, 2007. Print.

Summit, Jennifer. *Memory's Library: Medieval Books in Early Modern England*. Chicago: U of Chicago P, 2008. Print.

# Part I

## Introducing Archives

**Sarah Werner**

# Bringing Undergraduates into the Archives

If you want to teach undergraduates the value of researching primary materials in the early modern period, studying the history of books offers research opportunities and helps students learn how research can fundamentally alter and expand their knowledge of the period. A focus on books and early modern culture shifts attention away from interpreting a text to considering how its material forms raise questions about its production and affect its reception. By exploring those questions and then connecting them to textual interpretation, students gain a better understanding of how and what a text means and learn research and interpretive skills that they can bring to bear on other classes and research projects.

In this essay, I use my experience running the Folger Undergraduate Program to explore facets of teaching research skills. Although the parameters of these seminars were shaped by practical considerations specific to the Folger program, the advantages of doing primary research into books and the early modern period apply to a wide range of other classes. Between 2007 and 2013, the Folger Undergraduate Program offered two semester-length seminars in cooperation with George Washington University and Georgetown University. The seminars, titled Books and Early Modern Culture, used the framework of the history of books to teach research skills through a multidisciplinary lens. In the past few years, students have come from many different majors, including English, history, art history, classics, French, religion, philosophy, and music. Students in the seminar discuss a set of common readings that present three approaches to the field of book history: books as physical objects, books as exerting and reflecting cultural concerns, and books as vehicles for texts. In addition to these readings, students pursue independent research projects to explore how the theories can be put into practice. Early in the semester, each student identifies one book on which to focus. Over the course of the seminar, students write papers on their chosen book's author, printer, readers, and collectors, culminating in a biography of that book from inception to today. At the end of the seminar, each student has acquired an in-depth knowledge of one book's history, has learned to use some basic tools for researching early modern books, and has developed an understanding of how to approach reading and texts in other periods.

The Folger Undergraduate Program and the Folger Shakespeare Library have specific concerns that other courses in undergraduate book history or archival research might not. The program is designed to draw students from different disciplines: because schools pay to participate, the program's seminars must engage students from across the humanities in ways that not only motivate them but also fulfill requirements in their majors. This multidisciplinarity brings both benefits and challenges. Students are exposed to thinking that is unlike what they have encountered in discipline-bound courses and to a wider range of early modern books, a key element for understanding early modern print culture. But it is a challenge for both students and teacher that such diversity in thought and books offers little in the way of common methodology or knowledge to help move the conversation forward.

The Folger program suffers from an embarrassment of riches. Students in the seminars have access to materials that range from rare early modern printed works to a specialized collection of modern scholarship on the period. The materials are supported by a library staff made up of experts in early modern books. The resources of books and people greatly exceed what students typically have available to them at their home institutions. But this surfeit poses problems as well: How does the Folger Shakespeare Library balance the needs of access and preservation? How do students avoid the paralysis of information overload?

The seminars address both these challenges by carefully constructing assignments that teach basic research tools, applying them to specific problems, and relying on in-class conversations and readings to open up larger examination of the issues at stake. The seminar starts with consideration of what it means to study book history; we read essays by Robert Darnton, D. F. McKenzie, and Roger Chartier, then discuss some of the theoretical concerns that will gird students' explorations. (A recent syllabus for the seminar is online at www.folger.edu/undergraduates.) We move on to examine books as physical objects, learning some basics of how books were printed and of descriptive bibliography, supporting what students learn from reading Philip Gaskell's *New Introduction to Bibliography* with plenty of hands-on examination of books in class. At this point, students are asked to produce a physical description of a book they have chosen, describing all physical aspects of the book to the best of their abilities without worrying about precise bibliographic terminology. The assignment is fun and easy, and since students do not need to be able to read the text, it's a chance for them to handle books they might not otherwise be able to work with. But the assignment is also important, since it teaches the necessary skills of observation that will be important for researching printing and reception history.

Next the course moves from the physical object of the book to the roles of books in history, both as forces of cultural change and as markers of that change. In this section, students examine the commercial aspects of the book trade and the Stationers' Company and they turn to subjects that combine the concrete with such abstract concepts as authors and libraries. By this point, they have all chosen a book to study. While the class as a whole considers the economics of printing in early modern London and the relationship between authors and stationers, each student is doing research for a paper on the makers of a specific book, tracing its origins. Given the nature of the Folger's collections and interests students bring to the seminar, most books that are being researched were published in London in the sixteenth and seventeenth centuries. Students who can are asked to find the entry in the Stationers' Register (Arber; Eyre and Rivington) for their book, along with any previous and subsequent entries for that text. They also draw on catalogs and biographies of early modern printers and writers, such as A. W. Pollard and G. R. Redgrave's and Donald Wing's short-title catalogs, the *Bibliographie lyonnaise*, the *Oxford Dictionary of National Biography*, the various dictionaries of printers and booksellers, and relevant volumes from the *Dictionary of Literary Biography*. Although students first search for the details of who printed what and when (and where), that information is used to speculate about the context and popularity of their book. What does it reveal when we know that a book passed through many hands in the Stationers' Register? How does our context for a book change when we learn that it was printed by a stationer specializing in news books or in classical texts? Is the author a selling point for the book? Does the printer or another person function as an authorizing figure?

In their papers on the users of the book they have selected, students closely examine their book for signs of its intended audience and for traces of actual use during the early modern period and in later centuries. By studying both the physical book and its text—looking at its format and typography along with prefatory material and other textual clues—students guess who might have used the book and for what purpose. Classroom discussion, combining the specific examples of students' books with readings from William Sherman, Heidi Brayman Hackel, and Ann Blair, broadens the perspective. Readers of Mary Wroth's *Urania*, for example, surely used that book in a way that was different from the way people used a late-seventeenth-century etiquette manual or a 1558 psalter.

Course assignments also ask students to think about the afterlife of their book, considering who collected their book and what post-Renaissance editions of it might exist. These assignments don't directly involve the early modern period, but they are important in helping students conceptualize the shifting nature of books and the mediated form of edited or facsimile texts. For all the problems associated with *Google Books*, it is a valuable resource for these assignments. Information on book collectors is often easier to track down in nineteenth- and early-twentieth-century sources than in more recent ones: Thomas Pearson isn't a significant enough figure to appear in the *Oxford Dictionary of National Biography*, for instance, but he was an important eighteenth-century bibliophile whose books passed on to the Duke of Roxburghe and others. Biographic information about Pearson and descriptions of some of the books he owned (and marked with a distinctive stamp) are easily found through *Google Books* and can lead to a consideration of the politics of bibliophilia and how the early modern period came to be viewed in later centuries.

Assigning research exercises that draw both on practical skills and on historical and theoretical contexts allows students to learn how to do research with archival materials and understand why such research is valuable. The seminar that focuses on working with rare books and uses a multidisciplinary perspective offers important benefits to its participants and, in my experience, creates a ripple effect in bringing those new perspectives and skills to students in other classes. A student who is excited about the textual history of Spenser's *Faerie Queene* will ask questions about textual scholarship when studying Donne or Bacon.

There are practical challenges for teaching such a course. The first and most obvious is that access to materials is required. The Folger's seminars focus on rare books, not on facsimiles. Few colleges or universities have access to the quantity of rare books from the early modern period that the Folger Shakespeare Library has or access to the same well-known texts. But any book printed in the hand-press period can be a productive and interesting thing to study; indeed, it can be the lesser-known books that students respond to most, the thrill of discovery trumping the glow of fame. More important than which books are in a collection is the willingness of the staff to let students use those books. We have all heard stories about librarians who refuse to let patrons handle books, but at the Folger the different divisions of the library have worked together to put in place policies that allow undergraduates the same access to collections that other readers enjoy. Rare materials can be brought into our seminar room, which allows for careful training of students on how to handle rare materials (wash hands, be gentle, cradle carefully, and ask for help!). We ask them to observe book handling before they proceed with their own books, and we assist them the first time they use rare materials. When a large number of books are being handled, an assistant is present in the seminar room so that the teacher can focus on teaching. We also have a curator vet the books that students have chosen for their projects. If a book is not in good shape, a student may need to use a different copy or a different book. Sometimes the conservation staff will quickly stabilize a book so it can be studied. Such steps reassure all of us that the books are being taken care of.

Access to modern materials also is needed. Many basic resources are available in most college or university libraries or are available free online. The print edition of Pollard and Redgrave's *Short-Title Catalogue* (*STC*) covers works printed in England, Scotland, and Ireland and all works printed in English elsewhere between 1473 and 1640; the first two volumes list books, and the third contains indexes by printer and by date. Wing's catalog extends the *STC*'s coverage through 1700 and British America. The records of both the *STC* and Wing can also be found online in the *English Short Title Catalogue* (*ESTC*), which covers works printed between 1473 and 1800. While the *ESTC* is very helpful and easily accessible, it does not incorporate all the information found in the *STC*; in particular it does not include the *STC*'s helpful cross-referencing of works to their entries in the Stationers' Register. The transcripts of the Registers of the Stationers' Company are not held as widely as the *STC* and Wing, but many libraries should have both the transcript of the volumes from 1554 to 1640 (Arber) and the transcripts of 1640–1708 (Eyre and Rivington). Digital versions of all the volumes are available online, thanks to Columbia University's Butler Library. Other helpful print resources that can be found online are some volumes in the series of biographic dictionaries of printers (Aldis et al.; Duff; Plomer), and *ABC for Book Collectors* (Carter and Barker). The *Oxford Dictionary of National Biography* is, alas, expensive as an online resource, and not all institutions will subscribe. The *Dictionary of Literary Biography* includes volumes on writers, printers, and collectors that are extraordinarily useful. Some institutions might not have the print volumes, but there is an online subscription through the Gale Literary Resource database. Searching *Google Books* will often turn up nineteenth-century resources that are not easily traceable otherwise. The *Internet Archive* is another source of free digital books, and the quality of the digitization is often higher and includes books from sources other than *Google*.

With these resources widely available, students can do an extraordinary amount of research into the history of nearly all early modern English books, not only developing their research skills but also expanding their knowledge of the early modern period and their understanding of how books are made and used.

## Works Cited

Aldis, H. G., et al. *A Dictionary of Printers and Booksellers in England, Scotland and Ireland, and of Foreign Printers of English Books, 1557–1640.* London: Bibliog. Soc., 1910. *Hathi Trust Digital Library.* Web. 3 Mar. 2014. <http://hdl .handle.net/2027/mdp.39015014765203>.

Arber, Edward, ed. *A Transcript of the Registers of the Company of Stationers of London, 1554–1640 A.D.* 5 vols. 1894. Gloucester: Smith, 1967. *Columbia University Libraries Online Catalog.* Web. 16 May 2014. <http://clio.cul .columbia.edu:7018/vwebv/holdingsInfo?bibId=6177070>.

Blair, Ann. "Reading Strategies for Coping with Information Overload ca. 1550–1700." *Journal of the History of Ideas* 64 (2003): 11–28. Print.

Brayman Hackel, Heidi. *Reading Material in Early Modern England: Print, Gender, and Literacy.* Cambridge: Cambridge UP, 2005. Print.

Carter, John, and Nicholas Barker. *ABC for Book Collectors.* 8th ed. New Castle: Oak Knoll; London: British Lib., 2004. *International League of Antiquarian Booksellers.* Web. 3 Mar. 2014. <http://www.ilab.org/eng/documentation/29 -abc_for_book_collectors.html>.

Chartier, Roger. "Labourers and Voyagers: From the Text to the Reader." *Diacritics* 22.2 (1992): 49–61. Print.

Darnton, Robert. "What Is the History of Books?" 1982. *The Kiss of Lamourette: Reflections in Cultural History.* New York: Norton, 1990. 107–35. Print.

Duff, E. Gordon. *A Century of the English Book Trade: Short Notices of All Printers, Stationers, Book-binders, and Others Connected with It from the Issue of the First Dated Book in 1457 to the Incorporation of the Company of Stationers in 1557.* London: Bibliog. Soc., 1905. *Hathi Digital Trust.* Web. 3 Mar. 2014. <http://catalog.hathitrust.org/Record/001159969>.

Eyre, G. E. Briscoe, and Charles Robert Rivington, eds. *A Transcript of the Registers of the Worshipful Company of Stationers from 1640–1708 A.D.* 3 vols. London: Roxburghe Club, 1913–14. *Columbia University Libraries Online Catalog.* Web. 16 May 2014. <http://clio.cul.columbia.edu:7018/vwebv/holdingsInfo?bibId=6177199>.

Gaskell, Philip. *A New Introduction to Bibliography.* Oxford: Clarendon, 1972. Print.

McKenzie, D. F. "The Book as an Expressive Form." 1985. *Bibliography and the Sociology of Texts.* Cambridge: Cambridge UP, 1999. 9–30. Print.

Plomer, Henry R. *A Dictionary of the Booksellers and Printers Who Were at Work in England, Scotland and Ireland from 1641 to 1667.* 1907. London: Bibliog. Soc., 1968. Print.

Pollard, A. W., and G. R. Redgrave, comps. *A Short-Title Catalogue of Books Printed in England, Scotland, and Ireland and of English Books Printed Abroad, 1475–1640.* 3 vols. 2nd ed. Rev. and enl. by W. A. Jackson, F. S. Ferguson, and Katharine F. Pantzer. London: Bibliog. Soc., 1976–91. Print.

Sherman, William H. *Used Books: Marking Readers in Renaissance England.* Philadelphia: U of Pennsylvania P, 2008. Print.

Wing, Donald. *Short Title Catalogue of Books Printed in England, Scotland, Ireland, Wales, and British America, and of English Books Printed in Other Countries, 1641–1700.* 4 vols. 2nd ed. New York: MLA, 1982–98. Print.

**Heather Wolfe**

# Manuscripts and Paleography for Undergraduates

The production of manuscripts increased dramatically in early modern England, because of rising rates in writing literacy and, perhaps surprisingly, because of the greater availability of printed documents. The complementary technologies of printing and writing were partly defined by the limitations that each presented. Printed works were public and cheaper to produce in large quantities, while the circulation of manuscripts could be more closely controlled and tailored to a more private audience. An abundance of literary and nonliterary manuscripts, now available in digital or microfilm format, provides a broader picture of literary life in early modern England than if one were to limit oneself to printed primary sources and makes it possible to teach the two skills necessary for working with manuscripts from the period: familiarity with the handwritten world of early modern England and an ability to read English secretary script. Fully mastering secretary script requires in-depth training and practice, but students can gain a working familiarity with it in a session or two and learn how to interpret abbreviations, dating, and other scribal anomalies as they encounter them. They can also be introduced to italic or mixed hands instead of secretary hand if time is limited and exposure to the world of manuscripts in general is more important than attaining expertise with the handwriting of the period. There are plenty of letters and literary texts written in legible nonsecretary hands that will still give students the satisfaction of deciphering four-hundred-year-old handwriting and learning about manuscript culture in the process. Paleography, the art of deciphering historical manuscripts and writing systems, should not be taught in isolation: an understanding of manuscripts as physical objects as well as the context of their production and use is critical for interpreting the handwritten texts that one encounters, for making connections to related manuscripts or printed works, and for unraveling the often heavy-handed transformations of literary texts made by centuries of editors.

## Quick and Dirty Paleography

I have found that the best way to engage students in the joys of paleography is to distribute and discuss two cheat sheets—the secretary alphabet and common abbreviations—in the first session and then proceed to the reading of a manuscript as soon as possible. My favorite alphabet, from R. B. McKerrow's *An Introduction to Bibliography* and reprinted in Philip Gaskell's *A New Introduction to Bibliography*, is derived from manuscript letterforms. As a result, it is much more useful than the idealized woodcut alphabet, "The secretarie Alphabete," found in Jehan de Beauchesne and John Baildon's 1571 writing manual, *A Booke Containing Diuers Sortes of Hands* (*STC* 6446 and other editions), especially for letters like *e*, *h*, *r*, and *s*, which come in many variants. A list of abbreviations can be adapted from the introduction to Anthony Petti's *English Literary Hands from Chaucer to Dryden* or from one of the online paleography sites mentioned below. The medieval thorn that looks like a *y* but should be read and pronounced as a *th* is one of the easiest abbreviations for students to learn; one of the trickiest is the *-es* brevigraph, a looped stroke curving downward (and usually to the right) at the end of a word, which resembles both an *e* and an *s*. Students also need a basic set of editorial conventions for making transcriptions in class and for homework assignments and will benefit from a glossary of the basic features of early modern handwriting (e.g., minims, ascenders, descenders, lobes, spurs, crossbars, stems). Transcription conventions and glossaries are available from online paleography tutorials.

For the first reading exercise, supply students with a color or black-and-white photocopy made from a digital image or microfilm of a letter, poem, or will, written in a regular, uncrowded secretary hand. For example, the Folger Digital Image Collection (http://luna.folger.edu) includes a relatively easy letter (Folger MSS X.d.428 [11]; V.a.162, fol. 33v; and Z.e.40 [3]); alternatively, images and transcriptions can be used from one of the interactive paleography tutorials described below. Before commencing, tell them what the manuscript is and where it is currently located and make sure that both the repository name and shelf mark appear on the photocopy. Either go around the classroom having each student read a line out loud or break students into teams to transcribe a line or set of lines, and then have them share their transcriptions and questions with the rest of the class. Encourage them not to guess a word based on the first few letters but rather to break down confusing words letter by letter and even start from the end of the word if this approach is easier. If they are reading out loud, they should spell out each word so that everyone can follow along, and individual letterforms should be discussed if needed. I always find it useful to remind students to be patient with one another, since people grasp unfamiliar letterforms at different speeds and since some students are intimidated when put on the spot.

In addition to using the straightforward transcription of an easy and interesting manuscript, I have found two other exercises to be appropriate for students with little or no background in paleography. Students have seen plenty of movies in which actors in ruffs sign death warrants or dash off letters or write poetry with goose quills, pots of ink, and large sheets of paper. The physical labor of writing—the messiness of it, the noise of it, the difficulty of it—becomes readily apparent when they try it themselves. Have students try writing with quills on a firm angled surface using precut quills, ink, and rag paper. All these materials can be ordered online: Dennis Ruud sells hand-cut goose quills (www.dennisruud.com/quills .html), Twinrocker sells eighteenth-century-style paper made from cotton and flax (www.twinrocker.com), and Scribblers sells iron gall ink (www .scribblers.co.uk/acatalog/Iron_Gall_Ink.html). Useful instructions for preparing ink and quills and for writing can be found in printed form in "Rules Made by E. B. for Children to Write By," which appeared in various writing manuals in the early seventeenth century and in Beauchesne and Baildon. It may also be useful for students to read the online version of Martin Billingsley's *The Pens Excellencie* (1618), in which a spirited defense of handwriting and professional writing masters is followed by a series of exemplary plates and by instructions for forming letters, cutting quills, and holding the pen. Many early modern students learned to write by copying a set sentence many times on a sheet of paper, underneath an exemplar written by their writing master. Sometimes these sentences incorporated almost every letter of the alphabet, such as "Job a Righteous man of Uz waxed poor Quickly" (Folger MS X.d.243), which I have my students copy. When they are confronted with the labor of the physical act of writing, they develop a deeper appreciation for two-dimensional digital images of manuscripts and take a greater interest in the reasons behind different kinds of deletions and emendations.

Most students are unaware of the extent to which a literary text is processed before it reaches their scrutiny. I use sonnet 43 from the autograph manuscript version of Mary Wroth's "Pamphilia to Amphilanthus" (Folger MS V.a.104), written in a clear italic hand, to give them a sense of the process. After each student individually transcribes the sonnet, we discuss how students handled capitalization, punctuation, spelling, abbreviation, *u/v* and *i/j* graphs, corrections, deletions, interlineal insertions, and catchwords. We then compare the manuscript sonnet with the sonnet as printed at the end of *The Countesse of Mountgomeries Urania* (*STC* 26051) and six modern editions, including one digital edition. The discussion addresses a range of questions: What sort of differences do you notice between the autograph manuscript and the version printed in the first edition of *The Countess of Montgomery's Urania* (1621) and later editions? How might these differences affect your reading and interpretation of the sonnet? Is it possible for a compositor to alter the meaning of a poem? Which version do you think has more authority, the manuscript version, which has numerous corrections and was read by only a few people, or the published version? Should modern editors choose a single source text for their edition or instead combine features from many early versions? Should they modernize the spelling or alter the punctuation? How should modern editors represent the substantive changes or deletions in the manuscript version, if at all? How is a poem's meaning diminished or altered when read out of context or sequence? How would you edit the poem if it were your edition?

Teachers who want to introduce students to the paleographic basics of numbers and dates should provide them, from one of the online tutorials, with charts for numbers (roman, arabic, ordinal, Latin forms), money (l, s, d, for "pounds" [*libra*], "shillings" [*solidus*], "pence" [*denarius*]), and dating (regnal years, legal terms, saints' days, movable feasts, Old Style and New Style, English new year beginning 25 March, Latin and numerical forms of months [e.g., September, Septembris, 7$^{ber}$, 7$^{bris}$, vij$^{ber}$]). Students can practice deciphering numbers and prices by looking at financial accounts or inventories (for a basic roman numeral exercise, I use a summary of mortality bills for London in 1564 [Folger MS X.d.264]) and dates by looking at the subscriptions of letters (e.g., cut and paste an assortment of subscriptions from a digitized collection of letters such as the papers of the Cavendish-Talbot family or the Bagot family in the Folger Digital Image Collection).

Since paleography is not an exact science, I provide students with a list of important points to keep in mind when reading and transcribing early modern hands:

Forget what modern letters look like.

Forget how to spell and accept the fact that the same word could be spelled different ways in a document.

The *Oxford English Dictionary*, online or print, is your best friend, because it includes obsolete words and spellings.

Every person has a unique and inconsistent hand, and when the person is hurried or incapacitated, the hand degenerates.

Think of how the letters are formed—work out the directions of the pen strokes (the duct) and lifts—and try to reproduce those strokes in your mind, remembering that upstrokes are usually thinner and downstrokes thicker.

For difficult hands, or when comparing hands, compile your own alphabet by copying letters from the manuscript, paying particular attention to letters with unique ascenders, descenders, loops, and bowls.

Watch out for interference from letters with long ascenders and descenders in the lines above and below the line you are transcribing.

If you are not sure of a word, write the letters you know, put dots or *x*'s to indicate the illegible letters (and return to them later), and enclose the word in square brackets—do not guess a word on the basis of its first few letters.

Minuscules and majuscules are often used inconsistently.

Minim letters (*i*, *m*, *n*, *u*)—that is, letters formed by a series of single strokes (*i* is formed with one stroke, *m* with three, *n* with two, *u* with two)—are often indistinguishable from each other, so count the minims and try out different letter combinations until one works (for example, the word *minimum* has fifteen identical minims).

Four online English paleography tutorials allow for online transcription practice both in and out of the classroom and serve as excellent sources for creating handouts. *English Handwriting: An Online Course* (scriptorium.english.cam.ac.uk/handwriting) has twenty-eight transcription exercises, sortable by difficulty level and date. Students can make their own transcriptions and compare them with the model transcription; they can also take an interactive test. The United Kingdom's National Archives hosts *Palaeography: Reading Old Handwriting, 1500–1800: A Practical Online Tutorial* (http://www.nationalarchives.gov.uk /palaeography/). This tutorial includes interactive transcription exercises for ten documents arranged in order of difficulty, and a further practice section contains many additional noninteractive transcription exercises. *Scottish Handwriting.com: Online Tuition in the Palaeography of Scottish Documents* (www.scottishhandwriting.com/) provides a series of tutorials with examples, transcriptions, and a weekly poser. *Early Modern Paleography* (paleo.anglo-norman.org/empfram.html) includes nine examples of legal and manorial documents with full transcriptions and explanations. The transcription tutorial of the *Letters of William Herle Project* (http:// www.livesandletters.ac.uk/herle/), supported by the Centre for Editing Lives and Letters, has thirteen interactive transcription exercises. The Web site *Bess of Hardwick's Letters* (www.bessofhardwick.org/) provides eighteen transcription exercises. The Folger Shakespeare Library is developing an online interactive transcription database (*Early Modern Manuscripts Online* [*EMMO*]), that will allow learners to test themselves and teachers to view, compare, and correct student transcriptions through a collation function. Jean Preston and Laetitia Yeandle's invaluable *English Handwriting, 1400–1650: An Introductory Manual*, with thirty-five reproductions and transcriptions, is now available as a reprint on demand.

## Digital Images, Catalogs, and Databases

An increasing number of early modern manuscripts freely available in digital format can supplement the resources listed above for paleographic teaching and provide material for course work relating to manuscript and print culture and the production of literary texts. While downloading high-quality images from these sites is often not possible, the ability to zoom and pan across images often makes them easier to read online than in person. A few collections and projects are worth highlighting, and others will undoubtedly appear in the near future. The English Paleography (beinecke .library.yale.edu/digitallibrary/paleography.html) and Osborn collections of Yale University's Beinecke Rare Book and Manuscript Library (beinecke .library.yale.edu/digitalguides/osborn.html) include hundreds of descriptions and zoomable images. Cambridge University's *Scriptorium: Medieval and Early Modern Manuscripts Online* consists of images and detailed descriptions of twenty miscellanies and commonplace books (scriptorium.english.cam.ac.uk/manuscripts/). The Wellcome Library's *Recipe Books Project* contains images of seventy-five manuscript recipe books (library.wellcome.ac.uk/node9300909.html); when viewed alongside the roughly eighty recipe books included in the microfilm series *Receipt Books, c. 1575–1800, from the Folger Shakespeare Library* (www .adam-matthew-publications.co.uk/collections_az/Receipt-Books /contents-of-reels.aspx), they allow for intensive research on this female-dominated manuscript genre. The *Henslowe-Alleyn Digitisation Project* (www.henslowe-alleyn.org.uk/catalogue/catalogue.html), consisting of hundreds of images from Dulwich College, provides access to the most important archive on professional theater in early modern England as well as to extensive supporting material and is an invaluable resource for classes on early modern drama. The *Anglo-American Legal Tradition: Documents from Medieval and Early Modern England from the National Archives in London* (aalt.law.uh.edu/) includes thousands of images of court documents with links to the relevant records in the National Archives catalog (www.nationalarchives.gov.uk/catalogue/). The University of Pennsylvania's *Penn in Hand: Selected Manuscripts* (dla.library.upenn .edu/dla/medren/index.html) provides digital images of a handful of early modern English manuscripts, which can be reached by narrowing the search to "English, facsimile, and sixteenth and seventeenth century." The Folger Digital Image Collection contains thousands of early modern manuscripts.

In addition to free resources, a number of subscription-based digital image databases have a focus on early modern manuscripts. *Perdita Manuscripts: Women Writers, 1500–1700* consists of digitized microfilm images of over 230 manuscripts compiled by early modern British women, along with detailed indexing, biographical and bibliographic information, and contextual essays. *Literary Manuscripts: Seventeenth- and Eighteenth-Century Poetry from the Brotherton Library, University of Leeds* includes digitized microfilm images and original color images of 190 manuscripts, with essays and biographies, searchable by author, title, first line, verse form, manuscript genre, and shelf mark. The *Virginia Company Archives* consists of digitized microfilm images, some transcriptions, and contextual material relating to the Ferrar Papers (1590–1790) from Magdalene College, Cambridge. *State Papers Online* provides digitized microfilm and original color images of state papers from the National Archives and the British Library, as well as calendars and transcriptions of the Cecil Papers at Hatfield House. The manuscripts are fully searchable through their calendar entries and index points and are supplemented with essays. The Cecil Papers at Hatfield House have now been fully digitized and are available through ProQuest.

Teachers should introduce students to some of the most useful online manuscript catalogs, finding aids, and indexes, which can be used in conjunction with the image databases. For example, see the guide to the Osborn Collection at the Beinecke Library (beinecke.library.yale.edu/digitallibrary/osborn.html), the Folger Shakespeare Library catalog and finding aids (shakespeare.folger.edu and findingaids.folger.edu), and the British Library manuscripts catalog (http://searcharchives.bl.uk). Larger union catalogs are *A2A: Access to Archives: The English Strand of the UK Archives Network* (www.a2a.org.uk/), a database that holds items from 390 record offices and other repositories, including the National Archives, searchable by keyword, date, repository, and region, and *Archive-Grid*, which provides links to finding aids and collection descriptions for North American and British manuscripts and archives of all periods (www.archivegrid.org/web/index.jsp).

For poetic and other literary manuscripts, students should familiarize themselves with the *Union First Line Index of English Verse* (firstlines.folger.edu), an online database of the first lines of manuscript verse from a range of repositories (in addition to verse from selected books printed in England or in English from 1475 to 1700), searchable by first line, last line (in some cases), author, title, gender, repository, and shelf mark. It is also possible to create a list of all the poetry in a single volume by searching by shelf mark and then sorting the results by folio or page number. Peter Beal's *Catalogue of English Literary Manuscripts, 1450–1700* (www.celm-ms.org.uk/), a greatly enlarged and updated version of the printed *Index of English Literary Manuscripts*, is arranged by writer and includes valuable introductions and descriptions of all known manuscripts associated with each writer.

## Digitized Manuscripts versus the Real Thing

Students should keep in mind that they are often not seeing a manuscript in its entirety when viewing it online. Important information about ownership, dating, or handwriting on the binding, endpapers, or other parts of the manuscript may not have been digitized. The image should be viewed alongside the catalog entry for the manuscript (sometimes located separately from the digital image) to avoid confusion. For example, the recipient of a letter is usually identified in a superscription located on the address leaf of a letter rather than on the main leaf of the letter, and marks of ownership often appear on the endpapers or pastedowns of bound manuscripts rather than in the body of the manuscript. It is difficult to contextualize an image of a poem from a manuscript poetical miscellany unless the other poems in the volume, often written in different hands at different times, can also be consulted. If these seemingly extraneous leaves are not reproduced and if the metadata is inadequate, a digital image can become a highly unreliable source of information.

In an ideal world, digital images are a gateway to the manuscripts themselves, preparing students for forays into special collections libraries. Digital images are also valuable surrogates after the original manuscript has been consulted. Evelyn Tribble writes in this volume of the necessity of a "material substrate of knowledge about the book," to avoid the pitfalls of two-dimensional misinterpretation. When students are forced to grapple with the materiality of the text they are reading or transcribing, they begin to ask questions that are far more nuanced than if they have only ever seen digitized manuscripts. Take your students to your university's special collections library to look at an old manuscript. The curator or librarian will often be aware of random uncataloged fragments in addition to what might already be described in the catalog. Even better, consider adding seventeenth- or eighteenth-century manuscripts or manuscript fragments to your teaching collection. Inexpensive items such as receipts, deeds, and stray pages are available from booksellers if you ask about their unadvertised stock, and they are available on *eBay*. Even if the manuscript isn't English or early modern, it will rarely fail to make a lasting impression. Interaction with original manuscripts leads to discussions about format, genre, ownership, dating, and physical attributes, and it makes students aware of the importance of nontextual and paratextual features in determining the story of a manuscript and the trajectory of its text.

## Works Cited

Beauchesne, Jehan de, and John Baildon. *A Booke Containing Diuers Sortes of Hands.* London, 1571. Print.

McKerrow, R. B. "A Note on Elizabethan Handwriting." *An Introduction to Bibliography.* Oxford: Oxford UP, 1928. 341–50. Rpt. in *A New Introduction to Bibliography.* By Philip Gaskell. Oxford: Clarendon, 1972. 361–67. Print.

Petti, Anthony. *English Literary Hands from Chaucer to Dryden.* Cambridge: Harvard UP, 1977. Print.

Preston, Jean F., and Laetitia Yeandle. *English Handwriting, 1400–1650: An Introductory Manual.* Binghamton: Medieval and Renaissance Texts and Studies, 1992. Print.

**Shawn Martin**

# Images, Texts, and Records: Electronic Teaching in a Confusing Landscape

Electronic technology has made the process of finding resources for teaching much faster but also much more complex. Some electronic resources are freely available; others are restricted. Some are catalogs of books available in print; others make records and e-books available. Some digital databases provide access to images; others allow full-text searching. Online resources for the study of early modern literature such as the *English Short Title Catalogue* (*ESTC*); *Early English Books Online* (*EEBO*); *Eighteenth Century Collections Online* (*ECCO*); *Evans Early American Imprints* (*Evans*); *Women Writers Online*, created at Brown University; and the *Text Creation Partnership* (*TCP*), from the University of Michigan, offer tremendous possibilities but have some limitations. How are teachers to understand and navigate their options in their limited time? How can an electronic archive be used to set up a dialogue between new skills and old methodologies? How can students be taught about the potentials of electronic scholarship without losing the essentials of traditional humanistic inquiry?

## The *English Short Title Catalogue*

Most scholars who have studied early modern English literature and history are familiar with the *STC I* and *II* (Pollard and Redgrave) and the Wing supplement (Wing). Now available online (http://estc.bl.uk/), the *ESTC* provides instantaneous access to over 460,000 books published between 1473 and 1800. With the cooperation of the British Library, the Bibliographical Society, the Modern Language Association, as well as libraries around the world, the cataloging information is provided by experts and designed so that scholars and researchers can locate titles in any library. If one is looking only at bibliographic information, whether or not the purpose is to find and see the original book, the *ESTC* is unparalleled.

The *ESTC* gives a good overview of publication history, bibliographic standards, general deviations between editions (such as changes in title), and histories of library acquisition. Scholars considering a particular research library can get a quick glimpse of its holdings and assess whether it would be valuable for them to visit the library or not. The major drawback of the *ESTC* is that one cannot see the actual book through the database.

## *Early English Books Online*

Where the *ESTC* leaves off, *EEBO* begins. It has the information of the *ESTC* but in addition provides access to scanned images, in most cases full texts, of most of the books in the *ESTC*. *EEBO* provides instantaneous access to over 125,000 texts; enables teachers to assign a primary text for a course like Shakespeare; and allows students to find resources about Shakespeare, texts by rival playwrights, sources that Shakespeare used, and developments in early modern history to which Shakespeare may have been responding—avenues of information that were previously impossible. With *EEBO*, undergraduate students can do primary research that even a few years ago only doctoral students did.

Examples of creative teaching abound with the use of *EEBO*. A list of assignments and some syllabi that instructors are using are available at the *TCP* Web site ("Sample Assignments"). Hillary Nunn at Michigan State University, for example, has her students use *EEBO* to find background information on particular plays, including *As You Like It*, *King Lear*, *Twelfth Night*, *Winter's Tale*, *Measure for Measure*, *The Tempest*, and *Othello*. Students then present about the other books they found and explain how that information helps them understand the context of Shakespeare's plays ("Group Assignment"). Huston Diehl at the University of Iowa had her students consult any text in *EEBO* and ask questions about its themes and tell what in the text struck them as odd or different. This exercise led to student essays on how texts open a window into seventeenth-century culture ("Research Assignment").

A weakness of *EEBO* is that it does not provide full-text searchability, only catalog records with a series of images attached to them. Without such access, students cannot easily or comprehensively find out what people in the seventeenth century thought about events like the Great Fire of London or the political controversies going on in Europe.

### Eighteenth Century Collections Online and Evans Early American Imprints

*ECCO* and *Evans*, in providing access to texts, give a tremendous advantage to scholars in eighteenth-century studies and American literature, respectively. In both databases, publishers have employed optical character recognition (OCR) software to make not only the images and catalog records available but also the text of the works fully searchable. Yet OCR comes with a caveat. Often one will hear that it is 99% accurate, which sounds high but means that there will be one mistake per hundred characters. OCR also incorrectly scans when there are words in a language that has unfamiliar diacritical marks, when a page was crooked in the scanner, or when the typeface is unconventional.

OCR allows students to see quickly in their search how relevant for them a book may be. (For example, does a search for "Shakespeare" return one hit or one hundred?) Students using OCR may also find things they do not expect, like Shakespeare in a cookbook. The usefulness of OCR is limited if one is trying to teach a subject in which accuracy is important (linguistics, orthography, editing).

### Women Writers Online

Established at Brown University and based since 2013 at Northeastern University, *Women Writers Online* supports more in-depth teaching and research and offers tools that are essential for linguistic and editorial research. Its texts, transcribed by staff members and graduate students, are accurate. Perhaps even more important, *Women Writers Online* includes tags that show where paragraphs are, where items have been crossed out, where handwritten notes have been added, where linguistic variations between editions are located, and what parts of speech are in a given sentence. For graduate teaching, these features are essential. Graduate students often approach a text in a particular way, looking at one aspect of it and asking questions that a general *Google*-like search in *ECCO* or *Evans* is unlikely to answer.

Such electronic resources, however, are expensive to produce. As a result, there are few collections like *Women Writers Online*, and the ones that do exist tend to focus on canonical writers: for example, the MLA's two recent volumes (*Winter's Tale* and *Comedy of Errors*) in the New Variorum edition of Shakespeare provide the contents on CD as text-searchable PDFs with internal links; the MLA has also made the XML files and schema for these volumes available under a Creative Commons license. These editions are undoubtedly valuable but exclude lesser-known authors and obscure texts. The question arises: Is there a middle ground whereby it is possible to get some if not all of the advantages of full-text searching with scholarly apparatus?

### Text Creation Partnership

*TCP* is an attempt at striking this middle ground between OCR resources like *ECCO* and *Evans* and full-text searchability with tags from resources like *Women Writers Online*. *TCP* has mistakes but far fewer than OCR-accessible texts do. Its version of tagging is less complete than that of *Women Writers Online* but provides a structure that can be added to later. Currently there are *TCP* editions of over thirty thousand texts in the *EEBO*, *Evans*, and *ECCO* databases. More are being created and hopefully will be integrated into commercial products (as has been done with *EEBO*) in the near future. They are also cross-searchable, so students can look at how ideas changed not only in early modern England but also in the eighteenth century and in America.

The *TCP* approach supports undergraduate research with more accurate searching, and it can also be used for advanced teaching (Martin).

### What Are We Gaining? Losing?

The teaching possibilities of electronic resources like *EEBO*, *Evans*, and *ECCO* are tremendous. By using such resources, however, the academic community is losing something that has been a traditional aspect of humanistic inquiry. In the print world of the past, close reading of a text was always important. It was thought better to study one book in depth than skim a thousand. Electronic access encourages the opposite: the cursory reading of a thousand texts. Humanists also valued the artifactual value of a text, the ability to see a sixteenth-century book, say, and analyze its size and printing quality, factors that demonstrated how it was received and by whom. In a black-and-white scan and even more in a transcription, all that information is lost, and students lack the cues that are evident when one sees a physical book. Universities are gaining access to many texts but losing some modes of scholarship that traditionally were passed on to students. How should the academic community address this issue?

Archival research has been essential for humanities students and scholars for centuries. Electronic resources have changed that. Why should I look at the original if it is available in *EEBO*? More worrisome is the *Google*-generated syndrome of believing that if a text is not contained in an electronic database of some sort, then it does not exist. These two concerns have led to hesitation among some scholars. If one goes to an archive and sees a poorly printed octavo and a richly printed folio with hand-colored woodcuts, it is reasonable for one to deduce that the octavo may have been meant to be hidden in a pocket and the folio intended for display in a library or church. The possibility of making this deduction will be denied to a younger generation of scholars who turn increasingly to electronic resources and are not trained in the use of sources like print bibliographies. Finally, if scholars are using *EEBO* and not consulting books in the library, what purpose does the library serve (Hirtle)?

The role of libraries is changing. Special collections may be consulted less often as digitization increases. But if the use of some types of material declines, the use of others will increase. For instance, the Bodleian Library at Oxford University reports an overall decrease in paging of books that are included in *EEBO*; it also reports an increase in paging of manuscript material that has not been digitized (Ovendon). Students are perhaps enhancing their already advanced research with more inquiry into special collections.

In essence there are two kinds of research in which humanists engage. The first is informational, reading a book for its contents, for the words it contains. The second is artifactual. Electronic resources can revolutionize informational research but cannot begin to replace artifactual research. The key is to teach how to navigate this difference.

In an essay on the historical imagination, William Thomas states:

> The goal for historians working in the new digital medium needs to be
> to make the computer technology transparent and to allow the reader
> to focus his or her whole attention on the "world" that the historian
> has opened up for investigation, interpretation, inquiry, and analysis.
> Creating these worlds, developing the sequences of evidence and inter-
> pretation and balancing the demands and opportunities of the technol-
> ogy will take imagination and perseverance.

This argument can be taken a step further. It is incumbent on historians
of the electronic age to create new historiographies and new modes of
inquiry. It will also be incumbent on humanities teachers to navigate a
changing landscape in which the roles of scholar and student are increasingly merged. Educators must take an active role in steering this development in ways that will eventually enhance the mission of teaching and
learning.

The relationship between student and teacher is changing. The research once available to students only at the doctoral level is now available
to those at the undergraduate level. As some recent students—many of
them now young faculty members—have stated:

> The unpredictability that research in *EEBO* might bring, both to the
> classroom and to our research more broadly, ultimately brings about
> new insight not just into the early modern period, but also into the
> nature of literary scholarship. The conversations that *EEBO* and other
> digital resources provoke can provide a valuable means of exploring
> the ways that four hundred years' worth of scholars have engaged with
> texts, allowing users a deeper understanding of what generations of
> academics have considered worthy of study. This conversation in turn
> helps students—and beginning faculty—to see room for their own
> work within the wider discipline. Just as importantly, digital resources
> like *EEBO* allow students and teachers alike to see how earlier gen-
> erations of scholars have found new things to say about an old, but
> still evolving, body of literature. (Crowther, Jordan, Wernimont, and
> Nunn)

In the electronic age, it is not a matter of either-or. We should dis-
pense with the notion that the use of one type of resource necessitates
the loss of another. Electronic resources can significantly enhance informational uses of primary documents, yet they need to be balanced with
close reading and the artifactual value that print resources provide. The

humanistic methods that teachers are employing have not changed, only the mechanics they are using. The academic community needs to decide how best to employ these mechanics in order to provide the most effective teaching for its students.

## Works Cited

Crowther, Stefania, Ethan Jordan, Jacqueline Wernimont, and Hillary Nunn. "New Scholarship, New Pedagogies: Views from the '*EEBO* Generation.'" *Bringing Text Alive: The Future of Scholarship, Pedagogy, and Electronic Publication.* Spec. issue of *Early Modern Literary Studies* 14.2 (2008): n. pag. Web. 15 Feb. 2010. Spec. issue 17.

"Group Assignment." *TCP.* Text Creation Partnership, 2013. Web. 18 Oct. 2013.

Hirtle, Peter B. "The Impact of Digitization on Special Collections in Libraries." *Libraries and Culture* 37.1 (2002): 42–52. Print.

Martin, Shawn. "Collaboration in Electronic Scholarly Communication: New Possibilities for Old Books." *Journal of the Association for History and Computing* 9.2 (2006): n. pag. Web. 15 Feb. 2010.

Ovendon, Richard. "Being Digital in Bodley: Early Books and Research Libraries in the *Google* Era." (De)materializing the Early Modern Text: *Early English Books Online* in Teaching and Research Conf. Bath Spa U. 8–9 Sept. 2005. Address.

Pollard, A. W., and G. R. Redgrave, eds. *A Short-Title Catalogue of Books Printed in England, Scotland, and Ireland and of English Books Printed Abroad, 1475–1640.* 2nd ed. 3 vols. London: Bibliog. Soc., 1986–91. Print.

"Research Assignment—Primary Texts." *TCP.* Text Creation Partnership, 2013. Web. 18 Oct. 2013.

"Sample Assignments and Syllabi Assignments." *TCP.* Text Creation Partnership, 2013. Web. 18 Oct. 2013.

Thomas, William G., III. "Computing and the Historical Imagination." *A Companion to Digital Humanities.* Ed. Susan Schreibman, Ray Siemens, and John Unsworth. *Blackwell Reference Online.* Blackwell, 2004. Web. 27 Aug. 2014.

Wing, Donald Goddard, comp. *Short-Title Catalogue of Books Printed in England, Scotland, Ireland, Wales, and British America, and of English Books Printed in Other Countries, 1641–1700.* 2nd ed. 4 vols. New York: MLA, 1972–98. Print.

**Evelyn Tribble**

# The Work of the Book in an Age of Digital Reproduction

Some years ago, the library at my former university belatedly converted its online catalog from ancient green-screen, dirt-encrusted workstations to then-modern Pentium-class computers. These were placed throughout the stacks and set to the online catalog home page. While working in the library shortly thereafter, I noticed a student typing "What is mitochondria?" into the search box on the screen. Observing her frustration when faced with a result that informed her that "her entry" would be between "What is midrash?" and "What is modern architecture?," I tried to help. "You won't find an answer to that question there," I said. "That's the card catalog." Several minutes of comic cross-talk ensued, and it was only after the encounter that I realized the source of the young woman's confusion: I persisted in referring to what was obviously a *computer* as a *card catalog.* Had she ever seen a card catalog? Did she have any sense that the records "behind" the screen were once housed in sleek oak drawers, the mythical book *What Are Mitochondria?* represented by a typed card nestled between *midrash* and *modern architecture*?

I am not about to indulge in a nostalgic ode to the card catalog in the vein of Nicholson Baker, for all of us have come to recognize and appreciate the infinite malleability of the online search. Rather, my point is that those of us who once used card catalogs have a material substratum of knowledge about the kinds of records contained in it. The catalog itself—think of the Folger Shakespeare Library card catalog here—represents the contents of the library in a particular way, and an online catalog represents that representation. A database is an abstract concept, and making sense of it depends on how we represent it to ourselves. For many of our students, the arbitrariness and abstraction of digital resources—their flatness, so to speak—can be profoundly disorienting, in contrast to the reassuring solidity, materiality, and boundedness of a computer.

Internet resources such as *EEBO* (*Early English Books Online*) and Web-based digitization projects such as the University of Pennsylvania's *SCETI* (*Schoenberg Center for Electronic Text and Image*) offer enormous boons for researchers, and the essays in this volume testify to their rich pedagogical potential. Online editions of early books and manuscripts produced by scanning or key entry and markup greatly expand the range of materials available to students, allowing undergraduates to pursue genuine research.

But caution is required. The proliferation of digital resources makes acquaintance with the material objects—the books and manuscripts—that these images and records represent all the more necessary. To take an example of scanned text freely available on the Internet, I start from a surprising passage in James I's *Basilikon Doron*:

> I onely permitted semen of them to be printed, the Printer being first sworne for secrecie, and these semen I dispersed amongst some of my trustiest seruants, to be kept closely by them, lest in case by the iniquitie or wearing of time, any of them might have been lost, yet some of them might have remained after me.

Some years ago a graduate student posting on a discussion list inquired about this passage and its unusual use of a paternal procreative metaphor. The response from the members of the list came quickly: "semen" was a misprint of "seven," an error of a sort all too likely to occur from optical character recognition (OCR) scanning.

The disclaimer on the Web site from which the text came raises another issue:

> The text of books and articles presented on this website may contain errors.The electronic texts are provided for research purposes only. Before using any electronic text from this site in any scholarly work, check the electronic text against the printed original. ("Disclaimer")

Which printed original? *The Poitical* [sic] *Works of James I*, edited by Charles Howard McIlwain (Cambridge, 1918). The date 1918 is eloquent: materials published more than seventy-five years ago are in the public domain. Texts of this sort proliferate on the Web: translations of Plato from 1920, editions of Donne and of Spenser from 1896. There have always been bad editions; most of us who teach Shakespeare have watched students lug in books with puffy faux-leather bindings, a red ribbon, and a text last edited in 1850. But the free availability of online texts increases the importance of educating students about their origins and use.

Equally important is understanding the difference between a material object and the image of it. Computers tempt us to see the simulacrum as the thing itself, as perhaps better than the thing itself. New reading technologies such as the Kindle and the iPad are naturalizing screen-based reading, creating the widespread impression that books are in some essential way unchanged in the journey from print to pixel. But when we read online, we receive surface images only, and these are tailored to our screen. Without knowledge of the origins of the electronic images, we are apt to misinterpret them. To use such images in scholarly research, even at the undergraduate level, we must know what they are not telling us as much as what they are.

Most crucially, an image does not reveal the social embodiment of knowledge. Size is probably the most obvious of the missing elements. When images are made to fit our computer screens, screen size and aspect ratio become the determining factors, and duodecimo editions of the Psalms may look very like folio editions of John Foxe's massive *Actes and Monuments*. Moreover, size is a three-dimensional quality, and the bulk of a book can often tell us as much about its intended audience as the size of a page. The book on the desk is a whole; the book on the screen is a part, available one image at a time.

In writing of the "myriad transformations that occur when producing a facsimile in another medium," Diana Kichuk argues that a "digital veil of varying opacity" is placed between the reader and the text (297). In addition to poor or nonexistent measures of size and bulk, scans of microfilmed images often lack pages in the original, especially front and back matter; lose text to cropping; distort the shape of pages; and flatten out distinctions in hue, among other omissions (298–99).

The screen tells us that this is *the* book, not *a* book. However, *EEBO* and other digitization projects must choose one exemplar, and all copy-specific information belongs only to that particular object. Experience of any rare-books collection helps us see that *the* book is fiction: copy-specific evidence, including binding (the first level of evidence of reception), chain lines, annotation, inscriptions, doodles, provenance, dirt, damage, repair—all attest to the social network in which the object has been embedded and circulated. Handling the book provides a tactile mode of affiliation with it, a sense of the ways it might have been held and carried—a book for the pocket or a book for the pulpit.

None of these observations is meant as criticism of *EEBO* or other digitization projects. However, the limitations of the digital medium must be acknowledged. I suggest that the best way to confront these issues is to help students develop a material substrate of knowledge about the book. Many of the old bibliographic-methods courses that were once a staple of early postgraduate study and even advanced undergraduate course work have fallen by the wayside in the face of the need to introduce students to critical and theoretical methodology. But a combination of the old knowledges often conveyed in such courses and the new knowledges needed to traverse the Web is crucial. This combination should include

- knowledge of how texts are produced for the Web and of copyright issues that dictate the choice of source texts
- knowledge of methods of entering text, ranging from OCR with minimal proofing, as in the *Basilikon Doron* example, to double transcription with checking of anomalies, as recommended by the TEI guidelines ("TEI")
- basic familiarity with HTML and the ability to view and understand the source texts of a Web document
- most important, so far as is practical, experience viewing and (preferably) handling books of the handpress era

How might teachers help students gain this knowledge and experience? The first three items on the list can be handled through lectures, seminars, and readings and perhaps supplemented by an assignment asking students to track different versions of the same text. The final item presents difficulties. Obviously resource availability varies greatly; someone teaching in a large metropolitan area such as Philadelphia has access to numerous libraries and special collections that students might visit. Instructors at smaller or more remote colleges are not so fortunate. However, many libraries at liberal arts colleges have small collections of books from the handpress era. Librarians of such collections are often more willing to work with undergraduates than are larger-scale special collections librarians, who have many competing demands on their resources. A small-scale assignment in these circumstances might be to locate a text with an *EBBO* or *ECCO* (*Eighteenth Century Collections Online*) record that is in the college or university library. After a very basic introduction to books of the handpress era, including the distinction among folio, quarto, and octavo, students would begin by attempting to describe a book from the digital copy: its size, shape, intended audience, and format. They would then have the opportunity to examine the material book itself, looking for information about it not apparent from the image. How does the size compare with the impression of size given by the image? Can anything more be told about the book's intended readers? Is there any copy-specific information, such as binding, old library stamps, notes in the margin, and the like? Such marks do not have to be contemporary with the book; all books bear multiple material traces of their history. Mapping the two-dimensional image onto the three-dimensional object will provide at least the beginnings of an awareness of the true dimensions of the material text.

With more resources and more time, it is possible to go further. Time spent in special collections is an invaluable adjunct to digital resources. The primary advantage of the digital database is its ease of use: users can browse dozens of books quickly, skimming through many related texts and quickly assembling a broad range of knowledge about a subject. The physical library encourages depth, reflection, and a haptic engagement with the book. Moreover, students who use special collections have the opportunity to embed themselves in the tacit knowledge base that underpins all research libraries. The context in which the book exists is also the library itself, comprising both its institutional history and the people who manage and use it. A library is not just a repository of books, manuscripts, and objects: it is also a social network of knowledge. Much of this knowledge is hidden; public forms of information available in any library represent only a small fraction of what is known. A guided introduction to a special collection can furnish students with a context for work in a library and the courage to seek out the expertise of librarians and archivists.

Integrating the study of material artifacts and online resources provides students with the conceptual framework to use digitized material effectively—and to know when only the book itself will do.

## Works Cited

Baker, Nicholson. "Discards." *New Yorker* 4 Apr. 1994: 64–70. Print.

"Disclaimer." *Materials for the Construction of Shakespeare's Morals: The Stoic Legacy to the Renaissance.* Ed. Ben R. Schneider, Jr. N.p., 25 Oct. 2001. Web. 21 Oct. 2013.

James I. "James I's *Basilikon Doron.*" *Materials for the Construction of Shakespeare's Morals: The Stoic Legacy to the Renaissance.* Ed. Ben R. Schneider, Jr. N.p., 11 Mar. 2004. Web. 21 Oct. 2013. <http://www.stoics.com/basilikon _doron.html>.

Kichuk, Diana. "Metamorphosis: Remediation in *Early English Books Online.*" *Literary and Linguistic Computing* 22.3 (2007): 291–303. Print.

"TEI: P5 Guidelines." *TEI: Text Encoding Initiative.* TEI, n.d. Web. 5 Apr. 2013.

**Arnold Sanders**

# The Death of the Editor and Printer: Teaching Early Modern Publishing Practices to Internet-Raised Undergraduates

This volume's contributors share the hope that new online resources will help us teach early modern literature. Paradoxically, the technology that enables this goal may also disable our students in ways we are only beginning to detect. With the union of new digital technologies and traditional print and manuscript archives, we can help students recognize the dangers posed by the effect of online reading on their perceptions of documents. This essay argues that students can be prepared to interpret early modern literature by analyzing the printed books and manuscripts in which this literature first circulated and by learning the uses and limitations of online resources in that analysis. That my approach at Goucher College has been small in scale and often ad hoc in development allowed me to experiment with teaching methods to bring literature students to the archives for training.

Because students now learn to read and write online, their metaliteracy skills have been changed profoundly (Foster and Gibbons 63–71; Schirato and Webb 35–80; Lotherington). Most current undergraduates have never known an era when they did not create and read documents on computers, using keyboards and mice instead of a handheld pen on paper pages; they scroll through digital text more often than they turn paper leaves.

They are comfortable in a digital reading environment that sixth graders in a study described as visually painful; eighth graders in the same study thought online reading was normal. This difference suggests rapid adaptation to the new medium (Agee and Altarriba 386). Young readers learn to expend a lot of mental energy navigating hyperlinked documents that print authors would have organized for them (Kress 162). Cognitive studies of online readers reveal that they read more slowly on the screen than they do on the printed page, perceiving as "long texts" documents that print readers think are moderate or short (Dillon, qtd. in Schneider, "Hypertext Narrative" 200). As readers approach the screen's bottom edge, connection can be lost between sentences or paragraphs above and below; the result is anxiety and loss of textual coherence (201). Online readers also may have less ability to identify with fictional characters (Schneider, "Toward a Cognitive Theory" and "Hypertext Narrative" 202–03).

The greatest consequence of this new textual world is students' overwhelming preference for digital over paper texts (Carlson; McClure and Clink 126–28). As early as 2001, David Miall warned us of the "spurious interdisciplinarity" that online readers risk (1412). Student writers may cite more varied sources because of easier access rather than because they genuinely understand the disciplinary practice that grounds the arguments of a source. Digitally accessed scholarly texts also hide the supporting apparatus of expert knowledge, the social structures that print readers encounter in the front matter of scholarly journals, in editors' and authors' prefaces, and in the evidence of peer-reviewing.

Students are increasingly unsure about what constitutes a source. In a study by Nancy Foster at the University of Rochester, students tended to identify sources as documents, whereas faculty members identified sources as people who created the documents. My own undergraduate students sometimes identify as a source a digital library like *JSTOR* or a search engine like *Google*. Although students still appear to respect printed books, their familiarity with them and their ability to assess a source's authority seem to have declined over the past decade (McClure and Clink; Imler and Hall; Carlson). Like shoppers who expect eggs to come from Styrofoam cartons instead of hens, students expect articles and electronic books to arrive through a search window, a delivery mechanism that separates the text from evidence of its production by a human mind with scholarly training, from peers who care about that mind's training and accuracy, and from editors who repair the text's mistakes. This development may be the real "death of the author" that Roland Barthes announced, satirically, in 1967, and it also may herald the demise of editors and printers in students' perceptions of textual accuracy and authority.

As I designed assignments to introduce undergraduate students to archival research methods using early modern printed books and manuscripts, I had to adjust to their rapidly changing expectations. We have different ideas of what a page looks like; of how readers operate documents; of how writers create, preserve, and distribute documents; and of what determines a document's quality. I could not send students to work with a rare-book collection without first cultivating their curiosity about the means of production of handpress and manuscript books and giving them hours of hands-on contact with old documents that were not fragile. Because their previous training in literary interpretation concentrates on explication of the text, literature students often do not know what kinds of historical, social, and material questions to ask about an early modern book. Many who read Chaucer or Shakespeare in modern print editions have not encountered the texts of these authors in original spelling and punctuation, without explanatory footnotes, and with early modern readers' manuscript annotations. They have no idea how strong or weak old linen rag paper can be or that commonly the front board may be detached without rendering a book unreadable. They cannot feel an old binding's safe limits of operation as they can the cornering ability of an automobile at speed or the invisible edge of disaster through a video game console. Teaching from early print editions requires us to teach students' bodies as well as their minds (Shep).

I introduce early modern printed material to sophomores in the first half of an English literature survey (Beowulf to Dryden), at intervals that are significantly different in technology (1450–1500, 1600–50, 1650–1700). I show them digital images, handpress books and leaves, and economic data illustrating the shift from manuscript to print and from reading aloud to silent reading. This introduction is followed by an extra-credit assignment, which I also use for a Chaucer seminar, to interest students in Renaissance editions of Chaucer and in Renaissance historiography. At first I used digital surrogates more often than actual books or leaves and concentrated more on Chaucer in manuscript and print because of the availability of early modern Chaucer editions online. From William Caxton's 1478 and 1483 editions, available in digitized images from the British Library (www.bl.uk/treasures/caxton/homepage.html), students graduate to using our library's copies of editions by Thomas Speght (1598) and John Urry (1721). As they work with these editions, it is my openly stated intention to lure them into the extra-credit project "Getting to Know Some Old Things Very Well." I want to train them in rare-book and manuscript handling, using our oldest books from the James W. Bright Collection. The library's initiative to make sure all early printed books were properly cataloged allowed us to train another cadre of student workers to handle rare books, and they in turn became preliminary instructors for my literature students.

The first extra-credit sequence traces Chaucer's Renaissance rise to fame as the father of English literature and the emergence of the book as a commodity.[1] A second sequence represents early modern history and biography as Renaissance authors adapted medieval chronicles and saints' lives.[2] Some editions were produced after 1700, but they are still handpress artifacts. Just as Middle English scholars learned from Renaissance editors' and readers' receptions of medieval texts, so students of works written between 1473 and 1700 can learn from the construction and annotation of eighteenth-century editions. Also, because handmade eighteenth-century books are more common in small library collections than their early modern and incunable cousins, they offer more chances to teach with actual books instead of with digital surrogates.

Surprisingly, teaching undergraduates to use rare books and archival materials bears some similarity to teaching them New Critical close reading, which slows the grammatical operations of the text so that students can observe their motions. Archival printed or manuscript documents present physical puzzles that resist quick performance of the text with a layered bricolage of data, some intentionally assembled and some accidentally juxtaposed or removed before the document came to us. Only slow, patient observation will prevent the hasty assumption that a title page, library catalog entry, or bibliographer's record explains what we see. Students soon realize the scholarly weaknesses of studying only modern anthologies or student editions of a text.

In addition to the course-related projects to lead students to the rare-book room, we recruit students from other classes to study non-English manuscripts from the Renaissance, early modern period, and even the nineteenth and early twentieth centuries. Advanced students in French, Spanish, German, and Russian have volunteered to help us decode, transcribe, and annotate the documents, with the eager and welcome help of their language instructors. Manuscripts appeal powerfully to the emotions. Today's students see very few handwritten documents from other eras, and even though few of our manuscripts could be called early modern literature, they command interest because they encourage readers to imagine the hands and minds of their authors. Once students have learned paleographic skills in these languages, including typical scribal hands and abbreviation patterns, they often pursue further studies in early modern printed texts in those same languages. Commonplace books, tax records, marriage settlements, land sales, legal disputes, and cookbooks preserve copious written records in all the languages of Europe, and their current owners often have little interest in them because their contents now seem obsolete. Online auctions frequently offer them in troves, though usually with little evidence of provenance, which creates an additional layer of mystery for students to investigate.[3] Modern online tools, including genealogy databases, image banks, and *Google Maps*, help in the reconstructing of provenance, enabling students to locate people, places, and things named in the documents and to envision the cultures from which the documents emerged.

After several semesters using the extra-credit assignments in literature surveys and in my Chaucer seminar and the manuscript projects, I built up enough student interest to justify designing a new course, Archeology of Text (English 241; see http://faculty.goucher.edu/eng241). The course surveys the evolution of text production, storage, and distribution, moving backward in time from the digital era to handpress books and manuscripts, including manuscript annotations in early modern books. Laboratory experiences bring students into hands-on contact with the means of text production, storage, and retrieval. Even in the digital text portion of the course, they discover how little they know about the technology of digital surrogates. The digital era is filled with surprises, from ASCII code's origins in the teletype keyboard to the Rothenberg rule of digital media survival, which indicates a life span as short as five years for all types of media currently used (Rothenberg 3).

The most important innovation of Archeology of Text is the giving of a cadaver book to each student on the first day of class. Just as the human cadaver teaches both the anatomy of and respect for the bodies that medical students study, each cadaver book is dedicated to initial contact with students learning to use book cradles, snakes, nonacidic paper markers, and gentle touch. This strategy was suggested by a comment made by Matthew Bruccoli, a collector and bibliographer who said that for descriptive bibliographers "[t]here is no substitute for handling thousands of books at antiquarian book sales and book stores." To make up for the lack of experience handling thousands of books, the class gives students time to repeatedly handle the same old book with increasing knowledge and understanding, augmented by contact with other students' cadaver books. Careful supervision and repeated reminders during the first weeks result in almost no added damage to the books. The damage they already have suffered, as well as their overall fragile condition, gentles students' hands in preparation for their future work.

For the first five to ten minutes of each class meeting, students are asked to take notes on the physical appearance of the cadaver books. They become used to handling them, to seeing more details of their construction, and to using the sense of smell and even hearing to know them. Repeated contact with these books schools students in the care old books need. Booksellers' familiar notations, such as "detached front board," "loose title page," and "missing last gathering," become evidence of the books' wear after centuries of use, each reader's touch inconsequential in itself but as devastating over time as the effect of visitors' feet on the stairs to the Acropolis. Even during the first month's exploration of digital texts, the cadaver books teach students how old paper and leather behave.

Archeology of Text has six laboratory assignments to help students read early modern printed books and early modern and medieval manuscript hands.[4] In the first lab, each student produces a diplomatic transcription of a different laid paper leaf from a gothic-type edition of Caxton's Middle English *Golden Legend* translation (London: de Worde, 1527). The second pairs students to decipher five leaves of a nineteenth-century manuscript of Andrew Lang's classic essay on book collecting, "Elzevirs." The third is a whole-class attempt to decipher seventeenth-century inscriptions in the library's copy of George Wither's *Abuses Stript and Whipt* (London: Humphrey Lownes, 1617). The fourth challenges the class to transcribe an eighteenth-century vellum manuscript indenture in modern English. The fifth pairs students to transcribe one of seven seventeenth-century manuscript indentures in early modern English. In the sixth, pairs of students identify and date scribal hands writing in Latin and German in medieval parchment binding fragments.

In those labs, students become more engaged than ever and learn the value of preparatory readings. Although they have access to digital surrogates of all documents, they quickly realize that dependency on the digital is a trap. As much as the digital image's magnification and ease of access can communicate about a document, the digital image cuts us off from crucial observations of the substrate and letterforms seen in natural and augmented light.

Laboratory assignments help students grasp the importance of collaborative work in making documents meaningful. The course maxim is, "The more eyes on the artifact, the better we see it." Shared vision and interdependent effort after meaning are ways of escaping the isolation of competition and discovering the joy of a collegial environment. Each lab begins with the whole class's examining the artifacts and digital surrogates. The whole class works first with a projected digital image, and we make as much progress as we can. Then two or three students are given the document itself to solve problems we have discovered in the image. Other students with laptops and print resources are assigned to help them identify and define unfamiliar English and Latin terms, place-names, and personal names, using aids ranging from the *Oxford English Dictionary* to *Google Maps* and Andrew Zurcher's *English Handwriting, 1500–1700: An Online Course.*

Each lab teaches students to shift focus from global to local. We begin by describing the page and the text block, its lines and font or hand; then we consider individual letterforms and predictable, repeating letter groups (articles, prepositions, familiar nouns, and proper nouns). When close scrutiny leads to impasse, we step back and look at the document from a wider perspective: What is it saying, to whom is it speaking, and what kind of document is it (e.g., literary genre, manuscript type)?

At this point, students go off in pairs or trios to explore their own portion of the document or documents they were assigned. They often consult with one another, a strategy that yields insight into passages that were impenetrable and corrects mistakes. This group work prepares students to do collaborative independent research at the end of the semester.

The course's final month is spent in such research. Students use books from the Bright Collection, the Burke-Austen Collection, and archival documents in need of careful bibliographic description, improved cataloging, and digital imaging. Each project generates real-world scholarship that aids our rare-book collection and that students use in résumés and graduate school applications. Independent research also leads to internships at the Library of Congress, the Folger Shakespeare Library, and the Max Brödel Archives at the Johns Hopkins University Department of Art as Applied to Medicine. We expect undergraduate study of early modern documents to be not an end in itself but the beginning of a life of "getting to know some old things very well."

## Notes

1. In addition to the 1598 and 1721 editions of Chaucer, students following Chaucer's early modern reception could read the provocative introduction to Sir Francis Kinnaston's *Amorvm Troili et Cresidae: Libri duo priores Anglico-Latini* ("The Loves of Troilus and Criseyde: The First Two Books from English to Latin" [Oxoniae: Iohannes Lichfield, 1635]); Richard Brathwait's *A Comment upon the Two Tales of Our Ancient, Renovvned, and Ever-Living Poet, Sr. Jeffray Chavcer, Knight* (London: W. Godbid for Peter Dring, 1665); and Dryden's *Fables Antient and Modern* (London: J. Tonson, 1713).

2. Students interested in the history-chronicle sequence could read Richard Grafton's continuation of *The Chronicle of Ihon Hardyng* (London: Grafton, 1543); John Higgins's *The First Parte of the Mirour for Magistrates* (London: Thomas Marshe, 1574); Peter Heylyn's *The Historie of the Most Famous Saint and Souldier of Christ Iesvs: St. George of Cappadocia* (London: Thomas Harner for Henry Seyle, 1633); and William Clagett's translation *An Abridgement of the Prerogatives of St. Ann, Mother of the Mother of God* (London: R. Chiswell, 1688).

3. Our most recent find was a one-hundred-leaf, pre-1917 Bulgarian manuscript cookbook, extensively illustrated in a single hand and exclusively devoted to elaborate desserts. Because Bulgarian shares the Russian alphabet and both are related to Old Church Slavic, the Russian instructor hopes to lead her students to work with much older texts. The interdisciplinary opportunities of this line of investigation are both scholarly and delicious.

4. Laboratory materials were acquired for under $2,500 on the rare-book market with funds provided by an Innovation Grant from Goucher College. The indentures, in particular, are often found for sale on *eBay* at affordable prices, and they represent a wide range of scribal and personal hands. For useful advice on acquiring affordable materials to support rare-book study, see Buchtel; Cole. For more information on the six laboratory events and for digital images of the artifacts we worked with, open the links at the Web site for English 241, given above.

## Works Cited

Agee, Jane, and Jeanette Altarriba. "Changing Conceptions and Use of Computer Technologies in the Everyday Literacy Practices of Sixth and Seventh Graders." *Research in Teaching English* 43.4 (2009): 363–96. Web. 24 Aug. 2014.

Barthes, Roland. "The Death of the Author." 1967. *Image, Music, Text.* Trans. Stephen Heath. New York: Hill, 1977. 142–48. Print.

Bruccoli, Matthew. "The Collector-Bibliographer." Collectors and Collecting: Private Collections and Their Role in Libraries. U of Southampton and Goucher Coll. Chawton House Lib., U of Southampton. 20 July 2007. Address.

Buchtel, John A. *"Jane Eyre* on *eBay:* Building a Teaching Collection." Hawkins 51–57.

Carlson, Jake. "An Examination of Undergraduate Student Citation Behavior." *Journal of Academic Librarianship* 32.1 (2006): 14–22. *EBSCOhost.* Web. 25 Oct. 2013.

Cole, Jean Lee. "History of the Book in the American Literature Classroom: On the Fly and on the Cheap." Hawkins 58–64.

Dillon, Andrew. "Reading from Paper versus Screens: A Critical Review of the Empirical Literature." *Ergonomics* 35 (1992): 1297–326. Print.

Foster, Nancy Fried. "Understanding the Behaviors of Researchers and Students: An Anthropologist's Approach." The Architecture of Knowledge: How Research Programs and New Courses Are Built: CLIR 2007 Sponsors' Symposium. Cosmos Club, Washington, DC. 12 Dec. 2007. Address.

Foster, Nancy Fried, and Susan Gibbons, eds. *Studying Students: The Undergraduate Research Project at the University of Rochester.* Chicago: Assn. of Coll. and Research Libs., 2007. Print.

Hawkins, Ann R., ed. *Teaching Bibliography, Textual Criticism, and Book History.* London: Pickering, 2006. Print.

Imler, Bonnie, and Russell A. Hall. "Full-Text Articles: Faculty Perceptions, Student Use, and Citation Abuse." *Reference Services and Sources* 37.1 (2008): 65–72. *EBSCOhost.* Web. 25 Oct. 2013.

Kress, Gunther. *Literacy in the New Media Age.* New York: Routledge, 2003. Print.

Lotherington, Heather. "Emergent Metaliteracies: What the Xbox has to Offer the EQAO." *Linguistics and Education* 14.3–4 (2003): 305–19. Web. 25 Oct. 2013.

McClure, Randall, and Kellian Clink. "How Do You Know That? An Investigation of Student Research Practices in the Digital Age." *Libraries and the Academy* 9.1 (2009): 115–32. *EBSCOhost.* Web. 25 Oct. 2013.

Miall, David. "The Library versus the Internet: Literary Studies under Siege?" *PMLA* 116.5 (2001): 1405–14. Print.

Rothenberg, Joel. "Ensuring the Longevity of Digital Information." *CLIR Archives.* Council on Lib. and Information Resources, 22 Feb. 1999. Web. 6 Apr. 2013.

Schirato, Tony, and Jen Webb. *Understanding the Visual.* London: SAGE, 2004. Print.

Schneider, Ralf. "Hypertext Narrative and the Reader: A View from Cognitive Theory." *European Journal of English Studies* 9.2 (2005): 197–208. Print.

———. "Toward a Cognitive Theory of Literary Character: The Dynamics of Mental-Model Construction." *Style* 35 (2001): 607–40. Print.

Shep, Sydney J. "Bookends: Towards a Poetics of Material Form." Hawkins 38–43.

Zurcher, Andrew, ed. *English Handwriting, 1500–1700: An Online Course.* N.p., 22 Oct. 2013. Web. 25 Oct. 2013. <http://www.english.cam.ac.uk/ceres/ehoc/>.

**Patrick M. Erben**

# The Translingual Archive

For instructors introducing students to archival research methods, going beyond the monolingual orientation of available databases and research strategies may feel like an undue burden. This sentiment is in part based on the misconception that to teach or research translingual elements in early modern English literature, professors and students have to become experts in several languages, national literatures, and histories. In addition to anxieties over leaving behind one's comfort zone, the geographic and linguistic focus of *Early English Books Online* (*EEBO*) and other full-text online databases may create the false notion of monolingual, quasi-national English or American literary traditions in the early modern period. Reinforcing such a concept through archival research methods would deny our students access to a world that resembles today's in its concerns over globalization, diversity, and conflict.

Teaching early modern English literature through a translingual archive begins with several assumptions or definitions. My use of the term *translingual archive* emphasizes the exchange of books and ideas across linguistic and national borders throughout an early modern Atlantic world in which knowledge, literature, and texts were circulated, captured, and appropriated across cultures and languages. The concept of a translingual archive posits that students and scholars who are trying to understand the formation of English literature and culture in the early modern period should consider the influences of German, Italian, Dutch, French, Spanish, Portuguese, and other European literatures, which were frequently published in English translation. A translingual archive of early modern English literature also emerges when we understand the reception that works originally composed in English experienced through translation.

The focus of this essay is trifold: first, I survey historical and literary backgrounds that characterize the early modern age as a time profoundly occupied with linguistic multiplicity and attempts at mediating language difference. Second, I propose research methods encouraging students to explore the translingual and cross-cultural formation of early modern literature and culture in an Atlantic world context. While problematizing the use of English-language databases, I show how *EEBO* or *Early American Imprints* (known as the digital *Evans* collection) can reveal the translingual nature of early modern English literature and serve as starting points for research across languages. Third, I describe examples of student research assignments that use traditional archival materials and online databases to explore the multilingual nature of early modern English literature. I also suggest relinquishing the ideal of the professor-scholar as the supreme authority in all areas of knowledge and linguistic skill. A translingual approach to understanding the early modern world encourages teachers to harness the linguistic competencies present in the classroom, such as the expertise of bilingual students.

## Historical Currents: Multilingualism and Translation in the Early Modern Period

In introducing students to the relevance of translingual research in the early modern archive, it is useful to explain first the almost omnipresent encounter with multiple languages, as well as theoretical, philosophical, and theological questions about language, during this period. As Protestant churches moved scriptural authority to the forefront of their reformation efforts, "vernacular translation [became] the cornerstone of their creeds" (Sheehan 3). Scholars, theologians, and linguists debated how the divine word could be transferred into different human languages. The concern with translation and the anxiety over the transferability of divine meanings across human languages culminated in the vogue of polyglot bibles in the seventeenth century. Teachers can use *EEBO* to show Brian Walton's 1657 *Biblia Sacra Polyglotta* (known as "Walton's Polyglot Bible" or "London Polyglot"), which contains biblical text in various ancient and modern languages and a stunning array of typefaces. Similarly, students can research the large number of translations of Reformation authors and imagine the influence of translation on the English idiom and literary landscape. In America, biblical translation gained additional significance in the attempt to convert Native American peoples and in the movement of European immigrants to the New World.

In early modern Europe, the increasing use of vernaculars fostered the learning of many languages in order to participate in transnational conversations. On the one hand, Renaissance and humanistic society valued multilingual skill to create distinctions in literary artistry and emphasize erudition. On the other hand, language learning was touted as a solution to some of the most urgent problems of the early modern age. Jan Amos Comenius, a Czech linguist and educational reformer, devised didactic tools and popularized them during his stay in England during the 1640s. His works for practical language instruction—such as the *Janua Linguarum Reserata* (commony published in English as *The Gates of Tongues Unlocked and Opened*)—enjoyed the greatest popularity, with forty-six titles and editions published between 1631 and 1700. Comenius's *Janua Linguarum Reserata* used Latin in parallel columns next to English and French (or other vernaculars). During the civil war in England and the Thirty Years' War on the Continent, Comenius and other reformers hoped translingual communication would bring universal understanding and peace. This desire culminated in schemes to create universal languages in seventeenth-century England and across Europe (Eco 209–59; Large 19–42; Lewis 1–22).

Finally, "the discovery and conquest of America," as Ralph Bauer says, "was a thoroughly trans- (or, more accurately, 'pre-') national and translinguistic process" (8). His interpretation of Shakespeare's *Tempest* in the context of Iberian exploration accounts demonstrates how canonical texts of English literature reverberate with the many languages and literatures of the early modern world. Bauer has also amassed the impressive *Early Americas Digital Archive*, which helps students and scholars discover connections among themes, genres, and authors. Lisa Voigt, a Hispanist, demonstrates how the circulation, trade, and even forced capture of information and accounts about the New World among English, Spanish, and Portuguese imperial rivals created a translingual circulation of knowledge. In teaching translingual approaches, instructors can use Bauer's and Voigt's books alongside early modern collections of exploration and conquest accounts that have been considered quintessentially English, such as Richard Hakluyt's *Principal Navigations* or Samuel Purchas's *Pilgrims*, and interpret them in an interconnected and multivocal textual network.

## Translingual Research Methods

The research methods outlined here are designed to guide students with different research interests and varying linguistic skills in the process of discovering and interpreting the translingual archive of early modern literature. While translingual methods may seem to draw researchers into ever-expanding circles of literary influence, I suggest four related and focused approaches that provide entrance points into archival sources. My examples follow my research and teaching interests in German and English literary and religious connections in the early modern Atlantic world. Colleagues focusing on translingual connections between English and Dutch, Italian, French, Spanish, and Portuguese literatures use similar methodologies.

### Focus on a Genre and Its Translingual Influences

One of the most important translingual generic influences on English literature during the early modern period was the poetic and religious tradition of German hymnody and religious poetry. German religious poets and hymnists of the baroque developed a flourishing lyrical tradition that gave expression to the rising Protestant emphasis on a religion of the heart—that is, an emotive connection to Christ and a physically palpable understanding of his suffering and sacrifice. A starting point for exploring the influence of this tradition on the English religious lyric is Garold N. Davis's *German Thought and Culture in England*. Students interested in the transatlantic spread of this tradition can trace common tropes (such as images of liquefaction in describing the melting of the believer's stubborn soul and heart through the believer's desire for Christ) from Germany to England and to radical Protestant poetry in North America (e.g., the Puritan poet Edward Taylor). For tracing German literature in the early modern age, students may use three related databases, *VD* 16, *VD* 17 (databases of German-language prints in the sixteenth and seventeenth centuries), and *Deutsche Literatur des 18. Jahrhunderts Online / Eighteenth Century German Literature Online.*

## Focus on a Region and Its Archival Repositories

In exploring the translation and transmission history of certain texts and authors outside the print record, students may conduct research in traditional archives, specifically through a search of repositories in a specific geographic region. For researchers interested in translingual connections between English and German literatures, for example, eastern Pennsylvania offers one of the densest concentrations of archival repositories, reflecting the complicated and intersecting immigration history of this region. Beside larger archives such as the Historical Society of Pennsylvania and the Library Company of Philadelphia, researchers should pay attention to smaller regional or denominational collections. A regional focus reveals the manifold trans-Atlantic and translingual networks and paths of transmission that led to the development of bilingual and multivocal literary and religious traditions in a New World community consisting of German and English members.

## Focus on an Author

Focusing on an author allows researchers to trace the translation, dissemination, and adaptation of work across linguistic, cultural, and national boundaries. An excellent example for this approach is William Penn, a Quaker leader and the founder of Pennsylvania, because his activities as missionary, religious organizer, colonist, and politician took him and his literary influence across the Atlantic world. His writings in favor of religious liberty as well as his publications advertising his province to potential settlers (*Some Account*) met with widespread interest among sectarians and other Protestants across Europe. Penn's agents, translators, and publishers in Holland and Germany adapted his writings to the sensibilities and needs of non-English readers (*Nachricht*) and even admonished Penn to be more mindful of their cultural and religious perspectives. By constructing a textual concept of the province that would appeal to both English and German settlers, Penn gave the new community a translingual and transnational stamp.

## Focus on a Religious Denomination or Group

During the early modern age, many English and other European Protestant and even pre-Reformation religious groups experienced periods of persecution, exile, and migration. In search of more tolerant rulers and political systems, they carried their ideas and writings across linguistic and territorial borders, creating translingual networks. Dissenters and nonorthodox religious thinkers in England and on the Continent cultivated the exchange and translation of texts and corresponded about common religious ideas. Tracing the archival record of these migrations and networks allows researchers to understand how religious and literary motives, genres, and discourses affected early modern English literature.

One of the success stories of translingual integration and communal formation in the late early modern world is the Moravian Church, or the Renewed Unitas Fratrum (named after the Unitas Fratrum, a Bohemian church founded by Jan Hus, a pre-Protestant reformer). Even though the main period of the Moravians' expansion and founding of communal settlements and missionary stations across the Atlantic world falls well into the eighteenth century, the group's radical Protestant ideas and literary practices are thoroughly mystical and rooted in early modern aesthetics, especially the intense focus of Moravian poetics on the wounds and other physical features of the suffering Christ (Atwood; Fogleman; Peucker). Many Moravian hymns in fact follow the generic conventions of the Renaissance *blazon*, dissecting the body of Christ poetically to show each part's particular suffering and express the believer's intense, even amative emotions. The church's strong emphasis on missionary activity and global inclusiveness spawned many translations of Scriptures, hymnals, dictionaries, and other linguistic and devotional tools in manuscript and print.

## Student Assignments

In the classroom, my goal is to overcome students' fears about researching early modern English or American literature in a translingual or multilingual context. Ideally, assignments harness students' foreign language skills in working with primary source texts that are connected to early modern English and American literature yet in a language other than English. For both undergraduate and graduate levels, I set up the class as a learning community that researches and reenacts the translingual literary culture of the early modern Atlantic world. This means that some students will work on English texts, some will work on the translation and transmission of texts from or to English, and others—especially those with bilingual skills—will work on and even translate non-English texts that are part of or connected to English and American literature.

In order to demonstrate how different levels of linguistic competency cooperate, both then and now, in creating an interconnected literary world, I choose a thematic area that was characterized by a high level of translingual integration. Individual projects do not have to demonstrate the whole range of translingual connections; they can represent a piece in a puzzle that in toto captures the multifaceted voices participating in a key cultural debate or literary development. Graduate students should be encouraged to achieve a certain level of translingual integration in their work; it will serve them well in their dissertations and professional activities.

## Undergraduate Assignment

One of the best topics for helping students develop translingual archival research methods is the development of the antislavery movement in the mid to late seventeenth century. Though English-speaking writers such as George Fox (*Gospel Family-Order*) and Thomas Tryon (*Friendly Advice* and *Tryon's Letters*) took the lead in articulating a criticism of slavery and the slave trade, the origins and later adaptation of their principles were deeply rooted in a translingual religious rhetoric. English radical Protestants were deeply influenced by the stream of German mysticism that entered English culture during the radical atmosphere of the civil war and interregnum. Phillippe Rosenberg's article on Tryon points out how the writings of Jacob Boehme, a German radical mystic, shaped the antislavery sentiments of both Fox and Tryon. Some students can use *EEBO* and *Eighteenth Century Collections Online* (*ECCO*) to follow Rosenberg's sources and research the extent to which antislavery sentiments were debated in early modern England. Others can use *Early American Imprints* to trace the transatlantic dimensions of the developing discourse on slavery by examining the English writings of Pennsylvania Quakers such as George Keith (*Exhortation*) or by comparing those writings with the articulation of a so-called benevolent Christian slavery by Cotton Mather in Massachusetts (*Good Master*).

In the context of the polylingual immigration to Pennsylvania, antislavery took on even more translingual dimensions, which can be discovered by a combination of online and traditional archival research. In 1688, Germantown Quakers (who were actually composed of Dutch-

and German-speaking settlers) drafted and submitted to several Quaker meetings a manuscript protest against slavery (Hendricks et al.). Notably, the coauthors used English to appeal to most of their coreligionists. While rhetorically convincing, the protest preserves many of the linguistic features of second-language writers, thus making the document a prominent translingual and transcultural text. Francis Daniel Pastorius, one of its coauthors, continued to write poetry and prose (including a rebuttal of Mather's *Negro Christianized*) in opposition to slavery in his "Bee-Hive" manuscript, a commonplace book and poetic miscellany circulated among his influential English Quaker friends.

After discussing secondary sources such as Rosenberg's essay or Katharine Gerbner's article on the Germantown protest, I provide an overview of research methods using online databases such as *EEBO* and *ECCO*. Students select an author and text for which to write a critical-biographical introduction, situating the work in the context of early modern antislavery and providing an excerpt or translation of an excerpt as well as scholarly annotations. Thus the project introduces students to both archival research and textual editing methods. For those who do not have access to primary archives, I provide a microfilm copy of Pastorius's "Bee-Hive" manuscript or introduce them to the University of Pennsylvania Rare Book and Manuscript Library's "Bee-Hive" digitization project. Students with a solid knowledge of German may produce alternative translations of Pastorius's German-language antislavery poem "Allermassen ungebührlich ist der Handel dieser Zeit" ("Altogether reprehensible is the trade/conduct of this time"). In oral presentations, individual students or groups demonstrate how their author and text contributed to the overall discourse on slavery in the late seventeenth and early eighteenth centuries; they present short textual examples and reflect metacritically on the challenges they faced in the research and editorial process.

### Graduate Assignment

In the graduate unit, as in the undergraduate, I introduce translingual research and scholarly approaches by framing a thematic context that lends itself to exploring Atlantic world connections across linguistic, cultural, prenational, and religious differences. For instance, a unit on utopian and religious experiments works particularly well in setting up the exploration of literary negotiations in the context of Atlantic world migration, settlement, transculturation, and hybridization. The focus on migration and networks allows students to trace how literary types and practices were adapted, transmitted, and redeployed. Focusing on the establishment of specific religious or utopian communities provides concrete places, denominations, authors, and literary practices that students can then follow across different geographies of faith, literature, and aesthetics. Thus the approach lends itself to harnessing the methodologies of other disciplines, such as art history, anthropology, architecture, and theology.

Several graduate students traced the identification in the Moravian Church of the believer with the suffering body of Christ across different phenomenologies, including art, worship, music, and hymnody-poetry. When graduate students have a more extensive knowledge of literary history, they can follow the adaptation of this topos across English and non-English literatures, genres, and periods. Some students explored connections among medieval female mysticism in the works of Julian of Norwich, English metaphysical poets, and the hymns and poems of Nicholas Ludwig, Count Zinzendorf. They examined how Zinzendorf's poetics influenced, in the eighteenth century, the language of American Methodism, the Great Awakening, and the Romantic poetry of nineteenth-century American literature. In crossing languages, canons, disciplines, and periods, students apply translingual methods of archival research and scholarship to other boundaries that have dissected humanities scholarship on the early modern period and beyond.

Translingual approaches to research and writing create new paradigms of global, interconnected literary and cultural scholarship. In understanding the translingual nature of the archive, students will become cognizant of the many literary and cultural genealogies that constitute the early modern period.

## Works Cited

Atwood, Craig D. *Community of the Cross: Moravian Piety in Colonial Bethlehem.* University Park: Penn State UP, 2004. Print.

Bauer, Ralph. *The Cultural Geography of Colonial American Literatures: Empire, Travel, Modernity.* Cambridge: Cambridge UP, 2003. Print.

Comenius, Jan Amos. *The Gates of Tongues Unlocked and Opened.* London: Griffin, 1637. Print.

———. *Janua Linguarum Reserata.* London: Young, 1636. Print.

Davis, Garold N. *German Thought and Culture in England, 1700–1770: A Preliminary Survey Including a Chronological Bibliography of German Literature in English Translation.* Chapel Hill: U of North Carolina P, 1969. Print.

Eco, Umberto. *The Search for the Perfect Language.* Trans. James Fentress. Oxford: Blackwell, 1995. Print.

Fogleman, Aaron Spencer. *Jesus Is Female: Moravians and the Challenge of Radical Religion in Early America.* Philadelphia: U of Pennsylvania P, 2007. Print.

Fox, George. *Gospel Family-Order, Being a Short Discourse concerning the Ordering of Families, Both of Whites, Blacks, and Indians.* London (?), 1676. Print.

Gerbner, Katharine. " 'We Are against the Traffik of Men-Body': The Germantown Quaker Protest of 1688 and the Origins of American Abolitionism." *Pennsylvania History: A Journal of Mid-Atlantic Studies* 74.2 (2007): 149–72. Print.

Hakluyt, Richard. *Principal Navigations, Voyages, Traffiques and Discoveries of the English Nation.* London, 1599. Print.

Hendricks, Garret, Abraham Isacks op den Graeff, Derick Isacks op den Graeff, and Francis Daniel Pastorius. *Germantown Quaker Protest against Slavery. 1688.* MS 990 B-R. Quaker and Special Collections, Haverford Coll., Haverford.

Keith, George. *An Exhortation and Caution to Friends concerning Buying or Keeping of Negroes.* New York, 1693. Print.

Large, Andrew. *The Artificial Language Movement.* Oxford: Blackwell, 1985. Print.

Lewis, Rhodri. *Language, Mind, and Nature: Artificial Languages in England from Bacon to Locke.* Cambridge: Cambridge UP, 2007. Print.

Mather, Cotton. *A Good Master Well Served.* Boston, 1696. Print.

———. *The Negro Christianized.* Boston, 1706. Print.

Pastorius, Francis Daniel. "Bee-Hive." Ms. Codex 726. Special Collections, Van Pelt Lib., U of Pennsylvania, Philadelphia.

Penn, William. *Eine Nachricht wegen der Landschaft Pennsilvania in America.* . . . 1681. Frankfurt, 1683. Print.

———. *Some Account of the Province of Pennsilvania in America.* . . . London, 1681. Print.

Peucker, Paul. "The Songs of the Sifting: Understanding the Role of Bridal Mysticism in Moravian Piety during the Late 1740s." *Journal of Moravian History* 3 (2007): 51–87. Print.

Purchas, Samuel. *Hakluytus Posthumus; or, Purchas His Pilgrims.* London, 1625. Print.

Rosenberg, Phillippe. "Thomas Tryon and the Seventeenth-Century Dimensions of Antislavery." *William and Mary Quarterly* 61 (2004): 609–42. Print.

Sheehan, Jonathan. *The Enlightenment Bible: Translation, Scholarship, Culture.* Princeton: Princeton UP, 2005. Print.

Tryon, Thomas. *Friendly Advice to the Gentlemen-Planters of the East and West Indies.* . . . London, 1684. Print.

———. *Tryon's Letters, upon Several Occasions.* London, 1700. Print.

Voigt, Lisa. *Writing Captivity in the Early Modern Atlantic: Circulations of Knowledge and Authority in the Iberian and English Imperial Worlds.* Chapel Hill: U of North Carolina P, 2009. Print.

Walton, Brian. *Biblia Sacra Polyglotta.* London: Roycroft, 1657. *EEBO.* Web. 19 Nov. 2013.

**Katherine Rowe**

# Virtual Theater History: Interpreting the Space of Play in a Shakespeare Class

What can be archived? Until recently, the answer was any order of experience that leaves a material register or trace. Several essays in this volume consider the translation of such material traces—and their collections—into electronic formats. Yet digital media also expand the orders of experience that we can collect, catalog, and mine. This essay offers a case study of an emerging mode of archive: the virtual architectural collection dedicated to modeling, organizing, and preserving experiences of built space. As academics mine the scholarly possibilities of gaming platforms, archives of this kind are proliferating swiftly, from the *Rome Reborn* project in *Google Earth* to *Soweto76*, which is dedicated to the student uprisings in South Africa under apartheid.[1]

My text and also my scene of analysis are *Theatron³*, a historical collection of virtual theaters that illustrates the resources this new kind of archive can offer to literary studies. *Theatron³* has proved a tremendously effective tool for addressing a long-standing challenge in my introductory Shakespeare course. (The archive is currently on hiatus, but I have transported the assignment it fostered quite easily to other Globe Theater builds in the same virtual environment, described below.) Thus I begin (where all tech-in-the-classroom projects should) with a field-specific teaching task, in this

64

case one that has its own multimedia history going back at least a century. For several generations, Shakespeare teachers have used build-it-yourself models of the Globe Theater to give students some sense of historical play space. In my suburban United States high school, teachers assigned dioramas. At college, faculty members generally upped the production values, ordering photo-realistic kits by mail from educational suppliers.[2] In both cases, the routine was similar. Early in the semester we would gather to gaze earnestly down into miniature, half-timbered walls while our teacher described the heavens, speculated about the location of trapdoors in the stage, and observed the risks of cannons on dry thatch. Some sense of spatial presence was anticipated—perhaps an echo of Laurence Olivier's famous "thatch zoom" and "stall pan" from *Henry V* (1944). For several generations of filmgoers, that camera work conferred a quality of vivid, immersive presence on the distinctive architecture of the Globe (Rowe).

As a graduate student teaching assistant, I repeated the ritual. I trundled my discussion sections to Pusey Library, where the students gazed dutifully at C. Walter Hodges's conjectural model of the Globe, commissioned for the Harvard Theater Collection in 1980.[3] I lectured about groundlings and ticket price equivalents and noted the risks of cannon on dry thatch. Meanwhile, paper cutouts of the Globe migrated to the Web. And films such as *Titus* (dir. Julie Taymor, 1999) and *Shakespeare in Love* (dir. John Madden, 1998) began to reprise Olivier's camera work in an ironic mode.

As a student I enjoyed these field trips but had only a vague sense of their value for historicizing the experience of playgoing. As my graduate training fostered increasing skepticism about historical presence, I eventually abandoned them. When I became responsible for my own introduction to Shakespeare course, however, a compelling set of pedagogical interests in this Renaissance play space came into sharp focus.

Students today studying Shakespeare's plays for the first time describe a host of obstacles to a fluent reading experience: unfamiliar words, inverted syntax, evocative but ambiguous imagery, long speeches that travel through strange conceptual territory. Among the most significant obstacles, however, is one they rarely identify. Because the novel dominates United States secondary curricula, students generally come to college with limited reading experience of plays. Many struggle to orient themselves on pages that lack the familiar signposts of prose fiction. Speech prefixes tell them who is talking, but they lose track of who is listening. The lack of thick descriptions of interior life in many plays leaves students at a loss to guess a listener's emotional and physical response. When there is no exposition of action and setting, students have difficulty decoding basic information about a character's gesture, movement, and location. Plays, absent a governing narrative point of view, cause students difficulty decoding dramatic conflicts, which unfold through competing perspectives voiced by different characters. Character does not work the way they expect it to; it serves as a vehicle for those competing perspectives rather than as a unifying filter. Because a modern edition of a Shakespeare play comes in a package that looks like a novel, students may not be aware that they face these translation challenges.

In a Shakespeare play, the social use of space—how characters address each other, group, and separate—affects meaning in crucial ways. Considerable information about this use is present in the play text, but deducing it from lines of dialogue takes skill and practice. Without that skill, students cannot make the leap to interpreting the symbolic work of action and setting in a Shakespeare play. Gazing down at the bare play space of a Globe Theater model may help clarify this challenge, but miniature models provide few tools for tackling it. My initial solution was to turn to performance assignments. I developed a silly, enjoyable game that could be run in two class periods. Teams of students blocked a scene competitively. They had a day to prepare and a day to show off how many cues to action and location they could adduce from the play text as evidence for their interpretation. To frame this task, I assigned Andrew Gurr's terrific essay "The Shakespearean Stage." In semesters when I had actors in the class, the results were reasonably good.

Yet I quickly discovered what any theater professional knows, that physical environments shape understanding in profound ways. Although my classroom game helped students decode action clues from the text, they made spectacular errors. In the middle of a monologue they would send a character up from the (imaginary) stage to the (imaginary) Lord's Rooms (the stage gallery that served as Juliet's balcony)—an impossible scenario unless the player wears a mike and can deliver lines offstage. Moreover, they rarely shifted into higher intellectual gear to interpret action and setting in symbolic terms. Because English Renaissance public stages were unlocalized (bare, without scenery), setting can be a remarkably flexible device in a Shakespeare play: a rich source of symbolic juxtapositions and transitions from, say, wintry Sicilia to pastoral Bohemia. Yet my students rarely recognized the opportunities that unlocalized play spaces offer for this kind of symbolic work.

It was partly to help students over this interpretive hurdle and partly because of my own scholarly interests in cross-media adaptation that I began working with simulated theater spaces online. In what follows, I describe my students' work in the *Theatron³* Globe Theater and situate it in the (rapidly changing) landscape of virtual architecture initiatives. Virtual architecture projects come in three kinds:

> Three-dimensional graphical models, available online, in CD-ROM, or in DVD, allow for some user manipulation, providing controllable camera angles and sometimes player figures that can be positioned in space. They tend to use proprietary software and may not support social interactivity.[4]
>
> Projects that allow users to manipulate documentary footage from live performances are available on a Web site, in CD-ROM, or in DVD.[5]
>
> Architectural reconstructions in online games and virtual worlds offer varying degrees of free movement, authorship, and interactivity.[6] Unlike the resources described above, these may be extensible (designed for open-ended, collaborative world building) and persistent (what you build here lasts when you log off).

The *Theatron³* project, out of King's College London Visualisation Lab, belongs to this third sort of 3-D collection. Now on hiatus, at the time this essay was written it hosted scholarly reconstructions of twenty-five European theaters from antiquity to the twentieth century, in the virtual world *Second Life*. A commercial enterprise that combines social networking, 3-D design, and gaming, *Second Life* creates a powerful sense of proprioception (the sense of being in a body in space), making it useful as a teaching resource. Players interact through avatars in simulations (sims) that other users design and build. Imagine your avatar as a cross between a doll, a puppet, a car, a keyboard, and a telephone, and you will have a good sense of the interface *Second Life* offers for self-performance, communication, movement, and socializing.

Nine virtual theaters were available to be dialed up (rezzed) and entered from a central viewing platform at *Theatron³*. While a number of other Globes (and a Blackfriars Theater as well) are sometimes to be found in *Second Life*, including a serviceable Globe Theatre in Renaissance Island that I use as an alternative, the *Theatron³* Globe suited classroom work especially well. It was free, faculty members could reserve time slots as needed, and clear user instructions were available online. That the multimedia design is relatively uncluttered and quiet made it easy to explore with a group (fig. 1).[7]

**Figure 1.** In the yard at the *Theatron³* Globe Theater

In the *Theatron³* Globe, I wanted students to learn to parse action, re-action, and blocking from textual clues and then move on to interpret the symbolic uses of action and setting in the plays. I situated our work in the virtual theater early in the semester, concentrating on the opening scene of the second or third play we read, which is usually *Titus Andronicus*, whose first scene offers clear and interesting textual clues in a symbolically rich setting: a liminal space outside the city gates of Rome. The unit included background reading, an orientation in *Second Life*, group work outside class, a blocking report (textual analysis illustrated with screenshots), and a seventy-minute class discussion. By this discussion, the third of three, students have read the whole play.

For preparation I assigned Gurr's essay. Students set up a free user account in *Second Life* and read my instructions for new users. (Not all students own personal computers, so we had to ensure that the client software was also loaded on a few public workstations on campus.) I gave them a short list of other Shakespearean sims in *Second Life* and encouraged them to explore by themselves. (For this exploration, it helped to pair rookies with regular gamers.) We met for an online orientation session at the virtual theater, where I gave them a tour. I made sure they could move their avatars and use voice chat comfortably, and I answered any questions they had about the assignment.[8]

From this point until we met again in class, students worked independently in small groups, coming back to the virtual theater as needed

to write a blocking plan for the opening actions, marking their text to indicate locations that Gurr describes. I advised them to ignore the act and
scene divisions in their edition, explaining that many are modern interpo-
lations that may not correspond to Renaissance dramatic movements. I
posed a set of questions for them to work through as they composed their
blocking plans:

> How do the opening movements of the play set up dramatic conflicts
> and establish symbolic locations on the Globe's blank, unlocalized
> stage? To begin thinking about this question, position your avatars and
> move them as indicated in the text, marking the clues you identify.
> Note in your margins all the locations mentioned or implied in the
> opening scenes. Who addresses whom? Where (in both fictional and
> practical terms) is everyone? What reactions, gestures, props are speci-
> fied or implied, and how do you know? What clusters of conversation
> and action emerge, and how do they change?

As part of this assignment, students turned in short write-ups showing
their analysis, illustrated with screen captures as needed.

In class discussion, we spent about twenty minutes comparing their
discoveries, with the *Theatron*[3] Globe projected on-screen for reference.
Asked to list symbolically important locations, they typically mentioned
the gates of Rome, the Senate steps, the city itself, and a tomb, but
they missed the distant battlefield from which the Andronici returned.
We focused on points of disagreement regarding the final question I
set them: What clusters of dialogue and action emerge, and how do
they change? From points of disagreement, we shifted gears to interpretation, working out the different readings that might result from
different blocking plans. I asked students to speculate about how later
scenes return or refer to virtual settings established in the opening sequences. For example, a tomb where Titus buries his slain sons, presumably situated in a stage trap, will return later as a pit where a third son is
murdered.

In the final phase of discussion, I asked students to abstract some symbolic trajectories of movement from these opening exchanges. Conflict
far from Rome arrives at its walls to meet conflict inside; the play begins
as the two conflicts converge. Rome is at risk of falling, but to whom and
why? These actions might be staged as an external conflict passing into
the heart of Rome: a victorious civilization on the verge of collapse. Or, as
some modern stage directions indicate, they might be staged as opposed

but balanced forces entering and exiting by opposite doors: civility faces off against barbarity. Or both movements might converge: barbarousness fostered inside and outside Rome threatens the empire.

For newcomers to *Second Life*, navigating with an avatar may be a clumsy experience at first. Yet this clumsiness turns out to be a distinct advantage for the assignment. The minor difficulty of learning to move around with arrow keys and mouse—together with the powerful sense of architectural space conjured by the Globe's virtual galleries, stage, and yard—makes students proceed with greater deliberation. Having to choose where to position their avatars and expending effort to get the avatars there helped students appreciate the flexibility of an unlocalized stage space and the interpretive work needed when locations are invoked but then overlaid by other settings and actions as a play unfolds. After this assignment, student essays tended to show thicker textual references to action cues in the play text. The assignment also deepened their experience of live theater. Required to attend a performance in the weeks immediately after their work in *Theatron³*, then to debrief in a postperformance talkback, students remarked spontaneously on the movement of actors, blocking echoes, and the uses of stage space to conjure setting. The improvement in their spatial awareness was so marked, I assigned a midterm exam essay that asked them to apply what they learned about Shakespeare's symbolic use of space to the final scene of a different play.

I close with a few words about the strengths and limitations of the *Theatron³* collection and the other virtual Globes in *Second Life*. As yet, these virtual theaters lack the acoustic dynamics that would make them a good environment for training actors or for staging a performance assignment. The sense of physical proximity conjured in *Second Life* is particular to this virtual world—necessarily different from the complex physical and social feedback loops of an actual theater. That said, this collection offers opportunities to think about movement in architectural space comparatively, across long historical spans, in ways that actual theater spaces cannot support. A medieval-Renaissance drama survey might test Bernard Spivack's arguments about the evolution of the Vice character, for example, by comparing the possibilities of direct address to the audience from a medieval fairground booth or pageant wagon and from the Globe.

An unexpected payoff of this assignment is my students' increasingly thoughtful, analytic approach to online environments. Since I started using these virtual Globes, a number have gone on to write about other Shakespeare sims in *Second Life* in a critical mode, reading them as adaptations and interpretive works in their own right. Students come to the assignment fluent in social media but no more sophisticated in their understanding of digital tools than they are about a modern edition of a play. As N. Katherine Hayles reminds us, the transformation of material forms into electronic ones "is inevitably also an act of interpretation"; comparative work across media helps us understand our unspoken assumptions about and investments in both old and new media—letting us see their strengths and limitations with fresh eyes (89–90).

## Notes

1. On the emergence of three-dimensional archives in the arena of cultural heritage and on their practical research challenges, see Koller, Frischer, and Humphreys.

2. The earliest Globe model I have found is recorded in a 1930 photograph in the British Library. Conjectural cutout models were published by Waldo S. Lanchester in 1966 and reprinted in 1970. James W. Fitzgibbon designed a press-out model in die-cut paper (offering interchangeable historical stages) for the Folger Shakespeare Library in 1980. (Note that extant kits do not always indicate the source of their design or even which of the two Renaissance Globes they model.) Mail-order products are still widely available, including Shakespeare's Globe Theatre: An Authentic Card Model Kit of the Reconstructed Globe Theatre at Bankside, London, designed by Roger Pattenden in 1994.

3. Built by John Ronayne and John Mills, the model was commissioned by Stanley Kahrl, in memory of Alfred Harbage.

4. An example is the Learning Objects model of the Globe, out of Wesleyan University, with 3-D line drawings and simple cylinder figures that can be moved around for blocking exercises (learningobjects.wesleyan.edu/globe/). The Design Workshop Globe (greatbuildings.com/buildings/Globe_Theater.html) provides multiple camera angles but no blocking tools. It is part of a multimedia encyclopedia of architecture, the Great Buildings Collection, available online (www.greatbuildings.com/gbc.html) and on CD-ROM (edited by Kevin Matthews). Another 3-D general reference initiative is the emerging Encyclopedia of Egyptology at the University of California, Los Angeles (www.uee.ucla.edu/), which will allow users to scan through interactive topographic maps based on GPS data from archaeological digs.

5. For example, *The Chamber of Demonstrations* DVD, based on Martin White's reconstructions of the Jacobean indoor theater experience, out of Bristol: bristol.ac.uk/drama/jacobean/project1.html. This DVD allows users to manipulate four fixed camera angles to explore recorded performances of Jacobean plays.

6. Literary examples of online games are *The Faerie Queene Game*, out of Vanderbilt University, designed by Jay Clayton and Michael Hall for the *Neverwinter Nights 2* platform (a customizable, graphical, multiuser game). Its predecessor was *Arden I: The Shakespeare Game*, out of Edward Castronova's *Synthetic Worlds*

*Initiative* at Indiana University. Literary examples of virtual worlds are a host of fictional simulations in *Second Life*, such as *Foul Whisperings, Strange Matters*, a multimedia *Macbeth* installation (http://katerichards.net/art/foul-whisperings -strange-matters/).

7. For educational purposes, the simpler the design and the lower the demand on the server, the better a virtual space is for group work. Because movement and conversation in the graphically rich simulations of *Second Life* involve streaming instructions between each user's computer and a company server, multimedia-rich sims filled with many users (such as an undergraduate class) can become glitchy and slow.

8. *Second Life* supports both voice chat and text chat. Some time spent learning how to restrict conversation groups and manage voice chat is helpful.

## Works Cited

Gurr, Andrew. "The Shakespearean Stage." *The Norton Shakespeare*. Ed. Stephen Greenblatt. New York: Norton, 1997. 3281–302. Print.

Hayles, N. Katherine. *My Mother Was a Computer: Digital Subjects and Literary Texts*. Chicago: U of Chicago P, 2005. Print.

*Henry V*. Dir. and perf. Laurence Olivier. Two Cities, 1944. Film.

Koller, David, Bernard Frischer, and Greg Humphreys. "Research Challenges for Digital Archives of 3D Cultural Heritage Models." *ACM Journal on Computing and Cultural Heritage* 2.3 (2009): 1–17. Print.

Rowe, Katherine. "Shakespeare and Media History." *The Cambridge Companion to Shakespeare*. Ed. Margreta de Grazia and Stanley Wells. Cambridge: Cambridge UP, 2010. 303–24. Print.

Spivack, Bernard. *Shakespeare and the Allegory of Evil*. New York: Columbia UP, 1958. Print.

"Welcome Centre." *Theatron³*. Kings Visualisation Lab, King's Coll. London, n.d. Web. 14 Apr. 2013.

# Part II

## Building Archives

**Zachary Lesser**

# Teaching the Metadata: Playbook History in the Undergraduate Classroom

When I introduce undergraduates to *Early English Books Online*, their first response is often bewilderment. No matter how much preparation I have done—showing them how to use the interface, explaining the rudiments of early modern spelling and typography (the long *s*, *u/v*, *i/j*, and so forth)—*EEBO* can greatly confuse them. This confusion is not necessarily unproductive. My own response when I come across an early modern text on *EEBO* that is outside my area of expertise can be very similar. Sure, I can usually literally read the text (though not always, given *EEBO*'s highly variable reproduction quality), and I have more networks of knowledge into which to slot the unknown text than my students do. Still, I find myself not infrequently staring at the digital images of a sixteenth- or seventeenth-century book and thinking, "What in the world is this?" Indeed, it is often this question that keeps me interested in studying early modern culture, and some of my most exciting work has been done to answer it. But my undergraduates generally have neither the time nor, to be frank, the inclination to spend several weeks or months of research answering this question, and they usually lack the knowledge of the period that would allow them to see in the first place why an unfamiliar text might be exciting.

For this reason, most of my *EEBO*-based assignments guide students to texts that I have already decided are relevant: William Gouge's *Of Domestical Duties* (1622), when we read *The Taming of the Shrew*, and Robert Coverte's *True and Almost Incredible Report of an Englishman . . . Cast Away . . . in Cambaya* (1612), when we read John Fletcher's *The Island Princess*. But such assignments seem merely the virtual equivalent of a Norton Critical Edition, not truly designed to take advantage of the possibilities of *EEBO* or to involve students in using the digital archive as I do in my own research: peripatetically, sometimes serendipitously, winding my way through the vast array of early modern print forms by following leads wherever they take me.

For this reason, I sometimes give students a version of the old *Oxford English Dictionary* assignment that I inherited from my teachers, which asks students to choose a key word in one of the plays we are reading and trace its historical meanings through the *OED*. In my variant of this assignment, after students look up the word in the *OED*, they must also perform a search in *EEBO* to see how the word was actually used in early modern England. This assignment allows them to take advantage of the full-text search capability of *EEBO* (I am lucky enough to be at an institution that subscribes to it), which means they can follow a more random, less professor-driven path. (Those teaching at schools without access to the full-text *EEBO* might use *Literature Online* in a similar way, although *LION*'s restriction to literary texts is not helpful in this exercise.) That the assignment introduces students to a wide spectrum of early English print culture but through the fairly narrow lens of a single word makes the digital archive more comprehensible to beginners. After this exercise, I have students write a critical essay on the play based on their chosen word and its historical meanings, and occasionally the texts that they find through their word searches provide fulcrums for their arguments.

What the *OED* assignment gains in making a database comprehensible, however, is offset by loss of context. Students search texts but pay little attention to the books in which those texts are embedded. If *EEBO* does not reproduce many of the semiotic aspects of early modern books (their bindings, sizes, marginalia, color), the *OED* assignment increases this dematerialization by asking students to pull their key word from any kind of book, allowing them to dive into the text only at the point at which the word appears. For some purposes—for instance, understanding the historical uses of *bond*, a word central to *Merchant of Venice*—this dematerialization may not matter much. But I also want to introduce my students to the kinds of knowledge that can be gained from thinking about texts as books and from thinking about genres of books just as we encourage them to think about genres of texts.

*EEBO* is not particularly well equipped for genre-specific investigation. Since it attempts to account for all of early modern print culture, its search terms must appertain to most of its large number of records. Students are therefore confined to searches in the categories of author, title, subject, or imprint. The very comprehensiveness of *EEBO*, in other words, limits its searchability to a few fields. For this reason, although the user interface is fairly intuitive and in my experience students are generally able to use the database with only a few minutes of training, their activities in *EEBO* are relatively simple, as in my *OED* assignment: search for a key word, retrieve the texts in which it appears, read the surrounding context. Or as in an assignment for higher-level students: research a particular topic (say, usury) by searching for title or subject key words, retrieve the relevant texts, read them to provide a kind of new-historicist contextualization for a given literary text (say, *The Merchant of Venice*). The particularities of the material presentation of certain classes of books—which sermons indicate that they were preached at court? which playbooks include the name of a theater on the title page? which religious treatises are dedicated to women?—are difficult to perceive using *EEBO* without significantly more time and research skills than most undergraduates possess. Since my research focuses on the history of the book, particularly of playbooks, in early modern England, I want to get students involved, quickly and easily, in work that helps them understand how the material presentation of a book can illuminate its cultural meanings. For this purpose, *EEBO*'s search-and-retrieve design is limited.

It was partly for this pedagogical reason—and partly because most of the same difficulties also apply to scholarly research in this area—that Alan Farmer and I created *DEEP: Database of Early English Playbooks* (http://deep.sas.upenn.edu). Unlike *EEBO*, or the *English Short Title Catalogue* (*ESTC*) for that matter, *DEEP* does not aim for comprehensiveness. Precisely because it is limited in scope to playbooks printed in the British Isles through 1660, it is able to offer more sophisticated search capabilities, allowing even beginning students to undertake high-level research in the history of the book. Instead of providing digital facsimiles of books, *DEEP* focuses on metadata, information about each early modern playbook, such as whether it contains paratextual material of various kinds; what generic label appears on its title page and to what genre it has typically been assigned by modern scholars; and whether a playing company, theater, or author is named on its title page. *DEEP* also includes metadata about the play as performed on stage, such as the year of its first performance and its auspices (closet drama, professional drama, university drama). In this sense, *DEEP* is an analytic database, one designed to ask and answer the questions that interest scholars today, as opposed to a more archival database such as *EEBO*, which displays the books themselves in approximation of a rare-book library.

Because of its analytic nature and its focus on metadata, *DEEP* lets students jump more quickly into real research on early modern playbooks. Much of the guidance they need from their professors with a database like *EEBO* is already built into the structure of an analytic database like *DEEP*. The search terms themselves alert students to some of the ongoing areas of inquiry in early modern book history, although students will still need help perceiving why and how these inquiries matter for their understanding both of the plays and of larger cultural formations. What follows is an assignment that I have used in my advanced undergraduate classes to introduce students to the importance and excitement of research into the printed plays of Shakespeare and his contemporaries. With some adaptation, it should also work well in a graduate class, perhaps as a background exercise for a student presentation to open class discussion.

I structure this assignment as a scavenger hunt, dividing the class into small groups. Each group is responsible for a multipart question that I designed on the basis of my research (so I know in advance that it will produce interesting results). Here are examples:

1. How many professional plays were first produced before 1610 but not printed until 1630 or later?

   a. How many of these plays contain paratextual material?

   b. Using *EEBO*, read the paratextual material in a few of these plays, including addresses to the reader, prologues, epilogues, dedications, and so on. Do the paratexts indicate that the plays are old? In what ways do they indicate it?

   On the basis of your findings, what hypotheses might you formulate about these plays or about the ways that early modern theater changed over time? How would you continue your investigation into that change?

2. What was the first professional play to advertise a specific theater on its title page?

   a. Of all professional plays published from 1600 to 1640, how many advertised an indoor theater on their title page?

   b. Of these, how many indicated the playwright's elevated social status?

   c. Of all professional plays published from 1600 to 1640, how many advertised an outdoor theater?

   d. Of these, how many indicated the playwright's elevated social status?

What conclusions might you draw about indoor versus outdoor theaters from the difference you observe? How would you investigate further that difference?

3. Who published the first edition of *The Roaring Girl*?

   a. What other professional plays did this person publish? Can you find a common theme to these plays?

   b. Use the *ESTC* to search for this publisher. What was the most popular book this person published, in terms of number of editions?

   c. Look up this most popular book on *EEBO*; does the title page of the book resemble the title page of any of his plays?

What conclusions might you draw about this publisher, or about these plays? How would you investigate them further?

Each of these questions requires students to perform advanced *DEEP* searches that combine multiple categories. The answer to the first question, for instance, could be found by this search path: "Single-Play Playbooks and Plays in Collections," "Play Type: Professional," "Date of First Production: To 1609, "Date of First Edition: From 1630."

The three questions address different aspects of current scholarship on early modern book history. The first points to the use of paratextual material to investigate cultural transformations in the London theater: how did publishers, playwrights, and others understand the changing aesthetics of drama, and did they perceive or construct distinctions between different periods of drama? The second question considers the dynamics of playbook marketing: what was the relation, if any, between title-page features such as the attribution of a particular kind of theater and the attribution of a playwright's elevated status (e.g., "Gent.," "Master")? This question also asks students to think more broadly about how the data they find relate to differences between the indoor and outdoor theaters in terms of audience and repertory, an issue I generally raise early in the semester in a Tudor-Stuart drama class. The third question—which replicates some of the research underlying a chapter of my book *Renaissance Drama and the Politics of Publication*—asks students to consider the connections between a play that we are reading in class and other printed books, through the lens of a particular publisher and his most popular book. As a rule I structure the assignments so that students use *DEEP* first and then proceed to *EEBO* to look at facsimiles of the books they have isolated in their research. *DEEP* thereby helps them navigate a path through early modern print culture on the basis of a research agenda that is larger than simple key-word or subject searches.

After this assignment, the groups report back, and the whole class discusses their findings. I stress that this scavenger hunt is only the beginning of our investigation, and we work together to imagine avenues for further research. This discussion might or might not lead some students to their final papers, but the point is to get them working experientially, and at a level they can handle, with the kinds of research that scholars are currently doing. This assignment thus integrates an analytic database like *DEEP*, one that provides metadata about a narrow area of early modern culture, with an archival and comprehensive digital collection like *EEBO*. The combination offers a powerful way to introduce undergraduates and beginning graduate students to the research scholars do.

After this assignment, I might ask each group to create a question for one of the other groups. By exploring the available search terms in *DEEP* (currently more than twenty), students can get a sense of which aspects of early playbooks will reward study—more quickly than they can with a database like *EEBO*—and they can then frame a research project along the lines of the ones I have modeled for them. For example, modeling their question on the third one in my scavenger hunt but following the path not of the publisher but of the dedicatees of a certain group of plays would lead them through the archive in a way that closely resembles the research most of us do: we proceed neither randomly nor single-mindedly, without a clear sense of what we are expected to find yet with a definite direction. Because students have already been attuned to the genre-specific features of plays, they may begin to notice print elements that recur in other categories, so that they can critically bring together not only texts but also books.

Other trajectories for exploring the archive are valuable, whether through *EEBO* or through the rare-book library (if one is lucky enough, as I am, to work at an institution with strong special collections and with librarians who are eager to share those collections with undergraduates). But more and more I am designing exercises that work with analytic databases focused on narrower genres of books and their metadata, such as *DEEP*, the *English Broadside Ballad Archive* (http://emc.english.ucsb.edu /ballad_project; see the essay in this volume by Fumerton, Chess, Gniady, and McAbee), and *LEME: Lexicons of Early Modern English* (http://leme .library.utoronto.ca). Such exercises integrate primary sources with the developing scholarly knowledge about them, so that students do not have to reinvent the wheel and can see how scholarship builds on earlier work in the field.

### Work Cited

Lesser, Zachary. *Renaissance Drama and the Politics of Publication: Readings in the English Book Trade*. Cambridge: Cambridge UP, 2004. Print.

Sheila T. Cavanagh, Gitanjali Shahani, and Irene Middleton

# Engendering the Early Modern Archive

The *Emory Women Writers Resource Project* (*EWWRP*) was established in 1994 as a means to expand the body of electronic materials related to women's writing, while providing graduate and undergraduate students with direct experience in the process of creating an archive. Many students have been involved in its development, through text selection, editing, encoding, filming, grant proposal writing, and other intellectual and technical contributions. Some students have graduated to faculty positions, some to librarianships or other careers, and many have published articles, given conference papers, and developed dissertation chapters drawn from their work with the *EWWRP*.

The evolving archive is available for free at http://womenwriters.library .emory.edu/. A digital collection of over three hundred female-authored and female-centered texts, the *EWWRP* includes genres such as recipe collections, travelogues, novels, romances, broadsides, plays, prophecies, and pamphlets, from the sixteenth to the early twentieth century, ranging in subject matter from Native American writers to World War I poets to suffragists, abolitionists, and early modern women writers. Intended initially for pedagogical use, the archive now offers local and international scholars and students the opportunity to use previously inaccessible resources for a variety of educational purposes.

This essay, cowritten by the *EWWRP* director, Sheila T. Cavanagh, and two former *EWWRP* graduate fellows, Gitanjali Shahani and Irene Middleton, describes some of the prominent practical and theoretical issues that emerged during the creation and development of this collection. One issue has been the complex relation between gender and genre as shaped by the scholarly world's growing access to early modern archives. It is through the archives that we sought access to women's writing and in the process discovered a variety of genres, including advice books, conduct manuals, recipe books, and diaries, that have revealed to us the minutiae of women's daily lives. Assessing the ways in which these texts have informed work on early modern material culture, we simultaneously draw attention to their absence in the undergraduate classroom—an omission that archives such as the *EWWRP* hope to repair.

We approach these issues through a thematic focus on early modern women's work, by which we mean their literary productions as well as their labors in other realms, such as the domestic or commercial. Our analysis deals with the configuration of the literary and the nonliterary in such diverse publication venues as advice manuals, pamphlets, and book-length translations. By reading these different categories together, we examine the competing and conflating narratives by which notions of gender were constructed and negotiated in the early modern period. Our discussion is framed by the larger pedagogical question of how we might deploy these diverse genres to shape students' understanding of gender in the early modern period. We propose a teaching model that makes the archive an integral part of the undergraduate classroom by drawing on material available through ready-made resources like *Early English Books Online* (*EEBO*) and *Eighteenth Century Collections Online* (*ECCO*), but we also suggest strategies for instructors to create their own resources in accordance with specific institutional goals. We seek to create a pedagogical template by which instructors can customize the canon as much as they customize the archive. Rather than have students and instructors work with the archive or the canon as monolithic categories, we argue that multiple archives and canons can flourish in a classroom. Such an approach encourages students to reflect on the complex processes by which female-authored and female-centered texts are retrieved and transmitted from past to present and on their shifting position in such categories as archive and canon.

The *EWWRP* was founded, in part, to give students a guided learning experience in creating and maintaining a digital archive. Cavanagh assigns digital critical editions in a graduate-level course, and Shahani and Middleton have prepared digital editions for the archive under her guidance and with the assistance of the Lewis H. Beck Center for Electronic Collections and Services. Undergraduates have participated in almost every aspect of the archive's growth. We draw from these experiences to discuss here the pedagogical possibilities and challenges of building a digital archive.

When students are assigned to edit a piece of women's writing that will go into the *EWWRP*, they first must consider the goals of the archive and determine what texts will complement the existing collection. Middleton's recent additions, for instance, increased its coverage of the sixteenth and seventeenth centuries and expanded the genres of the collection to include romances and translations. Each addition was considered carefully. When determining whether to edit and publish Margaret Tyler's translation *The First Part of the Mirrour of Princely Deeds and Knighthood* (1578?), by Diego Ortúñez de Calahorra, and Henry Cogan's 1652 translation of Madeleine de Scudéry's *Ibrahim; or, The Illustrious Bassa*, Middleton wondered whether works written by one sex and translated by the other fit a women writers' project. Including them allows both translators and authors to appear in the list of authors' names, suggesting that a translator too is an author. The decision to add these texts highlights the importance of translation for early modern female authors and the growing association of chivalric romances with female readers. These choices also enabled Middleton to think about the position of translators during this time and to explore women's reasons for choosing translation as their mode of creative expression. For instance, the translator of the *Mirrour* dedicates the book to her former employer's son; it is unclear what her role was in the household, but she describes herself as a former "servant" to the employer (ii [dedication]). Tyler asks her readers to excuse her unorthodox subject matter: "y^e rather for that it is a womans work, though in a story prophane, and a matter more manlike then becometh my sexe" (iii ["To the Reader"]). She also raises the question of whether it is right for her to have translated a romance rather than

> penning matters of great weight and sadnesse in diuinitie or other studies, the profession whereof more neerely beseemeth my yeares, other some discoursing of matters more easy & ordinary in common talke, where in a gentlewoman may honestly employ her trauaile.

She argues that although this was "worke put vpon me by others," that "yet bicause the refusall was in my power, I must stand to answere for my easy yelding" (iv). Her words express the conflicted views about women writing and translating that were prevalent during this time. Its inclusion in *EWWRP* expands the definition of *women's writing* in ways that early modern scholars have yet to fully theorize, as does *Ibrahim*, whose translator is male. Such expansion suggests that the pedagogical values of creating an archive are wide-ranging.

Students encountering such texts on a daily basis may find, as Middleton did, that understudied women's genres counter many expectations of canonical literature. She discovered, for example, that *Ibrahim* inverts the traditional relationship between maid and mistress by giving the maid a more significant voice. While the plot of this romance revolves around the mistress, editing the volume emphasizes the quantity of text given to the maid, since the servant narrates most of the mistress's story. Only with knowledge of the canon can a student recognize the novelty of an unfamiliar text. Middleton, in preparing her editions, became well versed in a range of topics related to women and writing in the early modern period, both in canonical and less studied texts.

Shahani, a Joan Gotwals Woodruff Library fellow assigned to the *EWWRP* in 2005, also had the opportunity to address complex questions about editing texts and creating an archive. Like Middleton, she added to the early modern collection. During her research, she became intrigued by the work of a number of lesser-known women writers, such as Hannah Woolley and Amelia Chambers. First published in 1670, Woolley's *The Queen-like Closet* promises to open up a "Rich Cabinet" stocked with a variety of hitherto secret recipes to "all ingenious persons of the FEMALE SEX" (title page). Woolley sees her task as one of national importance. "I have taken this pains to impart these things for the general good of my Country," she informs her readers. She is aware that many women have been "forced to serve" as a result of the "late Calamities, viz. the Late Wars, Plague, and Fire," and she seeks to equip them with the skills they will need for this service (378–79). Herself a victim of this fluctuating social order, Woolley clearly hopes to profit from sharing her household expertise. Her domestic manuals frequently promote her products and services "at reasonable Rates" (*Supplement* A8r). In "An Advertisment," which opens *A Supplement to* The Queen-like Closet (1674), she offers "any Gentlewoman or other Maids, who desire to go forth to Service" the benefit of her instructions and her letters of recommendation, all for "a reasonable Gratuity" (A8r). The manuals themselves function as commodities for sale in a marketplace, sales from which she expects to garner an income. As John Considine notes in his entry on Woolley in the *Oxford Dictionary of National Biography*, she was one of the first Englishwomen to make an income (albeit an uncertain one) through her writing.

Woolley's corpus of domestic manuals, conduct books, and recipe collections, now easily accessible through databases such as *EEBO*, has received some attention in early modern scholarship, particularly in the work of Elaine Hobby and Wendy Wall. Yet Woolley remains conspicuously absent in the classroom. As other nonliterary and noncanonical texts that archival recovery projects brought to our attention have been treated, it would seem that the worth of her work is more contextual than textual. Shahani's decision to make that work readily accessible for pedagogical use reflects the project's aim to expand the categories of texts that receive classroom scrutiny. It was from this perspective that Shahani focused on domestic manuals and recipe collections such as *The Ladies Best Companion*, by Chambers, and the anonymously written *The Accomplished Ladies Rich Closet of Rarities*. Shahani's first assignment involved browsing the *English Short Title Catalogue* (*ESTC*) for works that could enhance the collection's strengths. The texts were then digitally captured and transformed by optical character recognition (OCR) software. The final step involved coding the text in accordance with the guidelines laid out by the Text Encoding Initiative consortium. Wherever appropriate, spellings were modernized and annotations—etymological, contextual, and historical—were provided. Her objective was to create open-access, fully searchable digital editions of little-known genres such as the advice book and the domestic manual for use in a variety of pedagogical situations.

The search for texts led Middleton in a different direction. Instead of using the *ESTC*, she identified longer works that *EEBO* had photographed but not yet made searchable. These texts were also not on *EEBO*'s list of forthcoming works. She found that neither *Ibrahim* nor *Mirrour* has an edition easily used in the classroom. For *Mirrour*, she retyped the text, because OCR would not function with the original, poor-quality black-letter printing. For *Ibrahim*, she had digital photographs made of Emory's 1652 first edition, which were then put through OCR. Both texts were edited against the original images to ensure a high-quality transcription.

Few students at any level have experience with the process of scholarly editing. Cavanagh's graduate course, therefore, incorporates library sessions to help train students about the issues involved in text selection and electronic processing. To prepare a text for inclusion in a database, they learn how to provide annotations appropriate to their audience (whether to gloss or give contextual information, for example) and how to preserve the text electronically. Some students will be comfortable with technological tasks at the outset; others may be skilled in conceptualizing the needs of potential audiences for the text. Cavanagh finds that small-group work and shorter editing tasks encourage peers to share and develop their respective areas of strength. Learning this material in stages is also useful, as students are introduced first to theories of editing and annotation, then taught the methodologies of digitization. Since this project requires significant intellectual and technological expertise, collaboration with experts in the library and elsewhere is indispensable.

These assignments are challenging for both the students and the instructor, yet they offer new kinds of engagement with early modern texts. Faculty members must be prepared to sacrifice some of their students' knowledge of the canon in favor of an in-depth, analytic study of an unfamiliar text that opens up questions about other generic, authorial, and critical issues that are not traditionally part of early modern classroom discussions. Designing effective assessment can be difficult because the assignment combines group work, the exercise of technological skills, and the mastery of multiple contexts, only some of which may be evident in the final product. Although undergraduates may not edit at a level that merits inclusion in an archive, they can assist with many aspects of the editorial process in the classroom, as part of a team, or through one of an increasing number of undergraduate research opportunities. At Emory, for example, undergraduates work with faculty members and graduate students on such projects through the Scholarly Inquiry and Research at Emory (SIRE) program.

The training process at the Beck Center expands on traditional classroom experiences. It encourages students to reflect on the complex processes by which female-authored and female-centered texts are retrieved and transmitted from past to present and on their shifting position in such categories as the archive or the canon. The archival methods imparted by Cavanagh, the technical expertise provided by project managers, the daily access to library personnel and equipment, and the lengthy partnerships established between students and other project staff members all create pedagogical possibilities beyond the practical limits of the classroom. Yet the value of the initiative lies in the fact that the resulting

digital editions are immensely useful tools for the classroom, both graduate and undergraduate.

The process of editing and the subsequent availability of new electronic texts make it possible to test the viability of bringing seemingly unorthodox genres, works created by women for women, from the archive
into the classroom. Faculty members and students might start such a study
by asking a series of questions: Widely read and frequently printed in their
own time, how might texts like *The Queen-like Closet* find a place in the
classroom? How might we convey to students the importance of the ideas
of women's labor, female community, and domestic wisdom that emerge
from these texts? Can those ideas be used to enrich discussions of more
frequently taught genres, such as drama? Should the works created for
women by women be taught as literary genres in their own right? What
does the introduction of these texts into the classroom imply for the canon
as a whole? Is it feasible to disseminate these texts in institutions that have
neither access to *EEBO* and *ECCO* nor the means to facilitate student
travel to such institutions as the Folger, the Newberry, or the Huntington
libraries?

Projects like the *EWWRP* can foster a variety of teaching models. They
allow students to become involved in the process of building an archive
at the same time that they afford students easier access to archives. They
facilitate individual internship opportunities as much as they facilitate large
classroom situations in which instructors and students can readily draw on
texts created by women like Woolley, Chambers, and Tyler. They can lead
to dynamic collaboration between disciplines and departments in order to
take advantage of specific institutional strengths and meet specific institutional needs. Their benefits often go beyond the founding institution, as
is the case with the *EWWRP*, which Shahani continues to use in devising
courses at San Francisco State University, which does not have access to
*EEBO* or *ECCO*.

As we continue to consider the role of archives in early modern pedagogy, we might revisit the idea of labor with which Woolley opens her domestic manual. "I have taken pains to impart these things," she writes—a
sentiment echoed by Chambers at the start of her manual, written over a
century after *The Queen-like Closet* in 1775. "I have undertaken this work
for the use of my Countrywomen, and am well convinced that it will answer the most valuable purposes, let their situation in life be either high or
low," Chambers says of her efforts (iii–iv). Her labor, like that of Woolley's, is crucial in that it caters to, even creates, a skilled female labor force

in a newly emerging marketplace. The writer of the domestic manuals, as much as the maids and mistresses she addresses, provides an important service in this market. Part of our labor in recovering these works is to pay homage to their labor in creating it.

## Works Cited

*The Accomplished Ladies Rich Closet of Rarities*. London, 1696. Ed. Gitanjali Shahani. *Emory Women Writers Resource Project*. Emory U. Web. 17 Jan. 2014.

Chambers, Amelia. *The Ladies Best Companion*. London, 1775. Ed. Gitanjali Shahani. *Emory Women Writers Resource Project*. Emory U. Web. 17 Jan. 2014.

Considine, John. "Wolley, Hannah (*b.* 1622?, *d.* in or after 1674)." *Oxford Dictionary of National Biography*. Ed. H. C. G. Matthew and Brian Harrison. Oxford UP, n.d. Web. 11 Mar. 2007.

Hobby, Elaine. *Virtue of Necessity: English Women's Writings, 1649–88*. Ann Arbor: U of Michigan P, 1989. Print.

Scudéry, Madeleine de. *Ibrahim; or, The Illustrious Bassa: An Excellent New Romance: The Whole Work, in Foure Parts*. Trans. Henry Cogan. London, 1652. Ed. Irene Middleton. *Emory Women Writers Resource Project*. Emory U. Web. 17 Jan. 2014.

Tyler, Margaret, trans. *The Mirrour of Princely Deeds and Knighthood*. By Diego Ortúñez de Calahorra. London, [1578?]. Ed. Irene Middleton. *Emory Women Writers Resource Project*. Emory U, Dec. 2008. Web. 17 Jan. 2014.

Wall, Wendy. *Staging Domesticity: Household Work and English Identity in Early Modern Drama*. Cambridge: Cambridge UP, 2002. Print.

Woolley, Hannah. *The Queen-like Closet; or, Rich Cabinet: Stored with Rare Receipts for Preserving, Candying, and Cookery*. 1670. London, 1675. Print.

———. *A Supplement to* The Queen-like Closet. London, 1674. Print.

**Patricia Fumerton, Simone Chess,**
**Tassie Gniady, and Kris McAbee**

# The *English Broadside Ballad Archive*: From Theory to Practice

This collaborative essay addresses, in four distinct sections, the theoretical, technical, presentational, and pedagogical challenges and advantages that have arisen in the construction and implementation of an online scholarly database, the *English Broadside Ballad Archive* (*EBBA*), which is hosted by the University of California, Santa Barbara. The goal of *EBBA* is to make early modern broadside ballads (ballads printed on a single side of a large sheet of paper) fully accessible as texts, art, tunes, and cultural records of the period. *EBBA*'s team focuses on the seventeenth-century heyday of the ornamental black-letter or gothic typeface ballad, replete with tune title, but also includes in the archive rarer sixteenth-century broadside ballads (of which only about 250 survive) as well as representative ballads of the eighteenth century. Expanding *EBBA* to look back to the sixteenth century as well as forward into the eighteenth has the advantage of allowing us to trace the development of the broadside ballad into and out of its heyday period.

## The Theoretical Challenge: Access to Constructive Deconstruction

Creating *EBBA* involves grappling with numerous conceptual challenges and opportunities. As with many digital projects, we are motivated first and foremost by a desire to create accessibility. In the simplest terms, we want to give students, scholars, and the general public access to digital facsimiles (in many sizes) of the largely inaccessible collections of seventeenth-century broadside ballads, such as the approximately 1,800 ballads assembled by Samuel Pepys and held at Magdalene College, Cambridge, and the approximately 1,500 ballads in the Roxburghe collection held at the British Library, London (both collections are now fully archived).[1] Access to these collections is routinely denied by the holding libraries, even to experts in the field.

The *EBBA* team encountered two roadblocks to the archiving of these collections. First, both Pepys and the many collectors of the Roxburghe album books, in their desire to preserve ballad culture, often destroyed it. The collectors trimmed almost all their broadsides, then often cut in half single sheets with two parts printed on them. They would paste the separated parts onto separate but facing album pages, or, as in volume 2 of the Roxburghe albums, the right half of the ballad would be pasted below the left half on a single album page. The collectors were determined to make the ballads fit into their bound album books. In the Pepys collection, trimming, cutting, and pasting forced the broadside ballad to conform to his personal aesthetic of how a book should look (Sidgwick xvi).

Second, Pepys's five volumes and Roxburghe's four volumes, although they preserved the ballads' many ornamental woodcuts (which most nineteenth-century and modern editors do not), ripped the ballads from their musical and cultural contexts. Pasted into albums, the ballads live on as partial forms of their original textual and artistic artifacts but not as lived song and history, which was how they were perceived in their time.

What to do? Pepys and the many successive Roxburghe collectors (Robert Harley, first earl of Oxford; James West, president of the Royal Society; Thomas Pearson; John Ker, third duke of Roxburghe; and Benjamin Heywood Bright) were significant historical figures, and their act of collecting ballads reflects values that they held and that were shared by many of their contemporaries. Yet the complete artifact and cultural experience of the broadside ballad were destroyed by these collectors in the very act of collecting.

The *EBBA* ballad team has responded to this problem by engaging in constructive deconstruction.

Whenever possible, we faithfully reproduce the image of the individual album pages or background sheets onto which the trimmed and often cut ballads were pasted. For the Pepys ballads, we worked from microfilm provided by the Pepys Library. Unfortunately, at the time the microfilm was made in the 1980s, the album books were unbound in preparation for rebinding, so we do not have images of the bound album pages. But for the Roxburghe ballads we were able to provide color album page facsimile images, especially valuable because they clearly show where the original ballad ends and the album page onto which it was pasted begins (e.g., http://ebba.english.ucsb.edu/ballad/31610/album).

We then disassemble the Pepys and Roxburghe albums: that is, we virtually unglue the ballads from the album pages and put those that had been cut in two back together again, whether they were originally two-part ballads or two separate ballads printed on a single sheet. The resulting image is a much closer approximation to the printed ballads as they came off the press and as they would have been hawked on the streets in seventeenth-century England (e.g., http://ebba.english.ucsb.edu /ballad/31610/image).

We also deconstruct our facsimiles in a third rendering of the ballads and reconstruct them as artifacts available to the modern reader-viewer: we preserve all the ornament in the originals but transcribe the often difficult-to-read font (especially when it is black-letter or gothic) into easy-to-read white-letter or roman type (e.g., http://ebba.english.ucsb .edu/ballad/31610/transcription). For the modern reader, furthermore, we add background essays on seventeenth-century ballad culture and on the individual collections and their collectors.

We then reconstruct the music for the ballads, using accurate tunes whenever they are available, researched by our expert team of ethnomusicologists, so that the reader can hear the ballads as well as see and read them. Finally, we perform one more act of constructive deconstruction: we rerender the ballad citation information and ballad texts into XML that conforms with the Text Encoding Initiative (TEI) guidelines and into MARC (machine-readable cataloging) records, so that they will continue to be available for future generations of digital readers-viewers.

In the opinion of the *EBBA* team, if a digital archive is to make traditional archives fully accessible, it must engage in such constructive deconstruction. Only then does the archive become fully alive.

## Digital Collecting: Creating a New Archive with Every Search

One of the curious aspects of creating digital facsimiles of the broadside ballads is the way in which digital archiving mirrors physical collecting. Our server houses all the images, citation data, tunes, and transcriptions in separate folders, much as the ballads were collected in separate volumes. However, the data are brought together by a *MySQL* (structured query language) server database that is accessed through PHP (hypertext preprocessor) pages on the Web, so that the archive is deconstructed and reconstructed differently for each user, each time a search is performed. For example, Pepys divided his collection not only into five albums but also into ten categories and a "Promiscuous Supplement." Should a user search for the Pepys category "Devotion and Morality," the results combine the ballads from volumes 1 and 2 that come under that heading, so that the user has crossed the volume boundary. The Roxburghe collection, reflecting its many owners, was constructed and reconstructed many times according to different schema, but on *EBBA* the user may create a tailored miniarchive of sorts. A broad keyword search may be refined by customization on the advanced search page, or an interest in a specific ballad may be broadened to include other ballads with similar aspects through any number of avenues, from a shared printer to a tune to a woodcut key word. For example, a search for *monster* brings up twenty-four results across all five volumes in the Pepys collection and two different printings of the same ballad in one volume in the Roxburghe collection.

To narrow the scope of this search, we might focus on one ballad that is multiply extant (http://ebba.english.ucsb.edu/ballad/20691/image). Entitled "Pride's Fall; or, A Warning for All English Women," the ballad details the trials of a vain merchant's wife who gives birth to a monster manifesting all the worst aspects of womanly pride. Of the three variants in *EBBA* at the time of this writing, two locating the birth in Geneva were issued by different printers (Pepys 2.66–67 and Roxburghe 3.64–65), whereas a Viennese modification to the story does not identify the printer (Roxburghe 3.806–07). All three editions use the same illustration depicting a pride-produced monster (described with a masculine pronoun in the text but costumed in all the most ostentatious male and female fashions of the day). This search identifies a ballad that must have been extremely popular, as it is estimated that only ten percent of ballads have survived, and these three variants, in addition to another edition with a different woodcut (in *EEBO* and held by the Bodleian Library), constitute a minicollection from which we may begin to hypothesize about the placement, categorization (in Pepys's case), and transmission history of one particular ballad. We could go on to look at other ballads concerning pride or fashion, or we could look at the conjunction of the word *monster* with other ballads dealing with childbirth.

Without the electronic resources of *EBBA* and *EEBO* it would be extremely difficult to make such connections. Even if a scholar wanted to trace the history of "Pride's Fall" through the Stationers' Register, only two entries can be found. This paucity of register entries supports Tessa Watt's assertion, in her book *Cheap Print and Popular Piety*, that only about sixty-five percent of ballads were registered (42). A scholar without access to expansive electronic sources would be hard-pressed to create these kinds of miniarchives or groupings, whatever their scope—from finding all the extant editions of one ballad to creating a compendium reflecting a particular researcher's interests in broadside ballad culture. Thus, by simply searching and researching the *EBBA* site to find ballads that fit their interests, scholars may reveal trends about ballad culture generally that would have been difficult to discern through the use of printed materials, and scholars may go on to create miniarchives meeting any number of needs.

## Presentational Approaches: Where Old Meets New

Today's digital archive of ballads mimics early modern ballad culture in many ways. Early modern collecting practices, such as Pepys's, are rearticulated in *EBBA*'s collection in the discrete categories of a database. Simply reading the ballads through *EBBA* is surprisingly analogous to the consumption of ballads in the early modern period. Reading through a digital interface, as Roger Chartier points out, is a "discontinuous reading process," based on fragmentary bits of information such as keyword searches or smaller pieces of information rather than on a coherent whole (142). Patricia Fumerton argues that this fragmentary nature of reading in a digital archive "actually approximates the early modern period's own access to its printed materials, which was never itself 'whole.'" The two ends of the historical spectrum thus come together. Their points of contact offer an effective strategy for making an archive like *EBBA* comprehensible to a wide audience, in which some people may have a better understanding of digital accessibility and others more knowledge of early modern textuality.

To be a viable and productive resource for a variety of students, a digital archive of early modern texts must be introduced in a way that navigates the complexities of providing a set of early modern material through state-of-the-art technology. Because to many students ballads are a genre that is unfamiliar and seems out of place in an academic context as well as in a technologically sophisticated context and because *EBBA*'s philosophy of constructive deconstruction may be too theoretically complex for most students, who know little about archival methods, strategies must be developed for introducing *EBBA* in the classroom. How does one explain what ballads are in a way that is succinct but captures their multifaceted nature? How might the use of a digital archive appeal to students interested in early modern literature? Discussing not only the connection between the historical and modern consumption of ballads but also how the creation and maintenance of the archive mimics the material production of ballads in the early modern period provides a way to introduce the archive and point to its use as a window to the early modern world.

To present *EBBA*, which has a number of interrelated elements designed for enhancing accessibility to the central texts, it is wise to start by walking the audience through the basic features of the site. Because ballads have been traditionally dismissed as objects of study, they require some basic introduction, and although many students are digitally savvy, few understand how to use a digital archive or translate experience from personal computer use to an academic task. Introducing the fundamentals of broadside ballads and introducing the features of a digital platform can be accomplished together as one clicks through the offerings of the site. Starting with collecting practices and the album page and moving to ballad facsimiles and format, facsimile transcriptions and black-letter font, recordings and ballad tunes, a demonstration that culminates with TEI XML encoding and the archive's search function builds on the lessons that each site feature teaches about ballad artifacts. This approach emphasizes the synergy between the curatorial goals of the early modern literature scholar and the skills of the Web programmer and designer.

After reviewing the different ways to access a text (album facsimile, ballad facsimile, facsimile transcription, tune recording, text transcription), one can step back and demonstrate the power of the search function. Examples that provide comparison across several texts can offer nuanced lessons about the ballads themselves. An advanced search by the key word *punishment*, in the most recent expansion of the archive, yielded

401 hits. Scrolling through these hits, one notices several similar woodcut impressions appearing many times, especially of women being burned at the stake for the crime of husband murder. Such depictions appear in a cluster of four ballads from the Pepys collection:

1.118–19 (http://ebba.english.ucsb.edu/ballad/20049/image)
1.120–21 (http://ebba.english.ucsb.edu/ballad/20050/image)
1.122–23r (http://ebba.english.ucsb.edu/ballad/20051/image)
1.124–25 (http://ebba.english.ucsb.edu/ballad/20053/image)

Their grouping evidences a subgenre of ballads, the good-night ballad, in which a criminal about to be executed laments his or her crime. (This popular form of ballad was frequently written in advance of an actual execution and sold at the event.) Variants of the same illustration appear in Pepys 1.120–21, "A Warning for All Desperate Women," and 1.124–25, "Anne Wallens Lamentation," demonstrating how the same or similar woodcuts were recycled. Such miniature lessons about early modern ballad culture result from demonstrations of special aspects of the digital archive.

## Pedagogical Approaches: Into the Undergraduate Classroom and Beyond

*EBBA* is an excellent testing ground for the theoretical, technical, and presentational questions that are increasingly emerging as technology becomes a more central part of early modern research. It can also serve as an invaluable resource for teachers. Broadside ballads, because they have for so long been hard to access and because of their status as cheap print ephemera, have traditionally been excluded from syllabi. Even if one wanted to include a ballad in a lesson plan or lecture, it is often unavailable in a version suitable for students (i.e., clean, legible). Ballads are rarely included in anthologies, and there are few edited print collections of them a teacher can use. But now that digitization projects like *EBBA* are making them easily accessible to scholars and students alike, what is the best way for us to bring ballads into the undergraduate classroom? How can students engage with them as material artifacts while at the same time considering them as texts? More broadly, how can ballads in the classroom inform the ways that we teach the early modern period?

Once students become comfortable with a digital archive, instructors can use *EBBA* in at least four major ways: to expand students' understanding of major cultural and historical themes of the early modern period, to encourage students to consider the canon from a new perspective, to expand their understanding of material print culture, and to enable them to find something new through their own research. These overlapping goals are evident in the following short examples of the successful use of ballads—and digital archives—in the classroom.

A discussion about gender politics in the early modern period might be enhanced by a look at the many ballads related to gender roles and to the status of women. A quick *EBBA* search for *women* shows a lesson on the taming of scolds (Pepys 1.454 ["The Cucking of a Scould"]); a report on witches (1.132–33 ["Damnable Practises / Of three Lincolnshire Witches"]); a discussion of women's pride (4.152 ["The Invincible Pride of Women"]); a defense of the often maligned women's fashion of wearing topknots (4.367 ["The Women and Maiden's Vindication of Top-Knots"]); a treatise for young maids, with instructions on choosing a husband (5.228 ["The Crafty Maid's Invention"]); and a lamentation about marrying the wrong wife (1.380–81 ["The Lamentation of a New Married Man"]), among many other topics. The sheer multiplicity of surviving ballads, combined with their frank discussion of many issues, makes them ideal jumping-off places for exciting classroom conversation. There are certainly other kinds of texts that touch on themes related to women's lives in the early modern period, but this array of entertaining and pithy ballads draws students into details of early modern culture and history. *EBBA* contains hundreds of ballads reporting on historic battles (Pepys 2.337 ["The Glory of Flanders"]), wars (2.276 ["The Triumph of Ireland"]), political decisions (2.374 ["Great Britain's Triumph"]), monarchs (2.233 ["A Loyal Song on King James"]), laws (4.309 ["The Chimney-Men's Grief"]), crimes (2.156 ["The Bloody Miller"]), and so forth. These short accounts of real occurrences can add to the data available from histories and other sources, and sometimes they provide several versions of the same event from different perspectives or in different narrative styles.

Ballads can not only complement lessons about cultural and historical issues but also serve as provocative companion pieces for canonical texts. Teaching *The Taming of the Shrew*, a teacher can call up a ballad from *EBBA* that tells its own version of the induction story of the play (Pepys 4.235 ["The Frolicksome Duke"]). The ballad informs the play and refocuses discussion toward the play's often overlooked induction. The *EBBA* collection has ballad versions of *Titus Andronicus* (Roxburghe 1.392–93; Pepys 1.86 and 2.184–85) and *King Lear* (Roxburghe 3.275).[2] Using ballads as complements to texts by canonical writers like Shakespeare allows students to compare famous works with those that are anonymous or written by obscure authors and therefore to get a sense of what rhetorical and stylistic choices make a well-known author different. The interplay and overlap between cheap and canonical can also open up discussions about influence, interpretation, genre, class, and audience. A comparative close reading of a part of a commonly taught text, such as the play within a play in *A Midsummer Night's Dream*, and a related ballad, such as Pepys 3.346, "Pyramus and Thisbe," can lead to rich discoveries for students. Further, this sort of investigation may unsettle familiar ideas about what marks literature and the literary and get students to think about what makes a text good or important.

Searchable digital archives can offer more in teaching than just a broader range of primary sources. The archive reminds students that early modern texts are also artifacts. Because of the archive's preservation of the entire ballad—text, woodcuts, tune, and information about provenance and the state of the ballad in a collection—*EBBA* lends itself to assignments that hone in on materiality and print culture. In one recent courtly literature course, a professor required that students search for ballads and fully annotate them into a scholarly edition complete with glossary, preface, and critical apparatus. The class's work was collected into an anthology, and there was a final capstone discussion about the differences between high courtly lyric and low ballad.[3] Other assignments could demand that students look closely at layout, woodcuts, and ornamental flourishes or at how collectors modified the ballads in their collections. Through assignments like these, students can learn the differences between edited and unedited texts and begin to consider material context as part of a text's meaning. *EBBA*'s recordings of ballad tunes remind students of orality and authorial intent; through hearing the music, they recognize that some texts are meant to be changed.

The search function of *EBBA* allows students to research and find ballads on their own, which gives them tremendous academic independence. Though most undergraduates cannot search the collections at rare-book libraries, they can experience the excitement and generative process of working with a large archive by mastering a digital archive. The openness of a real search mechanism means that undergraduates and researchers alike can stumble on important and never-before-studied primary sources. Because *EBBA* also allows students to see individual texts as intertwined, by revealing the connecting strands of recurring tunes, woodcuts, and themes, students can make connections between their new discoveries in an organic way that enables creativity and innovation. In this way, the modern interface of the *EBBA* collection makes old-fashioned archival research and discovery possible even for undergraduates.

We hope to provide a holistic vision of the challenges and opportunities that arise in creating an archive like *EBBA*. From the initial and ongoing theoretical questions that have shaped the format of the site, to the technical details that allow it to provide a new level of searchable and interactive digital material, to the ways that the site can be presented to users from all backgrounds and the ways that it can be applied particularly in the classroom, *EBBA* functions simultaneously as an early modern and modern cultural experience. The kinds of questions that we had to ask in creating *EBBA*, and the kinds of applications to research and teaching that we've already seen, reflect its place as a model for digitization projects, databases, and new media in early modern studies. By making the archive compliant with the TEI guidelines for XML, linked, and multiply searchable, we offer a level of access to cheap print broadside ballads that is remarkably current and always evolving as the technology evolves. By preserving as much evidence as possible of the material conditions of the ballads as they were collected, we also maintain a connection to the entire history of the ballads, from printing to collecting to archiving. The research and teaching possibilities of *EBBA* are vast; we have already seen an explosion of references to ballads in both research and teaching since the project's inception, and we expect to hear more about ballads in early modern studies as access continues to grow. In this way, through the very modern mechanism of the digital archive, broadside ballads are once again circulating as they originally did in the early modern period: cheaply, widely, and with reverberation.

## Notes

1. *EBBA* continues to expand, with new ballad collections and unassembled ballads being regularly added. But this essay confines itself mainly to the state of the database at the completion of the archiving only of the Pepys and Roxburghe collections. The Pepys Ballads at Magdalene College, Cambridge University, are cited throughout by volume, followed by page number. This procedure is also used to call up ballads at the Pepys Library, rather than by shelf mark. The four volumes of the Roxburghe Ballads at the British Library are contained within five physical volumes (volume 3 is divided into two separate books, numbered consecutively). Individual ballads, as with the Pepys, are cited by volume and page number.

However, the individual volumes of the Roxburghe Ballads also have their own shelf marks, ranging from C.20.f.7 for volume 1 to C.20.f.10 for volume 4.

2. For an in-depth discussion of Shakespeare's plays and their ballads, see Smith; Chess.

3. We are indebted to Simone Chess's colleague Jaime Goodrich, who taught this course using *EEBO*. An assignment of this kind is especially well suited to *EBBA*'s large database of ballads.

## Works Cited

Chartier, Roger. "Languages, Books, and Reading from the Printed Word to the Digital Text." Trans. Teresa Lavender Fagan. *Critical Inquiry* 31 (2004): 133–52. Print.

Chess, Simone. "Shakespeare's Plays and Broadside Ballads." *Literature Compass* 7.9 (2010): 773–85. Print.

Fumerton, Patricia. "Remembering by Dismembering: Databases, Archiving, and the Recollection of Seventeenth-Century Broadside Ballads." *Bringing Text Alive: The Future of Scholarship, Pedagogy, and Electronic Publication.* Ed. Shawn Martin. Spec. issue of *Early Modern Literary Studies* 14.2 (2008): n. pag. Web. 13 Mar. 2010.

Pepys Ballads. 5 vols. Magdalene Coll., Cambridge U, Cambridge. Print.

Roxburghe Ballads. 4 vols. in 5. British Lib., London. Print.

Sidgwick, F. Introduction. *Bibliotecha Pepysiana: A Descriptive Catalogue of the Library of Samuel Pepys.* London: Sidgwick, 1914. v–viii. Print.

Smith, Bruce. "Shakespeare's Residuals: The Circulation of Ballads in Cultural Memory." *Shakespeare and Elizabethan Popular Culture.* Ed. Stuart Gillespie and Neil Rhodes. London: Arden Shakespeare–Thomson Learning, 2006. 193–246. Print.

Watt, Tessa. *Cheap Print and Popular Piety, 1550–1640.* Cambridge: Cambridge UP, 1991. Print.

**Janelle Jenstad**

# Restoring Place to the Digital Archive: *The Map of Early Modern London*

A quick look at the *Oxford English Dictionary* (*OED*) shows that the term *archive* derives ultimately from the Greek ἀρχεῖον (*archeion*), meaning "magisterial residence," or place of government. My first experience of archival research took place at the Guildhall Library in London, an ἀρχεῖον in the original sense: on one side of the building, the Corporation of London conducted its daily business; on the other, researchers dug into its past. Trying to historicize references to merchants and goldsmiths in early modern city comedies, I read gossipy accounts of seventeenth-century guild business. While buying my lunch, I rubbed shoulders with the bankers of modern London. Then, in the early dusk of London winters, I walked the streets once inhabited by the men and women I studied, recognizing street names and building a mental map of my subjects' lives in Milk Lane, Cheapside, Paul's Chain, or Silver Street. The experience was synesthetic—and profoundly formative for a Canadian graduate student.

Today, an archive is both a place that preserves documents and the documents contained therein. With the advent of digitization, archival materials are increasingly detached from the ἀρχεῖον. My students do not need to be in London to read the print and manuscript traces of the early modern city. Having access to such archival riches changes the nature of their research in profound and positive ways, but digital archives do not help them build the spatial knowledge that I acquired by walking. To meet the challenge of teaching a body of literature peculiarly embedded in time and place to students who are neither of that time nor of that place, I developed *The Map of Early Modern London* (*MoEML*), which uses the capacities of digital media to re-create the archive in the sense of "place."[1] Taking a 1560s woodcut map of London as its platform, the site supports multiple layers of data and interpretation. All the pages in the site—encyclopedia-style descriptions of streets and sites, diplomatic transcriptions of texts about London, literary references, and editions of peripatetic texts—are linked to and from points on the map through underlying Text Encoding Initiative (TEI) markup that labels every street, site, church, ward, neighborhood, tavern, theater, company hall, identifiable person, civic institution, and primary or secondary source.[2] As contributors, research assistants, and technical assistants, undergraduate and graduate students have been involved in every aspect of creating the site, drawing on various archival sources to re-create the place of early modern London literature and culture both for themselves and for other students of the period.[3] Over the past decade, I have incorporated *MoEML* into my teaching of undergraduate courses on Shakespeare, Renaissance drama, and London studies and of graduate courses on London. In this essay I document the archival nature of the site, its current goals, and its pedagogical history and reflect on the place of students in the project's history. Even for readers who are not going to build databases, I want to stress by example the value of involving students in our research and encouraging them to think about their work as having real utility for scholars.

Civitas Londinum, or the Agas Map, first drawn in the 1560s, survives in three early-seventeenth-century copies, one of which was hanging in the manuscript room of the Guildhall Library when I was a graduate student researcher.[4] When I took a break from reading the manuscript records of various livery companies, I would stand before the map and travel the streets of sixteenth-century London in my mind, building a mental map of space, buildings, inhabitants, and historical events. As an archival document, it is a powerful tool for introducing London as an *urbs* (an aggregate of buildings; see Kagan 75), although the people of London are little in evidence (Jenstad). The map is useful not just because it spans London from the Tower to Westminster but also because it gives a vivid sense of the river traffic, the docks, the houses, the buildings, and the surrounding landscape. Wanting to share this evocative archival treasure with my students, I returned to Canada with photocopies of the seven woodcut sheets, assembled them into a poster six feet two inches long, covered them with adhesive shelf liner, and unfurled the map in many class sessions, drawing on it with soluble markers whenever I wanted to make a point about how London figured in the literature we were studying.

*The Map of Early Modern London* succeeded my low-tech efforts with markers. Through all its technological incarnations, the site's primary purpose has been to take the streets, buildings, monuments, and topography of London as the cataloging principle for an archive of texts and to provide for each place on the map a thick description that is both literary and historical. While the site itself is an archive—a database that is queried every time a page is rendered by someone's browser—it is an archive of marked-up transcriptions, editions, essays, and concordances, not of primary document images. The design of the project takes its inspiration from John Stow's *A Survey of London* (1598), whose purpose is to gather together the "originall, antiquity, encrease, moderne estate, *and description of that Citie*" (1: 1). Stow's labors were timely, for London's population quadrupled between 1500 and 1600, mainly because of immigration (Beier and Finlay 2–4). Many of his readers were, like my students, newcomers to London; few remembered the monuments that had perished or knew the history of those that had survived. The method Stow used was to read widely in the archive of papers that he collected and sometimes shared with other antiquarians, then organize this information into a ward-by-ward westward peripatetic. He walks the reader through each street along the horizontal axis of space, pausing at points of interest to traverse the vertical axis of history. He describes first his world (the rapidly growing "moderne estate"), then the world that was lost even then (the "originall" and antique). Although notorious for its calculated omissions and nostalgic coloring (Archer; Collinson 27–28), Stow's *Survey* does create a shared cultural memory by providing along that vertical axis a great deal of information about London's past, in the form of descriptions, etymologies, catalogs, narratives, lists, and chronologies.

*The Map of Early Modern London* likewise has two axes. Civitas Londinum is the horizontal axis of the project, on which streets, sites, churches, and wards are identified. The information and texts linked to the map form the vertical axis of history and narrative. The Encyclopedia tab leads to a descriptive gazetteer of streets, churches, sites, wards, livery companies, neighborhoods, and topographic features; to a database of historical and fictional people mentioned in the site; and to a glossary of topics and terms. The Library tab leads to diplomatic transcriptions of texts rich in London place references, an anthology of all the Elizabethan and Jacobean mayoral shows, and royal entries.[5] The Topics tab leads to articles on issues, people, and terms that recur throughout the site. The Stow tab will lead to all four editions of Stow's *Survey* (1598, 1603, 1618, and 1633) and tools for versioning and comparing the four editions. All these pages are linked to the map and to one another. Eventually Civitas Londinum will be linked to other historical maps and to a modern ordnance survey map by the technique of georeferencing points on all the maps and loading them into a GIS (geographic information system) program, so that the vertical axis will also be cartographic.

The most important component of the history-and-narrative axis is the descriptive gazetteer of locations. The essays focus on the period 1550 to 1650 but gesture backward and forward in time. We try to describe the past as Stow represents it, as Londoners knew it (the two are not always the same), and as modern historians and archaeologists have reconstructed it. We try to give a sense of what happened to a site in the Great Fire of 1666, the first of three reshaping events (the others are Victorian rebuilding and the Blitz), and of what is located there today, although historical GIS projects coming online will make it less necessary for us to provide a longer historical view.[6] The essays draw on various archival, early literary, and secondary historical sources, most of them digital.

In writing essays for our archive, we try to balance sources usually available only in academic libraries or through university library portals (*The Oxford Dictionary of National Biography*, the *OED*) with those freely available, such as the *Internet Shakespeare Editions*. Stow's *Survey* is the most important primary resource.[7] Until our own versioned edition of all the 1598, 1603, 1618, and 1633 *Survey* editions is available, Stow is available in various electronic forms. Our text of the 1598 *Survey* (STC 23341) is available on our site under the Stow tab. The 1908 Kingsford modernized edition of the 1603 second edition (STC 23343) has become available at *British History Online*, a nonsubscription database. Stow's *Survey* was updated periodically by other authors; comparing the various incarnations of the *Survey* is a useful way of tracking the history of a site or street.[8] We look primarily at the 1633 edition updated by Anthony Munday and Humphrey Dyson (STC 23345.5; transcribed by the Text Creation Partnership) and John Strype's 1720 post–Great Fire *Survey*, which incorporates Stow and usefully comments on changes since Stow's day; Strype is available in a fine electronic edition by Julia Merritt of the Stuart London

Project. Another digital resource we consult regularly is Richard W. Bailey, Marilyn Miller, and Colette Moore's edition of BL MS Cotton Vitellius F.v (popularly known as Henry Machyn's Diary [Machyn]). Searching records and full-text transcriptions in *EEBO* yields both the addresses of printers and booksellers and textual references that help us establish how a street or site figures in the cultural imagination. Most students will gravitate toward dramatic or poetic references, but some will dive gamely into religious or historiographic texts and teach themselves to read black-letter type. *British History Online* is a rich repository of secondary sources, many of them rare or long out of print despite their importance to London studies. Students might ignore these old books in a library, but digitization gives the books a legitimacy and accessibility that attracts them.

In the course of their research, students learn how to search effectively in a variety of databases, distinguish between primary and secondary sources, compare transcriptions to page images, and cite from early books. That these databases and other sources are listed in the guidelines given under the tab Contribute on *MoEML* obscures the extent to which students have expanded the critical range of the site. Each student has added items to the bibliography, which then becomes a better London bibliography for subsequent contributors.[9] Over time, contributors' essays have developed from redactions of a few print sources available in most university print reference collections to sophisticated syntheses and analyses of a wide range of print and archival sources, such as Marina Devine's essay "Cheapside Cross (Eleanor Cross)."

Students have often been the impetus for a new phase of *The Map of Early Modern London*. The first digitization of the map was made in 1999, by three undergraduate students who needed a project and a client in Writing Hypertext, a course at the University of Windsor.[10] Although at that time HTML (hypertext markup language) encoding and image markup tools were still relatively exotic in academia (and completely beyond my experience), I gave these three students the laminated map and wondered aloud if they could turn it into a digital map with hyperlinked streets. The project has been rebuilt four times with new technologies,[11] each incarnation refining the placement of map identifications[12] and adding new analytic and linking capabilities, but the goals I set in 1999 still pertain: to give historical information on landmarks that are relevant to the study of early modern London and situate them geographically on the contemporary rendering of the city known as the Agas map. Once the prototype was running on an intranet server at Windsor, I invited students to contribute projects that had some relevance to London culture. After a few early experiments that had students doing their own encoding and Web design, I learned that it was better to ask them to focus on the research and writing. Encoding took time away from the literary-critical and research outcomes for the course, the product did not always fit the Web site's style, and ultimately I felt unqualified to grade coding and design. The most enduring project format has proved to be three or more linked pages of historical background, followed by application to a literary or dramatic text. Laura Estill's 2003 piece on Whitefriars Theatre was a particularly successful example of a project emerging from a Renaissance drama course. The historical pages provided the context that allowed Estill to read *Epicoene* as a product for and of a particular theatrical market.

Because I did not set out to teach courses on London, early projects tended to deal with playhouses and playgoing.[13] I thought that the encyclopedia-style pages at the heart of the project were too important to be written by students and that the street and site essays ought to be written by me or other scholars, but the magnitude of the task meant that most of the links from the students' projects were pointing to blank placeholder pages containing only a map link.[14] The site was not yet fulfilling its mandate of giving historical information on landmarks. My students at Windsor, aware of the growing imbalance in the intranet site, came up with the solution themselves. One remarkable day, I was called to a meeting with my research assistant (Tara Drouillard) and the manager of the Hypertext Lab (Michael Davis). They made a strong case that I should teach a course on London and assign students the task of writing up street and site descriptions. At their urging, I proposed an honors seminar titled Representations of Early Modern London and required of each student two pages suitable for the *Map of Early Modern London* Web site. About half the pages produced by that 2002 class were publishable, and of those about half have been reencoded in XML (extensible markup language); examples are "Aldgate" and "Aldgate Ward," by Lacey Marshall, and "The Strand," by Neil Baldwin. The pages were welcome additions to the site, although all redact only secondary sources and Stow's *Survey*, in keeping with what was available at the time. I repeated the exercise in a graduate seminar at the University of Victoria in 2008, this time testing nascent versions of *MoEML*'s contributor guidelines. Devine's superb "Eleanor Cross" was a product of that course, as are the current guidelines, which I revised and expanded as I was marking the students' submissions. In the end, then, students have been key in developing the current format of the street and site essays that I was once reluctant to charge them with. Comparing "Abchurch Lane" (Jenstad and Chernyk) with "Billiter Lane" (Jenstad and St. Clair) will indicate the extent to which students like Devine, Amy Collins ("Pudding Lane"), Paisley Mann ("Love Lane, Thames Street"), and Paul Hartlen ("Tower Street") have raised the bar for contributions to the site.

Projects continue to be a major way in which undergraduates and graduates alike augment the vertical axis of the Web site and add depth to the thick description that *MoEML* tries to provide for each point on Civitas Londinum. Students have provided diplomatic transcriptions of early texts (Chernyk), compilations of London references in plays (Mann, "Extracts"), editions of street performances (Marshall and Campbell), biographies of early modern Londoners (of which Lo's splendid work "Henslowe's Diary" offers several examples), and explanations of terms that appear throughout the Web site (e.g., Mead-Willis). Beth Norris's "London Aliens" addresses an urban challenge that Stow overlooks, while Tara Drouillard's "Executions" and "The Prison System" explain some of the ways in which order was imposed on an often unruly urban population. Such projects—each with every street, site, and person tagged—form a complexly linked archive of primary texts and critical essays about London and a dynamic archive of literary references to specific places.

The importance of students to *The Map of Early Modern London* is clear. But how have the students themselves benefited from being contributors? Their understanding of textual cultures and generic conventions certainly changes when they confront the early print materials that inform their assignments, and they are better historicists for having read some of the nonliterary texts that dominate the early modern discursive field. They learn to research to the point of redundancy, to assess the credentials of their sources, and to distinguish primary from secondary sources and bibliographies from archives—skills that we all try to teach in different ways. But the principal benefit derives from their being treated as scholars and collaborators. Estill, who was a second-year student when she wrote the project on the Whitefriars,[15] writes that "working on the Map . . . made me feel like a scholar and pushed me to take my research skills to the next level" (Letter). Another student in Estill's class, Christopher Lawrence Menard, observes that *MoEML* "allowed us [even students who did not contribute directly] to feel a part of something bigger than ourselves." I have potential contributors submit a proposal, a site map listing pages and diagramming the links between them, and a writing sample before

I invite them to produce a major project in lieu of the standard research essay. The proposal anticipates later aspects of their scholarly lives (thesis prospectuses, fellowship applications, conference paper proposals), and its formal nature sets the tone for the level of work required. My feedback on structure and sources invites them into a scholarly dialogue and anticipates (in a small way) the peer review process.

Student contributors have always done far more research than is required for a term paper and take ownership of their writing in ways they do not when the assignment is a terminal exercise. After I have graded and returned a project, I issue a formal invitation to the student to publish his or her work on the Web site. The student and I then work together on revisions. The document will go back and forth between us as an e-mail attachment several times (exactly as in a revise-and-resubmit scenario), but the key part of the process is a coediting session in which we sit down together at one computer with two screens and two keyboards. While the session will explicitly address each student's particular learning needs (style, grammar, structure, integration of sources), the dynamic shifts quickly from teacher-student to editor-contributor. Such one-on-one teaching and mentoring is labor-intensive but immensely and immediately rewarding. I might correct a stylistic infelicity on the first page, the student will identify a similar problem on the second page, and by page 3 the student is typing in a revision before I have even read the page.

Students' taking ownership of their writing is intimately connected to their awareness of audience. Estill writes, "*The Map of Early Modern London* gave me an audience to write for and showed me that there could be real purpose for scholarly writing" (Letter). Web analytics software makes it possible to track some information about our readership: the more than 450,000 hits and 350,000 page requests per month come from over thirty countries; fewer than half the requests come from the .edu or .ac domains, which suggests that most of our American and British readers do not have university library cards. Students therefore perceive their work to be highly visible and take seriously their responsibility to the site's users. They owe scholars and other students the best scholarship available; they owe general users (many of whom are referred to *MoEML* by *Wikipedia*) a fair and accessible redaction of sources that are otherwise not available to them. In collating those sources and organizing the information gleaned therein, they learn something about the biases and narrative qualities of history, literary or otherwise. All contributors have to confront Stow's biases, even as they rely on Stow as a source and follow in his footsteps. Reading histories as they construct them makes them think about themselves as consumers and producers of the past. This awareness is reflected in the many essays that take their sources not as repositories of facts about London but as representations of London to be analyzed, compared, and contextualized.

When the site was launched on the Internet in 2006, my programmers and I needed to make a decision about the placement of student work in the site structure. From 2006 until 2010, students' projects were grouped under a tab entitled "Student Work." Segregating their work impaired the functioning of some searches and meant that valuable information was not immediately accessible from the map (the entry page for most visitors to the site). In 2010, all the students' contributions were transferred to the encyclopedia and library. Allowing student work to co-exist with the work of scholars enriches *MoEML*. Pages are labeled as a student project or graduate student project, but these labels function in part to put the contributor's work in the context of his or her career. Many student contributors have pursued graduate studies (or further graduate studies, if they were MA students), and some have entered the profession. While they are welcome to revise their projects and submit them for peer review, most seem content to let their work stand as evidence of early promise.

Anecdotal evidence and student feedback suggest that working on *The Map of Early Modern London* has been formative for students, just as my early research trips to London were for me. Although I designed the site for students who might never walk the streets of modern London or visit its libraries in search of the past, it is a happy fact that many contributors have eventually made their own pilgrimage to London. A few, like Lo, have even gone there to learn more about the people and texts they first studied for *MoEML*. Walking London's horizontal axis virtually on the site cannot entirely substitute for walking the streets. But it is also true that the streets of modern London have little in common—other than names, directions, and endpoints—with the streets of early modern London and that walking the streets now will not give one much sense of what transpired there in the past. I occasionally receive e-mail messages from people who have wandered around London while reading *MoEML* pages on a mobile device. If my students' work can be put to such uses, then they have truly re-created a historic place through a virtual archive.

## Notes

1. I have been using this hyperlinked map for various pedagogical purposes since 1999. It was made publicly accessible in 2006 at http://mapoflondon.uvic.ca.

2. We assign a unique ID to each of these items and mark up the items using a tag set derived from the Text Encoding Initiative.

3. Information about the research assistants and technical assistants can be found on the site (click on "About"). I focus here on students as contributors.

4. The map is now held at the London Metropolitan Archives.

5. Eventually, we will offer a complete edition of Stow's *Survey*, transcriptions of all the extant mayoral shows, and transcriptions from John Taylor's *Works*.

6. The most important venture is "Locating London's Past: A Geo-referencing Tool for Mapping Historical and Archaeological Evidence, 1660–1800," a collaboration of the Humanities Research Institute at the University of Sheffield, the Institute for Historical Research, and other parties.

7. Stow is such an important source that we will eventually provide a complete edition of the *Survey* that is marked up and keyed to the map.

8. See the list of editions in Mann, "Survey."

9. In 2013, we began adding a responsibility statement for each new item in the "Sources" database, as a way of acknowledging the sleuth work that goes into tracking down new sources.

10. The University of Windsor's English 26-208, Writing Hypertext, was designed and taught by Colin Atkinson, now retired. The three students were Jeremy Fairall, Matt MacTavish, and Dominic Carlone.

11. The redesign and reencoding were conducted at the University of Victoria, with technical support from the Humanities Computing and Media Centre (HCMC). Funding for training and employing technical assistants and research assistants has come from *TAPoR* ("Text Analysis Portal for Research"), the Social Sciences and Humanities Research Council of Canada, the Dean of Humanities, the Office of Research Services, and the Department of English. The HCMC and the Digital Humanities Summer Institute have trained and mentored my student assistants. Our most recent rebuild and relaunch took place on 9 December 2013.

12. Initially, we took our site identifications from Adrian Prockter and Robert Taylor's *The A to Z of Elizabethan London*, an atlas based on the Agas map. Over the past fourteen years, however, we have added many sites and identified many buildings not listed in Prockter and Taylor. Occasionally we challenged or modified their labels on the basis of our readings of Stow and other sources (as Paul Hartlen and I did in the essay about Tower Street).

13. Because of the time required to reencode the early HTML projects in XML, many have not been transferred to the new site.

14. The total number of sites, streets, buildings, and areas we have identified for description is just over a thousand.

15. Estill completed her PhD at Wayne State University with Arthur Marotti, went on to work as visiting assistant professor of English at the Université de Moncton, took up a Banting Postdoctoral Fellowship in 2011, and is now a tenure-

track professor at Texas A&M University, where she is the new editor of the *World Shakespeare Bibliography*.

## Works Cited

Archer, Ian. "The Nostalgia of John Stow." *The Theatrical City: Culture, Theatre, and Politics in London*. Ed. David L. Smith, Richard Strier, and David Bevington. Cambridge: Cambridge UP, 1995. 17–34. Print.

"Archive." *The Oxford English Dictionary*. 2nd ed. 1989. Print.

Baldwin, Neil. "The Strand." *The Map of Early Modern London*. U of Victoria, 2002. Web. 5 Nov. 2013. <http://mapoflondon.uvic.ca/mapoflondon/redesign /THES3.htm>.

Beier, A. L., and Roger Finlay. "The Significance of the Metropolis." *London, 1500–1700: The Making of the Metropolis*. Ed. Beier and Finlay. London: Longman, 1986. 1–33. Print.

Chernyk, Melanie. "The Marriage of London Stone and the Boss of Billingsgate." *The Map of Early Modern London*. U of Victoria, n.d. Web. 5 Nov. 2013. <http://mapoflondon.uvic.ca/mapoflondon/redesign/MARR1.htm>.

Collins, Amy. "Pudding Lane." *The Map of Early Modern London*. U of Victoria, n.d. Web. 5 Nov. 2013. <http://mapoflondon.uvic.ca/mapoflondon/redesign /PUDD1.htm>.

Collinson, Patrick. "John Stow and Nostalgic Antiquarianism." *Imagining Early Modern London: Perceptions and Portrayals of the City from Stow to Strype, 1598–1720*. Ed. J. F. Merritt. Cambridge: Cambridge UP, 2001. 27–51. Print.

Devine, Marina. "Cheapside Cross (Eleanor Cross)." *The Map of Early Modern London*. U of Victoria, 2008. Web. 5 Mar. 2014. <http://mapoflondon.uvic.ca /ELEA1.htm>.

Drouillard, Tara. "Executions." *The Map of Early Modern London*. U of Victoria, n.d. Web. 5 Nov. 2013. <http://mapoflondon.uvic.ca/redesign/EXEC1.htm>.

———. "The Prison System of Early Modern London." *The Map of Early Modern London*. U of Victoria, n.d. Web. 5 Nov. 2013. <http://mapoflondon.uvic.ca /redesign/PRIS1.htm>.

Estill, Laura. Letter to Robert Miles. 5 July 2009. TS.

———. "Whitefriars Theatre." *The Map of Early Modern London*. U of Victoria, 2003. Web. 22 Apr. 2013.

Hartlen, Paul. "Tower Street." *The Map of Early Modern London*. U of Victoria, n.d. Web. 18 Apr. 2013.

Jenstad, Janelle. "Using Early Modern Maps in Literary Studies: Views and Caveats from London." *Geohumanities: Art, History, Text at the Edge of Place*. Ed. Michael Dear, Jim Ketchum, Sarah Luria, and Douglas Richardson. New York: Routledge, 2011. 112–19. Print.

Jenstad, Janelle, and Melanie Chernyk. "Abchurch Lane." *The Map of Early Modern London*. U of Victoria, 2008. Web. 5 Nov. 2013. <http://mapoflondon .uvic.ca/mapoflondon/redesign/ABCH1.htm>.

Jenstad, Janelle, gen ed., and Morag St. Clair. "Billiter Lane." *The Map of Early Modern London*. U of Victoria, 2010. Web. 5 Nov. 2013. <http://mapoflondon.uvic .ca/mapoflondon/redesign/BILL3.htm>.

Kagan, Richard L. "*Urbs* and *Civitas* in Sixteenth- and Seventeenth-Century Spain." *Envisioning the City: Six Studies in Urban Cartography.* Ed. David Buisseret. Chicago: U of Chicago P, 1998. 75–108. Print.

Lo, Jennifer. "Henslowe's Diary." *The Map of Early Modern London.* U of Victoria, n.d. Web. 5 Nov. 2013. <http://mapoflondon.uvic.ca/mapoflondon /redesign/HENS2.htm>.

Machyn, Henry. *A London Provisioner's Chronicle, 1550–1563.* Ed. Richard W. Bailey, Marilyn Miller, and Colette Moore. Ann Arbor: U of Michigan P, 2006. *Michigan Publishing.* Web. 8 Jul. 2010.

Mann, Paisley. "Extracts from *If You Know Not Me You Know Nobody, Part 2.*" *The Map of Early Modern London.* U of Victoria, n.d. Web. 31 Oct. 2014. <http:// mapoflondon.uvic.ca/IYKN2.htm?name-GRES3>.

———. "Love Lane, Thames Street." *The Map of Early Modern London.* U of Victoria, n.d. Web. 5 Nov. 2013. <http://mapoflondon.uvic.ca/mapof london/redesign/LOVE1.htm>.

———. "A Survey of London and Its Revisions." *The Map of Early Modern London.* U of Victoria, 8 Oct. 2010. Web. 18 Apr. 2013. <http://mapoflondon .uvic.ca/render_page.php?id=STOW9>.

Marshall, Lacey. "Aldgate." *The Map of Early Modern London.* U of Victoria, 2002. Web. 12 Mar. 2014. <http://mapoflondon.uvic.ca/ALDG1.htm>.

———. "Aldgate Ward." *The Map of Early Modern London.* U of Victoria, 2002. Web. 12 Mar. 2014. <http://mapoflondon.uvic.ca/ALDG2.htm>.

Marshall, Lacey, and James Campbell. "Introduction to *The Triumphs of Truth.*" *The Map of Early Modern London.* U of Victoria, n.d. Web. 31 Oct. 2014. <http://mapoflondon.uvic.ca/TRIU1_critical.htm>.

Mead-Willis, Sarah. "Gossip and Gossips." *The Map of Early Modern London.* U of Victoria, n.d. Web. 5 Nov. 2013. <http://mapoflondon.uvic.ca/mapoflondon /redesign/GOSS1.htm>.

Menard, Christopher Lawrence. Letter to Robert Miles. 6 July 2009. TS.

Norris, Beth. "London Aliens." *The Map of Early Modern London.* U of Victoria, n.d. Web. 5 Nov. 2013. <http://mapoflondon.uvic.ca/mapoflondon/redesign /ALIE1.htm>.

Prockter, Adrian, and Robert Taylor, comps. *The A to Z of Elizabethan London.* London: Guildhall Lib., 1979. Print.

Stow, John. *A Survey of London: Reprinted from the Text of 1603.* Ed. Charles Leth-bridge Kingsford. 2 vols. Oxford: Clarendon, 1908. Print.

———. *The Survey of London. . . . now compleatly finished by the study & labour of A.M., H.D., and others.* London, 1633. *Early English Books Online.* Web. 21 Jan. 2014. STC 23345.

Strype, John. *A Survey of the Cities of London and Westminster: Containing the Original, Antiquity, Increase, Modern Estate, and Government of those Cit-ies.* London, 1720. Rpt. as *An Electronic Edition of John Strype's* A Survey of the Cities of London and Westminster. Ed. Julia Merritt. hriOnline, 2007. Web. 12 Mar. 2014. <http://www.hrionline.ac.uk/strype/>.

# Part III

## Teaching Texts

Jeremy Ehrlich

# "Magic in the Web": Online Resources for Undergraduate Shakespeare Courses

## "The Web ... Is of a Mingled Yarn, Good and Ill Together"

A *Google* search for "Shakespeare" turned up nearly 60 million hits on 26 June 2010. For good and ill, undergraduates at paper time will be online turning to these Web pages and to other electronic archives and resources to help them through their assignments. The rise of such sites offers a rich array of teaching resources, which nearly any approach to Shakespeare can put to use in the pursuit of appropriate pedagogy. In tapping into these resources, we can tap the power—and, indeed, the magic—of the Web and put it to use in a nearly infinite variety of ways.

With such a bewildering array of Web sites beckoning for attention, undergraduates are going to need direction and structure to make sense of it all. Just as our job as instructors is to pick out from many works the handful that will most illuminate our classes, so it is online. No class will want to lose the primacy of the Shakespeare text to the many online archives available for its study. Nevertheless, with careful planning and attention to course goals, any of a number of new tools can be worthwhile avenues of study for our students. By starting with the goals of our course

115

and questioning whether a given tool can help us better achieve them, we can incorporate those resources that are the most promising.[1] In this essay, I survey some useful archives with an eye toward practicality, hoping to ask two questions of each: How can this archive be applied usefully in the classroom? What kinds of pedagogically appropriate outcomes can I expect students to attain if I incorporate this technology?

### "What Is It Ye Would See? If Aught of Woe or Wonder, Cease Your Search": Online Concordances

Until recently, the lessons on language and imagery learned through a concordance took some concerted efforts to uncover. The rise of online concordances, however, has made them easily accessible.[2] The kinds of large-scale image study done in past eras are no longer in fashion, but the lessons to be learned about Shakespeare's language through the study of a concordance are at the fingertips of today's students. While students might sense that the language of *Macbeth* is darker than the language of other Shakespeare plays, they may have a hard time examining why that is so. With the advent of the electronic concordance, a number of useful avenues of inquiry into language use are now well within the grasp of most students.

The electronic concordance offers clear benefits over paper concordances: it can be operated much more quickly than a codex, instantly showing the passages in which a searched term appears.[3] A student puzzling over the mood and tone of *Macbeth* can quite quickly see how Shakespeare creates that tone and how his method is a departure from his writing elsewhere. In an investigation of the imagery of a Shakespeare play, I suggest taking students through a four-step process of concordance inquiry. Begin by selecting the imagery to be considered. Strong students will be able to generate their own lines of inquiry on the basis of their reading; weaker students will need some guidance. I like to get each student working on a separate image and give students time to report to one another on interesting findings. This reporting reinforces the usefulness of an inquiry and provides the opportunity for a finding to be confirmed as a pattern. If students do this work on their own, they can share their findings online just as easily as in a class discussion.

In *Macbeth*, possible image searches are *fair* and *foul*; *blood* and *bleed*; *night*, *dark*, and *black*; *day*, *light*, and *white*; *murder* and *murdering*; *drink* and *drunk*; *sight* and *sightless*; *life* and *death*; or *evil*. More challenging image sets include *desire* and *reason*; *witch, hag*, and *weird sisters*; *robe, garment*, and *clothing*; or *water/wine* and *milk/urine/blood*. A search for *like* will offer a useful lesson on the use of metaphor. Other search terms will, of course, present themselves to students. The first step is simply to experiment with the concordance by looking up the search terms. It will not take students long to realize that, for example, *black* and images of darkness far outnumber the instances of *light* and images of brightness. They quickly get a feel for the tone Shakespeare creates and begin to understand how the dark imagery of the play comes about. The second step is to examine the context in which their search words appear, which deepens analysis. Students may note that *desire* is nearly always used in a negative context and that the play is dripping with images of blood. At each step of the process, press them to draw conclusions about their discoveries. For example, what does it mean for the relationship between the Macbeths that desire is a negative force in the play? Two more layers of inquiry will help students draw further conclusions. Have them examine the other plays that Shakespeare was writing around the same time: how does *Macbeth* differ from them in language? Students may observe that the pattern of dark and light imagery does not hold in *King Lear* and *Antony and Cleopatra*, that indeed it reverses in some ways. Conclude with a look at the entire canon—a difficult search for certain common terms, of course, but often very revealing when the terms are unusual or when scanning is done quickly for large-scale patterns. Students will find that *blood* often refers to heredity, but that in *Macbeth* it refers only to the bodily fluid.

Sophisticated outcomes can come from this kind of exercise. Students may apply what they learn about diction, imagery, tone, and mood in any number of ways, including design and performance work. Some of Shakespeare's plays are more suited to this kind of project than others, of course, just as some word and image searches are more interesting on one level than on another. Once students understand the concordance and the kinds of conclusions searching it allows them to draw, they may well be able to mine the text for their own list of searches. In effect, they will have gained a tool to answer their own questions about the plays. Specific suggestions for image searches for nine commonly taught plays, along with hints for conclusions that students may draw from those searches, are available online ("Interactive Media Lessons").

Of course, the Web also allows us to combine electronic archives, aggregating their power for ever more sophisticated results. A more nuanced discussion of word meaning and lessons in etymology are available for students when their work is supplemented with the online *Oxford English Dictionary*. A concordance search in *Macbeth* for *weird* will direct them to *weird* (spelled a variety of ways, including *wayward*) in the *Oxford English Dictionary*, which will give them a much more complete sense of the range of meanings available to the word in the play. If they go back and search the canon for uses of *wayward*, they will gain an even wider understanding. Imagine how more sophisticated a set design or a performance of the witches' first meeting with Macbeth could be, for instance, with this exercise as background research. Instead of simply presenting strange witches, students might present a much more complex view of them.

### "What Is Your Text?": Multiple-Text and Other Primary Source Study

One of the great strengths of the Internet is its ability to aggregate large amounts of information, and in the Shakespeare classroom nowhere is that strength more apparent than in the wealth of resources available for primary source document study. Page images of nearly any document relevant to undergraduate study of Shakespeare are at today's students' fingertips. Primary source study is, of course, not new, but the availability of electronic archives facilitates a student's ability to find and use this material in ways that give this formerly rare teaching method a central place in the undergraduate classroom. As students learn specific lessons, they also increase their skill in using the archives for future projects.

I suggest the following assignments to tap into electronic text archives. After students read and reflect on the description of Cleopatra's barge in *Antony and Cleopatra*, send them to Plutarch to look up the passage from which Shakespeare draws much of his material for that speech.[4] It will give them a sense of what was important to Shakespeare in writing that scene. Ask them to analyze the changes he makes to Plutarch and reflect on the reasons for the changes. Have them perform the speech and write up an analysis of performance choices offered by Shakespeare's revision of the passage. Have them take another passage from Plutarch (or Holinshed) and rewrite it into a dramatic speech for a particular moment in a play. In each case, the use of the primary source will enrich the teaching of the play. While we might use print resources for an assignment of this nature, using electronic resources makes these texts easier to find and gives students the chance to examine entire texts, not the printed excerpts we used to assign.

Other fruitful areas of primary source study are available. Students have a great need for context before they can make sense of *The Taming of the Shrew*. Reading and comparing two 1617 works, Joseph Swetnam's *The Araignment of Lewd, Idle, Froward and Unconstant Woman* and Ester Sowernam's response, *Ester Hath Hang'd Haman*, can improve their understanding of Petruchio and Kate's society. Working electronically, students can examine the entire texts quickly and easily, not simply key excerpts. How would they perform Baptista after reading Swetnam and Sowernam? How should the wedding guests respond to Petruchio's behavior at the wedding? Is Shakespeare's play ultimately and unredeemably misogynist? All are useful questions that these sources can inform. Other dramatic texts help answer them. The anonymous 1594 *The Taming of a Shrew* contains a complete framing device: Christopher Sly does not disappear as he does in Shakespeare's *Shrew* but continues to comment on the action throughout the play. Students might examine the distancing mechanism of the framing device to examine whether it mitigates or increases the misogyny of the play. For teachers who find teaching the play distasteful, pairing it with the entire text or even just the conclusion of John Fletcher's *The Tamer Tamed* can be useful — not to mention a surefire way of generating heated class discussion. All these texts are available online.[5]

Students confronting otherness in the plays — in *Othello*'s racism or *The Merchant of Venice*'s anti-Semitism, for instance — will find a wide variety of documents through which to evaluate the cultural context in which Shakespeare was writing. Among many other early modern texts, the 1585 *The Work of Pomponius Mela* will give them an idea of Elizabethan attitudes toward Africans ("Concerninge"), while Pierre Boaistuau's *Certain Secret Wonders of Nature* will do the same for early modern attitudes toward Jews. These avenues of study develop in students a more nuanced view of the discussions going on in this period and, as a result, of Shakespeare's role in them. Students encountering *Macbeth* and wondering what James I's thoughts on witchcraft were can find them online with all convenient speed.

Many of these documents are already available in the undergraduate classroom, some excerpted as appendixes in the better print editions. The idea behind their electronic use in the classroom is to lower the barrier to students undertaking scholarly work. To truly harness the powers of the Internet for primary source study, however, and to make its ability to facilitate serious scholarship clear, students should engage in multiple-text study, mining different editions of early texts for their bibliographic lessons. Those who have no background in this kind of study might want to start with an educational Web site that limits the number of primary documents available to them, such as MIT's *Hamlet on the Ramparts*. Here students will find a wealth of material relating to the ghost scenes in *Hamlet*: film clips, visual art, adaptations, promptbooks, and early editions all make this site good for general research into these scenes. In its "Reading Room" section, students are able to compare many *Hamlet* texts: facsimiles of F, Q1, and Q2 (Folger or Huntington library copies); any of those texts as edited for *The Three-Text Hamlet*; the Arden edition; and the Folger edition. Any two of these texts can be placed side by side to allow direct comparison; each can also be placed next to visual art or film clips of the same scene. Comparing, students can make crucial discoveries about the provenance of the text they may know only as a single print edition, and they begin to learn about the wide range of information that a modern edition may conceal from them.

The Web has resources for more detailed multiple-text study. The British Library's site *Treasures in Full* has posted facsimile copies of its ninety-three Shakespeare quartos, and the site is designed for side-by-side comparison of different texts. For some students, simply looking at the texts and noticing how they differ will be a revelation. Others may want to jump into the work of examining the differences and trying to figure out their causes. To get students to engage in the activity of examining and understanding textual differences on this site, ask them to edit a scene of the play. The site, when used alongside digital images of the Folio, opens to students a whole range of ways of thinking about texts that can inform their work as editors. If editing a scene is beyond the purview of a course, students might critique the edition they are reading with reference to the original printed texts. Students can explain which character they think should read the "grey-eyed morn" speech, attributed to the Friar in Q1 and to both Romeo and the Friar in Q2, or pick three differences between texts of *Hamlet* in order to make an argument for their provenance.

For a completely different look at multiple-text study, and one available only online, I enjoy showing students the beautiful, fascinating, and virtually impenetrable *TextArc* (http://textarc.org). The software represents a text as a collection of words that are placed on the screen to represent their relative location in the text as a whole, brighter or dimmer depending on how frequently they are used, and to identify common connections among them. As a work of art, it represents a text in a way that is entirely new and visually stunning. But it is difficult to use for concrete literary analysis. The best way to use the site might be to compare the differences between *TextArc* presentations of similar texts. Q1 and Q2 *Hamlet*, two texts that have a specific relation to each other, show different displays in *TextArc*. *The Taming of a Shrew* and *The Taming of the Shrew* have a puzzling connection. When we compare the differences between the *TextArc* displays of the two *Shrew* texts with the differences between the *TextArc* displays of the *Hamlet* texts, we might find or not find a similarity between those differences. Perhaps a future student will be able to push this site from an aesthetically interesting visual display of text to a resource for analysis.[6]

## "I Were Loath to Link with Him": Working with Wikis

The first generation of the Internet had only existing archives to choose from, but Web 2.0 promotes the building of archives by a larger and socially networked community for a variety of specialized purposes. One way this change has come into play is through the creation of a wiki, a Web site that allows all users to edit its content. *Wikipedia* is the most commonly known example of the technology, but wiki sites are in wide use across the Internet. A wiki is the most anarchic of all of the different forms of online collaboration available today. Yet the benefit of teaching from a collaborative Web 2.0–style archive is considerable. The Library of Congress associate librarian for library services proposed in a 2004 address that commercial search services like *Google* might work better for conveying information to students than traditional library cataloging—that the power of the aggregation of information, in other words, could be greater than that of a single (presumably better-informed) individual (Marcum).

A type of classroom assignment that works ideally with this technology involves the group-created annotation of a particular text or piece of text. Together, a group of students can annotate a piece of text in far more detail than students can accomplish if they work alone. Each student builds on the work of the others to explicate a passage or a particular view of it. Adding glosses, interpretation, and a variety of links to related information, an average effort by each student can create a remarkably thorough group project. Because an open-ended assignment may be too difficult, the teacher should provide structure—requiring, for instance, that each student supply a certain number of notes that comment on or extend other students' notes. In this way, students who need structure in the assignment will have it, while those who can take an idea and run with it have a format in which they can do that too.

Setting up a wiki site for the classroom is not difficult; the software is available from a variety of locations on the Internet (see www.wikimedia .org). Although undergraduates may need help in navigating the software and in setting the specific goals of their annotations, the potential benefit of a wiki classroom is great (Farabaugh). For commuter students who cannot spend much time together working outside class, a wiki can facilitate many kinds of collaboration.

## "Never Fear the Net": Student-Generated Web 2.0 Archives

A technology that easily creates its own electronic class performance archive is video. Classrooms have used performance techniques successfully for many years, but these techniques face the challenges of a lack of class time and the general problem of shyness. One way around both problems is to incorporate performance on video. With or without their own digital performances as material, students can be motivated to create Shakespeare-related mash-ups. These are artistic creations of today's students that incorporate multiple sources of video and sound in order to make something entirely new. Students' facility with the form can lead to creative ways of presenting information. A mash-up might use sound as a design element, for instance, excerpting pieces of music for particular spots in the play. It might posit a new way of thinking about what performance of a text means in the digital age. Student mash-ups can work as criticism of a piece of text, just as Charles Marowitz rearranged many Shakespeare plays to produce works of art that acted as criticism of those plays. In Marowitz's day, such work was radical, but online now it is common. Short essays can accompany any of these projects, permitting students to put their argument in a more traditional format.

## "Magic of Bounty!"

Universities eager to incorporate educational technology have often put the technological cart before the pedagogical horse, hoping that learning would be the result. Any incorporation of electronic archives into the classroom must of course be used with skillful pedagogy to reach the goals of the course. When used appropriately, they can be a powerful tool. In many ways, Internet Shakespeare is to Shakespeare as modern performance is to performance. Modern performance of Shakespeare is not simply similar to performance, it is genuine performance and is also a way to understand performance. Similarly, networked Shakespeare archives are not only as genuine as traditional archives but also provide a way to understand archives in general. And that, in short, is the magic in the Web. "If this be magic, let it be an art / Lawful as eating."

## Notes

1. For help in thinking about curriculum design with this kind of backward model, see Wiggins and McTighe.

2. As of this writing, there are no scholarly editions of Shakespeare available for search, so students will need explicit instructions about dealing with noise in their results that may be generated by the lack of high-quality editing with the available concordances. Luckily, some scholarly editions are beginning to appear on *Internet Shakespeare Editions*, and more are on the way.

3. My current favorite electronic concordance is *Open Source Shakespeare*, followed by *Shakespeare Searched*. Unfortunately, no free scholarly edited concordance is yet available online. Thus students will need to understand the differences between the texts that they find online and those that they read in their course texts as well as the limits to the work that they can do with online resources. Nevertheless, the benefits of an electronic concordance outweigh the drawbacks, and the quality of this resource will only improve with time.

4. Students will find the scene on pages 981–82 of the 1579 editions of North's translation of Plutarch's *Lives*, STC 20065 and 20066, both available on *Early English Books Online*. This assignment can work for other pieces of Shakespeare's text. The passages from Holinshed's *Chronicles* describing King Duffe's murder and the meeting of Macbeth and the weird sisters are available online through the Folger.

5. For recent print editions, see Miller; Daileader and Taylor.

6. Any student who makes this discovery should contact me or the creator of *TextArc*, W. Bradford Paley. Paley has posted *TextArc* editions of the Q1 *Hamlet* and *The Taming of a Shrew* on his Web site to be compared with the more familiar *Project Gutenberg* texts already available there (http://textarc.org/custom/Erlich).

## Works Cited

Boaistuau, Pierre. *Certain Secret Wonders of Nature*. *Folger Shakespeare Library*. Folger Shakespeare Lib., n.d.

"Concerninge the Situation of the World." *Folger Shakespeare Library*. Folger Shakespeare Lib., n.d. Web. 28 Aug. 2014. Excerpt from *The Work of Pomponius Mela*. 1585. <http://www.folger.edu/eduPrimSrcDtl.cfm?psid=155>.

Daileader, Celia R., and Gary Taylor, eds. *The Tamer Tamed; or, The Woman's Prize*. By John Fletcher. Manchester: Manchester UP, 2006. Print.

Farabaugh, Robin. " 'The Isle Is Full of Noises': Using Wiki Software to Establish a Discourse Community in a Shakespeare Classroom." *Language Awareness* 16.1 (2007): 41–56. *Informaworld*. Web. 14 Aug. 2010.

Holinshed, Raphael. *Chronicles of England, Scotland, and Ireland. Folger Shakespeare Library*. Folger Shakespeare Lib., n.d. Web. 14 Aug. 2010.

"Interactive Media Lessons." *Lesson Plans Archive*. Folger Shakespeare Lib., n.d. Web. 14 Aug. 2010.

James I. *Daemonologie, in the Forme of a Dialogue, Divided into Three Books. Folger Shakespeare Library*. Folger Shakespeare Lib., n.d. Web. 6 Nov. 2013. <http://www.folger.edu/eduPrimSrcDtl.cfm?psid=169>.

Marcum, Deanna B. "The Future of Cataloging: Address to the EBSCO Leadership Seminar." *Library of Congress Professional Guild*. Lib. of Congress Professional Guild, 15 Aug. 2005. Web. 14 Aug. 2010.

Marowitz, Charles. *The Marowitz Shakespeare*. London: Boyars, 2000. Print.

Miller, Stephen Roy, ed. The Taming of a Shrew: *The 1594 Quarto*. Cambridge: Cambridge UP, 2008. Print.

Shakespeare, William. *The Winter's Tale. Open Source Shakespeare*. George Mason U, 2003–14. Web. 12 Mar. 2014.

Sowernam, Ester. *Ester Hath Hang'd Haman; or, An Answere to a Lewd Pamphlet. The Araignment of Lewd, Idle, Froward and Unconstant Woman. Folger Shakespeare Library*. Folger Shakespeare Lib., n.d. Web. 6 Nov. 2013.

Swetnam, Joseph. *The Araignment of Lewd, Idle, Froward and Unconstant Woman. Folger Shakespeare Library*. Folger Shakespeare Lib., n.d. Web. 6 Nov. 2013. <http://www.folger.edu/eduPrimSrcDtl.cfm?psid=50>.

Wiggins, Grant, and Jay McTighe. *Understanding by Design*. Alexandria: Assn. for Supervision and Curriculum Development, 2005. Print.

**Rebecca Laroche**

# Early Modern Women in the Archives

Although my position at the foot of the Rockies has many amenities, one cannot expect a relatively new, smaller, yet rapidly growing regional comprehensive research university in the Southwest such as the University of Colorado, Colorado Springs, to have early modern rare books and manuscripts or even access to extensive databases such as *Early English Books Online*. As a researcher I depend on regular trips to archives in the United States and Great Britain, where I get my *Short Title Catalogue* fix and have learned to transcribe to beat wildfire. But back in my classroom, I simply cannot countenance keeping my students in the dark about the magic that can happen when our current conceptions and glossy editions meet old books and original handwriting. Even more imperative is the need to tell students about the extensive work that remains to be done in understanding early modern women's contributions to the culture that formed a Shakespeare. I want them to know, also, from where I derive my passion for the field. So with gender-focused databases, our quick-acting interlibrary loan office, certain kind reference librarians, and a good dose of Western ingenuity, I have developed strategies to bring the archives—and the traces of women's lives and writing there—to my Colorado undergraduates.

Research in early modern women writers reached its teenagehood in the dawn of the Internet. As a result, online databases have become central to the field's self-conception, and, in the classroom, they can convey the wealth of resources and the need for ongoing scholarship. While not a direct link to the archives, *Women Writers Online* (*WWO*) is but one degree removed, and it was this project in its early stages that showed me, a graduate student of the early 1990s, the extent of the archival work left to be done. Searchable transcriptions of print texts by women with helpful introductory material, *WWO*, simply in its browse list under Texts, shows students that writings by women were not limited to devotional tracts or works by a handful of aristocrats, nor were these writings wholly suppressed, so it allows undergraduates to cast off their preconceived notions of the limits and suppression. In my early modern courses, I have students read extensively from the online editions in *WWO* as well as from other databases and Web sites that include manuscript texts.

Giving access to the archives in the form of high-resolution images of unique manuscripts are two databases now available through Adam Matthew Publishing: *Defining Gender, 1450–1900* and *Perdita Manuscripts: Women Writers, 1500–1700*. Indeed, the resolution is so fine for many of the manuscripts that students are able to transcribe directly from them, a task that inevitably shows undergraduates the rewards and challenges of archival research (see Heather Wolfe's essay in this volume). *Defining Gender* contains print texts that delineated the roles of women, such as *The English House-wife*, by Gervase Markham; thus it provides key lessons in the construction of gender.

*Perdita Manuscripts* stems from *Perdita*, a free online index that lists many women's manuscripts in repositories throughout Europe and North America. As with the lessons of *WWO*, the *Perdita* index reveals to students the lost knowledge of how many women could write and, again, how much work there is left to do with those writings. This index not only gives a lesson in scholarship on women but also makes undergraduates aware of how canonical works of Philip Sidney and John Donne existed only in manuscript during the poets' lifetimes and how these texts have undergone intense editorial scrutiny. In showing our students the many works by women that have not made it into print or even undergone a full transcription, especially writings that have been rediscovered only recently, we can demonstrate to students the influence that feminist scholarship has exerted and the need for its persistence. We may take this lesson for granted, but for our undergraduates coming directly out of a canon-driven and contemporary reading experience it is still very much essential.

The recent scholarship on Elizabeth Isham, a seventeenth-century memoirist whose detailed and expressive autobiography appears in an on-line edition and is only now being examined in scholarship (Clarke and Longfellow; see also Stephens), demonstrates the potential of archival research, as the fact that Isham's text was obscured in the Princeton archives and brought to light only in the past decade underlines the *now* that is women's history.

Examples like Isham require us to look at online library catalogs differently and to acknowledge the extensive feminist contributions that have been made by librarians and archivists. In bringing to the forefront texts formerly obscured in the catalog and in providing provenance records, the project of making catalogs available through the Web has been democratizing in a way that our attention to expensive databases may eclipse. As this online cataloging has largely been undertaken since second-wave feminism, female names have been entered alongside male ones. Yes, the researcher without easy access to an archive depends on online catalogs, but I contend that these records may also be teaching tools. As demonstrated by Georgianna Ziegler in key forums, the Folger Shakespeare Library's catalog *Hamnet* sets the standard in that it is searchable not only by title, keyword, and author but also, in an advanced search, by a name—"Anne" or "Catherine" yielding particularly good fruit—in the provenance records. In expanding undergraduates' notions of what women read as well as what they wrote, we remove the limits put on women's knowledge. Certainly, we can direct our students to recent scholarship on women's reading and book collections (Morgan; Brayman Hackel; Roberts; and Snook). But in creating adept researchers, we also introduce students to the libraries of Frances Wolfreston (Morgan), Lady Anne Clifford (Spence 189–92), and the countess of Bridgewater (Brayman Hackel 244–53, 258–81), and we have students conduct their own search for an example of woman's book ownership in *Hamnet*.

Of course, each of these examples assumes ready access to computers and their networks. But students can taste the archives also through modern editions in microfilm and print facsimile reproductions. There are impressive collections of women's manuscripts in microformat (see Hoby; Pennell), and a printout of a key page or a library lesson in microfilm reading can illustrate much to students about the nature of manuscript research. Relatively inexpensive (when compared with database subscriptions), the Ashgate Early Modern Englishwoman series, although certainly one step away from archives, brings the archival experience closer than modern editions may.

I suggest a lesson plan that draws on the above resources at the same time that it extends them. Isabella Whitney's *A Sweet Nosgay* (1573) is one of the few full-text editions found in *Women Writers Online*. The first Englishwoman to publish her secular poetry, Whitney deserves a place in classes on early modernity. My lesson highlights the framing metaphor of her work: she provides a metaphoric preventive medicine to her readership that staves off a plague-like disease of the mind. In using such a metaphor, she does not express anything untoward but rather reflects contemporary medical practice by women. Other texts on *WWO*, such as *A Choice Manual* (1653), by Elizabeth Grey, countess of Kent, though published much later, show continuity between Whitney and seventeenth-century works. In *Defining Gender*, Markham's *House-wife* and several women's recipe books, which include many medicines, exemplify the regular medical practice of women.

In general, medical recipes, or receipts, provide an immediate way to show students the extensiveness of women's medical practice and how it was entwined with their reading and writing practices. The *Perdita* index lists 304 examples of such receipts, some of which are reproduced in *Perdita Manuscripts*. With this topic, another resource arises, the *Wellcome Library*'s microfilms (Pennell), now online editions, of its remedy book collection. Most of this collection can be found in the Gale microfilm collection, edited by Sara Pennell, but the exciting recent news is that many of its seventeenth-century English receipt books can be found for free through its collection of electronic texts. The quality is clear enough for a transcription assignment. Another microfilm collection through Adam Matthew holds all the Folger recipe book holdings, and the Folger site has free images of several recipes online (Laroche, *Beyond Home Remedy; Sarah Longe's Recipe Book*; Smith; Wall, "On Food"). In hard copy, Elizabeth Spiller has selected and introduced the works of the sisters Elizabeth Talbot Grey and Aletheia Talbot Howard for the Ashgate facsimile series.

Other works that substantiate the presence of women's medical practice are Margaret Hoby's diary, Lisa Cody's facsimile collection of print medical texts by women in the Early Modern Englishwoman series, and the medical content in Isham's memoir. Hoby's early-seventeenth-century diary describes an extensive charitable practice by a gentlewoman of York.

Cody's collection, largely seventeenth-century, again demonstrates the continuity of women's practice. Isham's interest in medicine, as found in her memoir and other manuscripts, has been outlined by the *Constructing Elizabeth Isham* collective (DiMeo and Laroche).

As students do selected readings from these archival materials, they complete research homework, either individually or as a group, in which they search online catalogs for evidence of women's ownership of print medical texts. Having thus established in their minds women's medical practice as context, they can now return to Whitney's text, where the presence of women's medicine is undeniable, even from the title. In her address to the reader, the poet describes her collection of poems, her "nosegay" (sig. A7v), as "vertuous flowers"; students will have seen that *virtue* has particular medicinal valences. Whitney's nosegay provides a "defence" against the infectious "stynking streets or Lothsome Lanes" of London and is meant for the "health, not for [the] eye" of the reader (sigs. A6v, A7r). By the time the students encounter the poem called "a soveraigne receypt," which comes after Whitney's versified *sententiae* taken from Hugh Plat's "ground," *The Floures of Philosophie* (1572), the purpose of the lesson seems clear (sigs. C5r, A7v). Her metaphor is neither random nor unsubstantiated but wholly rooted in the historical moment.

If one ends the lesson here, students will leave the classroom with a solid and contextualized appreciation of Whitney's poetry, but the variety of archival materials should do more than articulate one truth about women's practice and Whitney's invocation of it. They raise an essential aspect of her text. If the medical metaphor is not unprecedented, what does Whitney gain through it? I suggest to my students that there's something more than authority and domesticity at work, as many have argued (Walker 161; Wall, "Authorship" 75; McGrath 151). When students articulate the details of the poet's self-positioning, they may come to notice lines in the address whose importance escaped them before, and they may comprehend key aspects of Whitney's persona.

I have argued elsewhere that Whitney may be in dialogue with satirical aspects of small print medical texts from the years surrounding her production (*Medical Authority* 146–65). It may be possible to make this point only in an upper-division or graduate-level seminar, but for the lesson plan in this essay, as in any course on early modernity, much is gained by getting one's students to realize the specificities of the poet's situation. As we find out from her poem to her married sister, who has children, Whitney is not married and has no children. Her address and the final poem, her "Wyll and Testament," tell us that she lives in London and is about to leave it for healthier environs. Finally, she is unemployed, "servicelesse," and poor, "very weake in Purse" (sigs. A5v, E3r). "As a poor, single woman who explicitly claims to write for money" (Ellinghausen 1), Whitney's persona does not occupy the position of many of the women who have been uncovered through the archives. Those whose biographies we know, Hoby and Isham, are far from poor, and Isham, even though she is single, is the female head of a large household for much of the narrative she relates. What is more, Whitney's text is not a domestic manuscript, like many of the recipe books we examine: hers is in print and publicly circulating. Unlike the countess of Kent's *Choice Manual*, it appeared during Whitney's lifetime because its author was publishing for monetary gain.

The difference in economic and marital status is pointed in these lines toward the end of the address to the reader:

Wherfore, if thou it hap to weare
and feele thy selfe much worse:
Promote mee for no Sorceresse,
Nor doe mée ban or curse. (sig. A8r)

In further illuminating these lines, we may introduce students to another work in *WWO*, *The Wonderful Discoverie of the Witchcrafts of Margaret and Phillip[a] Flower* (1618), which relates the trial and punishment of two women who had been in service in a lord's household early in the seventeenth century. This text provides students with information about the 1563 plague, the renewal of the witchcraft statutes, and the resulting surge of witchcraft trials in and around London. Whitney's expressed fear is not that of a gentlewoman practicing charitably or of a householder who takes care of her family. As a woman who offers a preventive medicine to a susceptible public, however metaphoric the medicine, she is vulnerable. Thus, through the archives and the foils and counterpoints found in them, students discover the uniqueness and nuance of a woman poet's persona.

## Works Cited

Brayman Hackel, Heidi. *Reading Material in Early Modern England: Print, Gender, and Literacy.* Cambridge: Cambridge UP, 2005. Print.

Clarke, Elizabeth, and Erica Longfellow, dirs. *Constructing Elizabeth Isham.* Centre for the Study of the Renaissance, U of Warwick, 5 Apr. 2011. Web. 29 Apr. 2013.

Cody, Lisa Forman, ed. *Writings on Medicine.* Burlington: Ashgate, 2002. Print.

DiMeo, Michelle, and Rebecca Laroche. "Elizabeth Isham and Medicine." *Constructing Elizabeth Isham.* Centre for the Study of the Renaissance, U of Warwick, 15 Feb. 2012. Web. 7 Nov. 2013.

Ellinghausen, Laurie. "Literary Property and the Single Woman in Isabella Whitney's *A Sweet Nosegay.*" *Studies in English Literature* 45.1 (2005): 1–22. Print.

Grey, Elizabeth, countess of Kent. *A Choice Manual; or, Rare and Select Secrets.* London, 1653. *Women Writers Online.* Brown U. Web. 29 Apr. 2013.

Hoby, Margaret. "The Diary of Lady Margaret Hoby. 1599–1605." *Medieval and Early Modern Women.* Marlborough: Adam Matthew, 2002–04. Reel 9. British Lib. Egerton MS 2614.

Laroche, Rebecca. *Beyond Home Remedy: Women, Medicine, and Science. Folger Shakespeare Library.* Folger Shakespeare Lib., n.d. Web. 20 Jan. 2011.

———. *Medical Authority and Englishwomen's Herbal Texts, 1550–1650.* Burlington: Ashgate, 2009. Print.

Markham, Gervase. *The English House-wife.* London, 1668. *Defining Gender.* Adam Matthew. Web. 29 Apr. 2013.

McGrath, Lynette. *Subjectivity and Women's Poetry in Early Modern England.* Burlington: Ashgate, 2002. Print.

Morgan, Paul. "Frances Wolfreston and 'Her Bouks': A Seventeenth-Century Woman Book Collector." *Library* 6.2 (1989): 197–219. Print.

Pennell, Sara, ed. *Women and Medicine: Remedy Books, 1533–1865, from the Wellcome Library for the Understanding and History of Medicine.* Reading: Primary Source Microfilm, 2004. Microfilm.

Roberts, Sasha. *Reading Shakespeare's Poems in Early Modern England.* Basingstoke: Palgrave, 2003. Print.

*Sarah Longe's Recipe Book. Folger Shakespeare Library.* Folger Shakespeare Lib., n.d. Web. 1 Feb. 2010.

Smith, Emily Bowles. "'Let Them Completely Learn': Manuscript Clues about Early Modern Women's Educational Practices." *A Manuscript Miscellany.* Folger Shakespeare Lib., n.d. Web. 1 Feb. 2010.

Snook, Edith. *Women, Reading, and the Cultural Politics of Early Modern England.* Burlington: Ashgate, 2005. Print.

Spence, Richard. *Lady Anne Clifford, Countess of Pembroke, Dorset and Montgomery, 1590–1676.* Stroud: Sutton, 1997. Print.

Spiller, Elizabeth, ed. *Seventeenth-Century English Recipe Books.* Aldershot: Ashgate, 2008. Print.

Stephens, Isaac. "The Courtship and Singlehood of Elizabeth Isham, 1630–34." *Historical Journal* 51.1 (2008): 1–25. Print.

Walker, Kim. *Women Writers of the English Renaissance.* New York: Twayne, 1996. Print.

Wall, Wendy. "Authorship and the Material Conditions of Writing." *The Cambridge Companion to English Literature.* Ed. Arthur F. Kinney. Cambridge: Cambridge UP, 2000. 64–89. Print.

———. "On Food for Thought." *Photo Gallery: 2011 Shakespeare's Birthday Lecture. Folger Shakespeare Library.* Folger Shakespeare Lib., n.d. Web. 29 Apr. 2013.

Whitney, Isabella. *A Sweet Nosgay; or, Pleasant Posy.* London, 1573. *Women Writers Online.* Brown U. Web. 1 Feb. 2010.

*The Wonderful Discoverie of the Witchcrafts of Margaret and Phillip[a] Flower.* London, 1618. *Women Writers Online.* Brown U. Web. 29 Apr. 2013.

Ziegler, Georgianna. "New Avenues to Teaching and Research." *Attending to Early Modern Women—and Men.* Stamp Student Union, U of Maryland, College Park. 11 Nov. 2007. Address.

**Peter C. Herman**

# Opening Up *The Roaring Girl* and the Woman Question with *EEBO*

When I was an undergraduate in the waning days of the New Criticism's hold on English departments, the thought of using a primary source in the classroom was a nonstarter for a variety of reasons. First, my teachers all believed in the sanctity of the words on the page. Primary sources (like editing issues, such as the two texts of *King Lear*) just were not something undergraduates needed to worry about. At the same time, I now recognize that technology, or lack thereof, also influenced the pedagogical focus on the text itself (presented of course in a modern edition). Books printed in the sixteenth and seventeenth centuries were not easily accessible. One either had to find one's way to a rare-book room or resort to the STC microfilms. It took a fair amount of time, travel, and effort to bring such books into the classroom, and obviously time spent on nonliterary texts took time away from Spenser or Shakespeare. The new historicism, which reinvigorated the use of history and primary sources in scholarship, changed all that. And it did not take long for the intensified scholarly focus on history in books and articles to manifest itself in the classroom. Both the Longman and the Norton anthologies now include copious amounts of archival materials, and Bedford–St. Martin's Press publishes the Texts and Contexts editions of Shakespeare that pair numerous and varied primary sources with each play.

Laudable as this development may be, the presence of early modern texts in teaching editions inevitably presents the past as if the texts were published today. That is to say, the archive is presented in an edited, footnoted version that perforce erases many traces of the past, including the original title pages, layout, erratic spelling, and idiosyncratic punctuation. However, *Early English Books Online* (*EEBO*) presents a remarkable opportunity for students and teachers outside the immediate vicinity of the Folger, Newberry, and Huntington libraries (not to mention the Bodleian) to use the same early modern texts that are used by those more geographically fortunate. To be sure, there is a difference between accessing an electronic file and handling the book itself. One misses the heft and feel in the hand of the actual artifact (I will never forget my surprise at how small and unimpressive the first edition of *Paradise Lost* seemed). *EEBO* also has two other drawbacks that must be admitted at the outset: it is expensive and the catalog is neither as complete as the *English Short Title Catalogue* (*ESTC*, available through the British Library's Web site and running through to 1800) nor as detailed as Alan Farmer and Zachary Lesser's essential *Database of Early English Playbooks* (see Lesser's essay in this volume).[1] But the perfect should not be the enemy of the good. *EEBO*'s catalog is certainly complete enough for the purposes of teaching undergraduates, and the ease with which one can access reproductions of early modern books can bring students and their teachers vastly closer to primary sources than anyone would have thought possible in the years before the digital revolution. In this essay, I show how one could use *EEBO* to open up not only Thomas Dekker and Thomas Middleton's *The Roaring Girl* (1611) but also the world of early modern publishing.

Rather than go directly into the play itself, I set the stage, as it were, by looking at two primary sources that suggest the horizons of expectation for Dekker and Middleton's audience, and I look at them using the lens of what has been variously called "the new philology" (Marcus 17–30), "the New Textualism" (Lesser 11), and the "New Boredom" (Kastan 212), which focuses as much on the materiality of the text, the supposedly mundane details of book publication, as on the play itself. Instead of using contemporary, edited versions of these texts, I open up *EEBO* and summon Joseph Swetnam's *The Arraignment of Lewd, Idle, Froward and Unconstant Women* (1615) and Rachel Speght's response, *A Mouzell for*

*Melastomus* (1617). I chose these books for two reasons.[2] The first is that they are roughly contemporaneous with the play.[3] The second reason we will get to shortly.

I have the class compare and contrast their title pages, which I remind the class functioned as the covers of books do today: they not only announced basic information about the book's contents, they also guided the prospective customer's interpretation of the work. There are clear similarities between the title pages of *Arraignment* (fig. 1) and *Mouzell* (fig. 2): both use a variety of fonts for the title, and in both the key term ("Araignment," "Mouzell") is printed significantly larger than the rest of the words, causing them to jump out at the viewer. Students also quickly notice differences. The cover for *Arraignment* includes an illustration of a nicely dressed woman holding what appears to be a large plant. Given that the book's title also advertises a "[c]ommendation of wise, vertuous and *honest Women*," it would seem that one of those women adorns the cover. The title-page illustration, in other words, works to blunt the book's polemical misogynist edge, a purpose further evidenced by the final words of the title, "Pleasant for married Men, profitable for young Men, and *hurtfull to none*," although the exclusively male readership seems to reinscribe the misogyny. When we turn to the title page of *A Mouzell for Melastomus*, students realize each title page has something the other doesn't. *Mouzell* lacks an illustration on the title page, but its title page, unlike that of the *Arraignment*, pointedly reveals the text's author. About two-thirds of the way from the top of the page, set off by borders and using large, italic type, is the announcement "*By Rachel Speght*." In a period with very few published women authors, when women were supposedly enjoined to silence, the emphatic revelation of the author's full name (no initials, as is common for other works by women) cannot be accidental; it continues the book's polemical aim, to rebut the "*Irreligious and Illiterate* Pamphlet made by *Io. Sw.* and by him Intituled, *The Arraignement of Women*."

We then flip through the books themselves, and once more students discover differences, in both layout and theme. The antiwoman tract begins with an epistle to the reader, then launches into the main body of the argument. Speght's *Mouzell for Melastomus*, on the other hand, has a much more elaborate design. The "Epistle Dedicatorie" by Speght to "all vertuous Ladies Honourable or Worshipfull" is followed by her acrostic poem on "Ioseph Swetnam" and underneath a list of errata, then a preface (also by Speght), and then a poem "In praise of the Author and her Worke" by one "Philalethes" (sigs. A3r, B1r, B4r). The page layouts are very different.

# THE
# ARAIGNMENT
## OF LEVVD, IDLE, FRO.
### ward, and vnconſtant women : Or
*the vanitie of them, chooſe you whether.*

With a Commendation of wiſe, vertuous and
*honeſt Women.*

Pleaſant for married Men, profitable for young Men, and
*hurtſull to none.*

LONDON
Printed by *George Purſlowe* for *Thomas Archer,* and are to be ſolde
at his ſhop in Popes-head Pallace, neere the Royall
Exchange.  1615.

**Figure 1.** Title page of Joseph Swetnam's *The Araignment of Lewd, Idle, Froward and Unconstant Women*, 1615 (British Lib. copy, *EEBO*)

A

# MOVZELL FOR

## MELASTOMVS,

The Cynicall Bayter of, and foule
*mouthed Barker against*
EVAHS SEX.

Or an Apologeticall Anſwere to
*that Irreligious and Illiterate*
Pamphlet made by *Io. Sw.* and by him
Intituled, *The Arraignement*
*of women.*

By *Rachel Speght.*

PROVERBS 26. 5.
*Anſwer a foole according to his foolishneſſe, left he bee wiſe in
his owne conceit.*

LONDON,
Printed by *Nicholas Okes* for *Thomas Archer*, and
are to be ſold at his ſhop in Popes-
head-Pallce. 1617.

**Figure 2.** Title page of Rachel Speght's *A Mouzell for Melastomus*, 1617 (Harvard Univ. Lib. copy, *EEBO*)

Placing them side by side, students see that while Speght's pages have borders enclosing the text that also separate the biblical marginalia from the main body, Swetnam's compositor does not include any marginalia or set the text off in any way. What do the differences in how the pages are composed contribute to the meaning of each text? What effect, I ask the class, does the presence of biblical marginalia have on the authority of Speght's argument? What does their absence say about *Arraignment*? It does not take long for students to see that Speght's book was designed to emphasize her authority. Perhaps knowing that a female author arguing against misogyny has a higher bar to surmount to convince readers of her point, whoever came up with the descriptive title discredits her antagonist by accusing him of being both "*Irreligious and Illiterate.*" With regard to the former term, Speght seeks to prove through copious biblical citation that misogyny has no biblical warrant, and thus she displays a greater mastery of biblical texts than Swetnam (who also cites the Bible frequently, but his compositor does not identify the quotes in the margins). The argument between the two is not restricted to the words in the manuscripts delivered to the printer; it also informs the production details of each book.

At this point in the discussion I give a brief lecture on the division of labor in the early modern printing industry (using Blayney as my source) and ask the students to look at the bottom of the title pages. Usually they are surprised to see that although there are different printers (George Purslowe for Swetnam, Nicholas Okes for Speght), the bookseller-publisher, the person who is responsible for the acquisition and sale of these books and who takes on the risk but also earns the reward, is the same man: Thomas Archer. Speght and Swetnam, in other words, may be enemies in one sense, yet their quarrel redounds to the profit of the man who publishes both. The Swetnam-Speght controversy thus starts to seem contrived, almost a publicity stunt, less a cultural battle and more a marketing ploy. But given how unusual it is for a publisher to publish works on both sides of a controversy (Lesser 118–19), I suggest to students that there may be more here than merely a stunt designed to sell more books and increase Archer's profit.

We turn to the framing of Dekker and Middleton's play. Once more, using *EEBO* (having retrieved the play from the database and projected it on the screen), I ask the students to examine the title page, and they realize the second reason why I chose to open the class with Speght and Swetnam: Archer published *The Roaring Girl* as well. The same man, or perhaps more to the point the same firm (I continuously remind the students that, then as today, publishing was a commercial enterprise), published a play challenging gender norms, an attack on women, and a defense of women in refutation of that attack. Adding to the financial aspects of this cluster of texts, I note that in the epilogue to *The Roaring Girl* (the speaker is not identified in the quarto but ascribed to Moll in some modern editions),[4] the audience is invited to return to the theater: "*The Roring Girle* her selfe some few dayes hence, / Shall on this Stage, give larger recompence" (sig. M3v). Not stated but assumed is that Moll will not be appearing for free, that the audience must "recompence" the theater by buying a ticket before they can behold "*The Roring Girle* her selfe." It would seem that the purpose of the woman question is as much to make money as to defend or attack misogyny.

At this juncture in the class, we take advantage of the "Imprint" option on the advanced search page of *EEBO* to see what else Archer published over the course of his career. The results regularly surprise students (they certainly surprised me the first time I ran this search). Of the ninety-six items listed, Archer published only six plays: Dekker and John Webster, *The Famous History of Sir Thomas Wyat*, better known to contemporaries as *Lady Jane* (1607, 1612); *Everie Woman in Her Humor* (1609); Robert Armin, *The Two Maids of More-clack* (1609); Dekker and Middleton, *The Roaring Girl* (1611); Webster, *The White Divel* (1612); and John Marston, *The Insatiate Countess* (1613, 1616). Given that *EEBO* ascribes to Archer ninety-six publications (including reprints), looking over the list drives home to students that despite our privileging of early modern drama, "printed plays never accounted for a very significant fraction of the trade in English books" (Blayney 385). Also, looking at all the title pages of the plays published by Archer, one can see that he developed something of a house style that would make his products immediately distinguishable in the marketplace: he tends toward a clean title page, with a word or phrase printed in large, boldface type; and it is interesting that five of his six plays identify the author or authors.

Then there is the question of content. What, I ask the class, do the titles of these plays all have in common? Students answer that all the plays concern women and the "woman question" (Lesser 116). More specifically, the two following *The Roaring Girl*'s publication in 1611, Webster's *The White Divel* and Marston's *The Insatiate Countess*, concern female sexuality but in complicated ways.[5] Webster's play may be full of misogyny (e.g., Brachiano's declaration after he hears Vittoria wailing over his imminent demise, "How miserable a thing it is to die / 'Mongst women howling!" [5.3.36–37]), yet it is the men who reveal themselves as homicidal maniacs (e.g., Lodovico's "Oh, could I kill you forty times a day / And use't four year together; 'twere too little" [5.6.195–96]). It would be hard to see this play as proving *Arraignment*'s view of women. Similarly, Marston's Countess Isabella may fall in love at the drop of a hat, thereby ostensibly proving the title's validity, but in the subplot the two husbands, Claridiana and Rogero, jump at the chance to have sex with each other's wives (e.g., Claridiana's declaration: "Beauteous Thais [Rogero's wife], I am all thine wholly, / The staff is now advancing for the rest, / And when I tilt, Rogero, aware thy crest" [2.4.12–14]).

Next I go over with the class the rest of Archer's publications (which one can retrieve, organize and download from *EEBO*).[6] What does this list look like? I ask the class. What sorts of books make up the bulk of his publications?

On the one hand, it's clear that Archer was a down-market publisher (Melchiori describes him as something of a bottom-feeder, specializing "in derelict plays belonging to companies recently disbanded" [3]). There are no large folio volumes, very few religious texts, and certainly no Latin works in his catalog. Instead, Archer focuses on international news. His first publication available in *EEBO* is *A True and Perfect Relation of the News Sent from Amsterdam, the 21. of February, 1603* (the *ESTC* lists two earlier publications, a proclamation from the Netherlands concerning trade and a travel narrative about the adventures of two pilgrims in and around Jerusalem). The publications immediately following *The Roaring Girl* are a reprint of the pilgrim travel narrative and *A True and Almost Incredible Report of an Englishman, That (Being Cast Away in the Good Ship Called the* Assention *in Cambaya the Farthest Part of the East Indies) Travelled by Land through Many Unknown Kingdoms, and Great Cities*. Later, in the 1620s, I tell the class, Archer and another publisher, Nicholas Bourne, produced "the first English serial newspaper" (Lesser 125). Furthermore, students also generally notice that Archer published some familiar literary names before he got to *The Roaring Girl*: in 1604 he brought out Dekker's *Newes from Graves-end* and in 1607 Samuel Rowlands's *Diogines Lanthorne*. Again, using *EEBO* (with help from *Literature Online*), we quickly realize that these are London satires denouncing the sins of the age in an almost nihilistic fashion. Dekker blames the plague on, inter alia,

The Courtiers pride, lust, and excesse,
The Church mans painted holinesse;
The Lawyers grinding of the poore,
The Souldiers staruing at the doore,
Ragd, leane, and pale through want of blood,
Sold cheape by him for Countries good.
The Schollers enuy; Farmers curse. . . . (sig. D2r)

There is more than just opportunistic publishing going on here.

When I ask students to sum up the sensibility evinced by Archer's list, they respond that while the man clearly chose to publish books he thought would sell, there seems to have been an almost avant-garde sense guiding his choices. A pioneer of the news trade and in literature, he preferred works that went out of their way to challenge convention (while also being profitable). He was not a man who published only those works that would reassure readers; instead he sought out plays and poems that criticized early modern London's culture instead of reinforcing the status quo. At the same time, Archer's list reveals the limitations of going against cultural expectations. Again, using *EEBO*'s database as our guide, students see that although Speght's book exists in only one early modern edition, Swetnam's *Arraignment* was republished sixteen times between 1615 and 1682. Eight of those editions were by Archer, and so we need to remember that misogynistic text was the best seller, not the book by a woman author challenging misogyny. Even so, the controversy itself had become part of the work's packaging, as it were. T. Cotes, the publisher of the 1634 edition of Swetnam's book, changed the illustration from an idealized woman to a man sitting at a desk surrounded by very angry, remonstrating women (fig. 3).

Having invoked the magic of *EEBO* to explore the resonances of Archer's list, the semiotics of his title pages, and the economics of the Swetnam-Speght controversy, the class can now turn to an investigation of *The Roaring Girl* itself.

THE
ARRAIGNMENT
of Lewd, Idle, Froward, and
Vnconstant Women:
*OR,*

*The vanitie of them; chuse you whether.*

W i t h

A Commendation of the Wife, Vertuous, and
Honest Women.

*Pleasant for married-Men, profitable for Young-
Men, and hurtfull to none.*

Printed at London by *T. C.* and are to be sold by *F. Grove,* at his Shop, at
upper-end of Snow-hill, neere the Sarazens head without New-gate, 1634.

**Figure 3.** Title page of Joseph Swetnam's *The Arraignment of Lewd, Idle, Froward
and Unconstant Women*, 1634 (Bodleian Lib. copy, *EEBO*)

## Notes

1. Further, on 1 January 2013, the first set of twenty-five thousand *EEBO* texts with searchable transcriptions will be made freely available through the *EEBO-TCP* project.

2. While I use *book* for the sake of convenience, I recognize that this term implicitly erases the distinctions between the physical object and its electronic counterpart, which is a PDF file of a scanned image on microfilm and thus three times removed from the original artifact.

3. The two popular works dealing with cross-dressing women, *Hic Mulier; or, The Man-Woman* and *Haec Vir; or, The Womanish Man*, were published in 1620, nine years after *The Roaring Girl.*

4. Bevington's edition ascribes the speech to Moll (1452); Carroll and Jordan do not (1488). The difference between the quarto and Bevington's edition provides another teachable moment for illustrating why it is important, as Marcus terms it, to "unedit" early modern texts. Why, one can ask the class, does Bevington alter the text? What is at stake with having Moll speak these lines and not somebody else?

5. The title page of *The Insatiate Countess* reproduced in *EEBO* has a black slash across the place where the name of the author, Marston, ought to be. Archer published this play after Marston renounced the theater, and Marston apparently asked to have his name removed from the play. Archer published another issue of the play, also in 1613, only this time the title page claims that the play was written by "Lewis Machin and William Bacster" (Melchiori 3). Like the problem with the ascription of the final speech in *The Roaring Girl*, the different title pages provide a teachable moment for illustrating the problems of authorial ascription in this period. I am grateful to Zachary Lesser for his help with this point.

6. The *ESTC* list consists of 129 items and therefore is much more complete than *EEBO*, which reproduces 96 of Archer's publications.

## Works Cited

Bevington, David, gen. ed. *The Roaring Girl. English Renaissance Drama: A Norton Anthology.* New York: Norton, 2002. 1371–452. Print.

Blayney, Peter. "The Publication of Playbooks." *A New History of Early English Drama.* Ed. John D. Cox and David Scott Kastan. New York: Columbia UP, 1997. 383–421. Print.

Carroll, Clare, and Constance Jordan, eds. *The Roaring Girl. The Early Modern Period.* New York: Pearson, 2006. 1416–88. Print. Vol. 1b of *The Longman Anthology of British Literature.*

Dekker, Thomas. *Newes from Graves-end.* London, 1604. *Early English Books Online.* Web. 19 Apr. 2010.

———. *Newes from Graves-end.* London, 1604. *Literature Online.* ProQuest. Web. 19 Apr. 2010.

Dekker, Thomas, and Thomas Middleton. *The Roaring Girle; or, Moll Cut-Purse.* London, 1611. *Early English Books Online.* Web. 19 Apr. 2010.

Kastan, David Scott. "Shakespeare after Theory." *Opening the Borders: Inclusivity in Early Modern Studies: Essays in Honor of James V. Mirollo*. Ed. Peter C. Herman. Newark: U of Delaware P, 1999. 206–24. Print.

Lesser, Zachary. *Renaissance Drama and the Politics of Publication: Readings in the English Book Trade*. Cambridge: Cambridge UP, 2004. Print.

Marcus, Leah S. *Unediting the Renaissance: Shakespeare, Marlowe, Milton*. New York: Routledge, 1996. Print.

Marston, John. *The Insatiate Countesse*. London, 1613. *Early English Books Online*. Web. 19 Apr. 2010.

Melchiori, Giorgio. Introduction. *The Insatiate Countess*. By John Marston et al. Ed. Melchiori. Manchester: Manchester UP, 1984. 1–50. Print.

Speght, Rachel. *A Mouzell for Melastomus*. London, 1617. *Early English Books Online*. Web. 19 Apr. 2010.

Swetnam, Joseph. *The Arraignment of Lewd, Idle, Froward, and Inconstant Women*. London, 1615. *Early English Books Online*. Web. 19 Apr. 2010.

———. *The Arraignment of Lewd, Idle, Froward, and Inconstant Women*. London, 1634. *Early English Books Online*. Web. 19 Apr. 2010.

Webster, John. *The White Devil*. Ed. Elizabeth M. Brennan. New York: Norton, 1978. Print.

———. *The White Divel; or, The Tragedy of Paulo Giodano Urini, Duke of Brachiano*. London, 1612. *Early English Books Online*. Web. 19 Apr. 2010.

**Joshua Eckhardt**

# Teaching Verse Miscellanies

While my campus library does enable me to teach some excellent rare books (such as printed books by Samuel Johnson and James Boswell and, especially, more recent artists' books), it has only a few holdings that pre-date Johnson. It has none of the early modern verse miscellanies, in either print or manuscript, that I wanted to teach in my first graduate seminar and later in my first senior seminar. It does not even have a subscription to *Early English Books Online*. When I began to consider teaching miscellanies, I learned that my campus library also lacked most of the twentieth-century printed editions of these anthologies, so the prospect of a course on the miscellanies seemed remote. Yet my associate chair, Nick Sharp, encouraged me to focus the graduate seminar on my research and to follow through on the quite simple ideas that I had for making such a seminar feasible. This essay briefly conveys my ideas and narrates how I taught verse miscellanies with very few resources. It thus offers a model that could work on a great many campuses. I taught early modern litera-ture less from the archives than far from them, in a place that even many modern editions and facsimiles of such literature had not yet reached. One could teach other sources with the methods that I used, but I propose that verse miscellanies, regardless of how specialized and arcane they may seem to some, lend themselves particularly well to the classroom, offering what modern anthologies do and much more, without the obfuscations and anachronisms found in those anthologies.

I realized that many would consider my courses too specialized even for a top PhD program in English and particularly unsuitable to my department's terminal master's program and undergraduate curriculum. I also knew that it would have been safer to choose a single modern anthology than several miscellanies for a course textbook. Instead of crowding major authors with minor ones, anonymous writers, miscellany compilers, and stationers, I could have stuck to the big names. I was writing a monograph that turned attention from major authors to verse collectors, from canonical to noncanonical poems, yet I found myself teaching to all levels of our undergraduate population either a major author alone—for example, Shakespeare—or an author-organized Norton anthology. I considered it risky if not foolish, but I wanted to teach a course that was not derivative, not a version of a course better taught elsewhere. I believed—and eventually demonstrated—that early modern verse miscellanies are richer and more historically accurate than the modern poetry anthologies that succeeded them.

First, I needed help getting twentieth-century editions of miscellanies on campus: from our collection librarian for humanities, Kevin Farley, who graciously located and purchased for Cabell Library some of the out-of-print books that the library lacked, and from our dean, Robert Holsworth, who responded to my letter explaining the situation with a small but generous and sufficient fund for buying the rest of the books that neither the library nor I owned. I then made some of the texts available to the students by resources that were available on campus at no additional cost: a course reserve list of library books; a decent scanner and computer; and *Blackboard*, a password-protected Web site. I was mindful of copyright law, giving students online access to image files of the brief excerpts that copyright allows and requiring them to visit the library to read the unscanned portions. The verse miscellanies I taught had thus been doubly remediated: first, when a twentieth-century editor produced a transcript or facsimile of the early modern book; second, when I scanned it. Although I focused attention on the original medium of these miscellanies, I did so mainly through the lenses of twentieth-century transcripts and twenty-first-century PDF files. This method of providing texts does not amount to much of a technological achievement, yet it kept textbook and photocopy costs to a minimum and had students go to the library to share a single copy of a physical book—much as scholars do in rare-book rooms.

## Print and Manuscript Verse Miscellanies, 1557–1682: A Graduate Seminar

The description for this course claimed that it would accomplish more than a standard survey of early modern poetry. The course covered canonical early modern English poetry (e.g., Wyatt, Surrey, Sidney, Spenser, Shakespeare, Jonson, Carew, Herrick, Dryden, and Rochester); provided a closer look at figures more prevalent in miscellanies, especially Raleigh, Donne, Corbet, and Strode; and in addition considered the compilers and other producers of the miscellanies. It analyzed the interplay of canonical literature with a wealth of noncanonical verse. By comparing manuscript and print miscellanies, it interrogated the distinctions that scholars have made between manuscript culture and print culture. It allowed us to read a poem in its various manifestations in different miscellanies, surrounded by different poems, in order to see its contexts.

The syllabus surveyed 125 years' worth of verse miscellanies by taking on at least one per week.

| | |
|---|---|
| Week 1 | *Tottel's Miscellany*, ed. Rollins (I would now use Marquis); Marotti; Hamrick |
| Week 2 | Arundel Harington manuscript, ed. Hughey; Woudhuysen; Love; McKitterick |
| Week 3 | *Paradise of Dainty Devices*, ed. Rollins |
| Week 4 | Cambridge University Library manuscript Dd.5.75, ed. May |
| Week 5 | *Brittons Bowre of Delights*, ed. Rollins; *Phoenix Nest*, ed. Rollins |
| Week 6 | *England's Helicon*, ed. Rollins; Woudhuysen |
| Week 7 | Texas Tech manuscripts PR 1171 D14 and PR 1171 S4 (known as the Dalhousie manuscripts), ed. Sullivan, *First and Second*; Wolf; Hobbs, *Early* and "Early"; Beal, "Notions"; Marotti |
| Week 8 | Harry Ransom Humanities Research Center, University of Texas, Austin manuscript, HRC 79, ed. Farmer; Cogswell; Croft; Bellany; McRae |
| Week 9 | Pierpont Morgan Library manuscript MA 1057 (also called the Holgate Miscellany), ed. Denbo |
| Week 10 | Stoughton manuscript, ed. Hobbs, *Stoughton Manuscript* |
| Week 11 | *Witts Recreations*, ed. Gibson; Smyth; Marotti; Raylor, *Cavaliers* |
| Week 12 | *Musarum Deliciae* and *Wit Restor'd*, ed. Raylor; Smyth |

| Week 13 | *Harmony of the Muses*, ed. Sullivan; Smyth |
| Week 14 | *Parnassus Biceps*, ed. Beal; Smyth |

Each week we began class with a student presentation, which I asked students to submit in writing and, as is done in most conference presentations, to limit to twenty minutes. I wanted students to try their hand at one of the academic genres in which scholars present new ideas. After asking questions of the presenter and discussing the issues that were brought up, we would discuss secondary literature, if any; take a break; and return for a poetry reading. For this second half of the meeting, I asked students to bring a short list of their favorite poems from that week's miscellany, to each read one of them aloud, and to explain why they chose the poems they did. These readings made the course easier for the students but more challenging for me: students routinely chose poems that forced me to expand my view of an individual miscellany. For their final project, they expanded their presentation essay, situating the miscellanies they discussed in the history of verse miscellanies.

## Manuscript Verse Collectors: A Senior Seminar

Although they were undergraduates, my senior seminar students did more to prepare for work in the period than had my graduate students. All but one had studied or was studying early modern literature with me in one, two, or even three other classes. So they were committing much of their university education to early modern literature, and we knew what to expect from one another. For them, I narrowed the seminar's focus to three manuscript verse miscellanies, partly to make sure that the course required less work than the graduate seminar but also because I knew that these students could do extensive work with a miscellany in the time allotted. I chose three of the manuscripts that I had taught to the graduate students: one of the Dalhousie manuscripts from Texas Tech (PR 1171 D14), in Ernest Sullivan's edition (*First and Second Dalhousie Manuscripts*); the largely political miscellany at the Harry Ransom Center (HRC 79), edited by Norman Farmer; and Michael Denbo's dissertation edition of Morgan manuscript MA 1057.

Further distinguishing the senior seminar from the graduate seminar, I minimized the number of assigned secondary sources, recommending additional sources for individual student projects. I set shorter lengths for both the class presentation and the term paper. But I added an assignment: an annotated modernization of one poem, in which students had to transcribe a poem and then rephrase it in contemporary English, adding annotations as needed to clarify the text. This assignment rewarded a kind of close reading and textual analysis different from that required by the presentation and term paper. Students did not have to make an argument but had to understand and respond to virtually every word of an early modern poem in its original spelling.

My senior seminar students undertook the most thorough reading of the poems of Corbet and Strode that I have witnessed. One student, writing on the wide range of funeral elegies in Morgan manuscript MA 1057, recognized the sharp contrast between Donne's respectable and Francis Beaumont's downright Baudelairean elegy on Lady Markham. Another insisted that we keep discussing George Morley's elegy on King James, which we read in the Morgan manuscript, until we discovered that Morley wrote it in direct response to the libels that we encountered in the Harry Ransom Center manuscript. Thanks to these students, I will never again pass over the Beaumont and Morley poems without recognizing how they engage contemporary verses.

The students in both my seminars studied many poems they could have found in other courses and other anthologies. The verse miscellanies that we read presented poems without the modern canon's focus on major authors, select genres, and single, authoritative texts, offering instead many versions of a famous poem as well as a wealth of noncanonical and anonymous texts, understudied genres, minor authors, and a more complicated, accurate picture of the collaborative process of literary production and dissemination.

## Works Cited

Beal, Peter. "Notions in Garrison: The Seventeenth-Century Commonplace Book." *New Ways of Looking at Old Texts: Papers of the Renaissance English Text Society, 1985–1991.* Ed. W. Speed Hill. Binghamton: Center for Medieval and Renaissance Studies, State U of New York, 1993. 131–47. Print.

———, ed. *Parnassus Biceps; or, Several Choice Pieces of Poetry, by Abraham Wright: Together with Pages from British Library Additional MS 22608.* Aldershot: Scolar, 1990. Print.

Bellany, Alastair. "Raylinge Rymes and Vaunting Verse: Libellous Politics in Early Stuart England, 1603–1628." *Culture and Politics in Early Stuart England.* Ed. Kevin Sharpe and Peter Lake. Macmillan: Basingstoke, 1994. 285–310. Print.

Cogswell, Thomas. "Underground Verse and the Transformation of Early Stuart Political Culture." *Political Culture and Cultural Politics in Early Modern England: Essays Presented to David Underdown.* Ed. Susan D. Amussen and Mark A. Kishlansky. Manchester: Manchester UP, 1995. 277–300. Print.

Croft, Pauline. "Libels, Popular Literacy, and Public Opinion in Early Modern England." *Historical Research* 68.167 (1995): 266–85. Print.

Denbo, Michael Roy. "The Holgate Miscellany (The Pierpont Morgan Library— MA 1057): A Diplomatic Edition." Diss. City U of New York, 1997. Ann Arbor: UMI, 1997. Print.

Farmer, Norman K., Jr., ed. "Poems from a Seventeenth-Century Manuscript with the Hand of Robert Herrick." *Texas Quarterly* 16.4 supp. (1973): 2–185. Print.

Gibson, Colin, ed. *Witts Recreations: Selected from the Finest Fancies of Moderne Muses.* Aldershot: Scolar, 1990. Print.

Hamrick, Stephen. "Tottel's Miscellany and the English Reformation." *Criticism* 44.4 (2002): 329–61. Print.

Hobbs, Mary. "Early Seventeenth-Century Verse Miscellanies and Their Value for Textual Editors." *English Manuscript Studies* 1 (1989): 182–210. Print.

———. *Early Seventeenth-Century Verse Miscellany Manuscripts.* Aldershot: Scholar, 1992. Print.

———, ed. *The Stoughton Manuscript: A Manuscript Miscellany of Poems, by Henry King and His Circle, circa 1636.* Aldershot: Scolar, 1990. Print.

Hughey, Ruth, ed. *The Arundel Harington Manuscript of Tudor Poetry.* Columbus: Ohio State UP, 1960. Print.

Love, Harold. *Scribal Publication in Seventeenth-Century England.* Oxford: Clarendon, 1993. Print.

Marotti, Arthur F. *Manuscript, Print, and the English Renaissance Lyric.* Ithaca: Cornell UP, 1995. Print.

Marquis, Paul A., ed. *Richard Tottel's* Songes and Sonnettes: *The Elizabethan Version.* Tempe: Arizona Center for Medieval and Renaissance Studies–Renaissance English Text Soc., 2007. Print.

May, Steven W., ed. *Henry Stanford's Anthology: An Edition of Cambridge University Library Manuscript Dd.5.75.* New York: Garland, 1988. Print.

McKitterick, David. *Print, Manuscript and the Search for Order, 1450–1830.* Cambridge: Cambridge UP, 2003. Print.

McRae, Andrew. *Literature, Satire, and the Early Stuart State.* Cambridge: Cambridge UP, 2004. Print.

Raylor, Timothy. *Cavaliers, Clubs, and Literary Culture: Sir John Mennes, James Smith, and the Order of the Fancy.* Newark: U of Delaware P, 1994. Print.

———, ed. Musarum Deliciae *(1655), and* Wit Restor'd *(1658).* Delmar: Scholars' Facsims. and Rpts., 1985. Print.

Rollins, Hyder Edward, ed. *Brittons Bowre of Delights, 1591.* Cambridge: Harvard UP, 1933. Print.

———, ed. *England's Helicon, 1600, 1614.* 2 vols. Cambridge: Harvard UP, 1935. Print.

———, ed. *The Paradise of Dainty Devices, 1576–1606.* Cambridge: Harvard UP, 1927. Print.

————, ed. *The Phoenix Nest, 1593*. Cambridge: Harvard UP, 1931. Print.

————, ed. *Tottel's Miscellany, 1557–1587*. 2 vols. Rev. ed. Cambridge: Harvard UP, 1966. Print.

Smyth, Adam. *"Profit and Delight": Printed Miscellanies in England, 1640–1682*. Detroit: Wayne State UP, 2004. Print.

Sullivan, Ernest W., II, ed. *The First and Second Dalhousie Manuscripts: Poems and Prose by John Donne and Others: A Facsimile Edition*. Columbia: U of Missouri P, 1988. Print.

————, ed. *The Harmony of the Muses, by Robert Chamberlain*. Aldershot: Scolar, 1990. Print.

Wolf, Edwin, II. *The Textual Importance of Manuscript Commonplace Books, 1620–1660*. Charlottesville: Bibliog. Soc. of the U of Virginia, 1949. Print.

Woudhuysen, H. R. *Sir Philip Sidney and the Circulation of Manuscripts, 1558–1640*. Oxford: Clarendon, 1996. Print.

W. Scott Howard, Peggy Keeran, and
Jennifer Bowers

# Archives on Trial: Executing *Richard II* and *Eikon Basilike* in the Digital Age

> They shall be satisfied. I'll read enough / When I do see the very book indeed . . . (Shakespeare, *Richard II* 4.1.273–74)

> Yet since providence will have it so, I am content so much of My heart . . . should be discovered to the world . . . (Eikon Basilike 159)

This essay offers a transferable model for an interdisciplinary literary studies course that investigates dynamic reciprocities between two foundational works: Shakespeare's *Richard II* (1597) and *Eikon Basilike*, the so-called king's book, purportedly written by Charles I during the months of his captivity leading up to his execution on 30 January 1648. As the above quotations illustrate, both texts challenge the divine right of kings in a cultural context marked by a steady progress toward limited monarchy and by the technologies of the times, which engendered public demand for greater access to information about liberty and license, Providence and Parliament, sovereignty and secularism in a rapidly changing world.

*Richard II* and *Eikon Basilike* provide myriad opportunities for exploring a rich, dialectical theme at the heart of literary studies in the digital age: how and why new technologies both celebrate and challenge the sovereignty of the text and of the archive; how and why interactively designed forms of access to information remediate the very objects of knowledge we value as well as the fields of study within and against which we place those artifacts.[1] *Richard II* and *Eikon Basilike* are especially well suited to this lesson because they are assemblages, even in some ways archives unto themselves; they are constituted by various source documents and printed in many editions. Since both works have a controversial scene or prayer that is present in some editions and omitted in others, even undergraduates may begin to discover the synergies between texts and technologies by comparing editions.[2] Both works highlight the political and precarious nature of knowledge when archives are themselves placed on trial—that is, executed through increasingly diversified points of access.

This essay draws on our research and teaching experiences in two courses at the University of Denver. Students worked with a generous selection of print and electronic texts, reference works, databases, and archives. The first course, Archives on Trial, was taught by W. Scott Howard, Peggy Keeran, and Jennifer Bowers; it was offered to both undergraduate and graduate students as an interdisciplinary experience and cross-listed in English and Digital Media Studies. Archives on Trial met in a smart classroom; we designed two digital tools (a research guide and a wiki) for assignments, dialogue, research, and presentations beyond our standard face-to-face meetings. The second course, Digital Archives, was taught by Howard as an English course and included two research presentations, by Keeran and by Bowers. Digital Archives was designed for undergraduates as a blended learning experience: an electronic class delivered via *Blackboard* that also involved alternating face-to-face and synchronous *Wimba* e-classroom meetings. Digital Archives reconfigured the first course for a new audience and occasion and accordingly employed a greater amount and variety of interactively designed digital tools and assignments.[3]

Notwithstanding those differences, both classes delivered a consistent methodology: an exploration of texts and contexts that define key issues and events from earlier times and that also provoke critical reflection on the diversified media (print, visual, electronic) that shape fields of knowledge.

## Methodology

Our courses examined the transformation of literary texts into cultural documents (and of cultural documents into literary texts) when those materials are taught, researched, and interpreted within and against the resources of subscription digital projects, specialized digital collections, and digital libraries. Our students searched in *Early English Books Online* (*EEBO*) and *Eighteenth Century Collections Online* (*ECCO*) to find a variety of documents concerning the ongoing *Eikon Basilike* authorship controversy, and they used the *Bodleian Library Broadside Ballads* to find differing accounts of King Charles's last words. In *British History Online*, they searched the *Journal of the House of Lords* for records of the impeachment of Queen Henrietta Maria; in the *John Milton Reading Room*, they consulted a hypertext edition of *The Tenure of Kings and Magistrates* for Milton's argument in favor of executing Charles I. Such an array of resources cultivates a rich learning environment in which archival research is grasped as immediate and integral rather than as remote and mysterious. By interweaving intellectual inquiry and the research process, our classes made central the discovery and interpretation of primary and secondary sources, thus helping our students understand the complexity of early modern print and visual cultures.

At each step along the way, we examined every resource, including printed books, vis-à-vis a three-point, recursive analysis.

> Access: What is the resource and where is it coming from? Who is the target audience? What degree of authority informs the resource? How and why has the point of access been constructed?
> Form and Content: How and why does the design of this resource make a contribution to a particular field of knowledge?
> Integration: How and why does the medium of information shape not only the message but also the changing field or fields of knowledge and object or objects of investigation?

We engaged our students on these three levels in order to address the fundamental matter of remediation: manuscripts, databases, and digital classroom tools are not neutral spaces; they all distinctively shape "the information [they convey] and [are shaped] in turn by the physical and cultural worlds in which [they function]" (Bolter and Gromala 77). Whether our students were interpreting King Richard's allegorical musings on the reflected image of his face (4.1.273–303) or navigating the British Library's *Treasures in Full: Shakespeare in Quarto* or deciphering King Charles's self-fashioned iconography[4] or comparing *Project Canterbury*'s digital edition of *The King's Book* (based on a so-called advance copy of the first edition) with versions on *EEBO*, we hoped they would gain a more complex and nuanced understanding of how literary works and digital archives are not static objects but dynamic sites where interactive design conditions the possibilities for collaborative and constitutive inquiry in and beyond the classroom.

## Resources and Strategies

After our students had completed reading Charles Forker's 2002 Arden edition of *Richard II*, including his substantial introduction and appendixes, they examined a variety of digital editions of the play: the six quartos through *Treasures in Full* as well as *EEBO*; out-of-copyright, scanned texts of the play available through *Google Books*; numerous e-book versions of *Richard II* from *Project Gutenberg*; and a digital transcription of the play available from the University of Virginia Library's *Electronic Text Center*. We investigated these versions of Shakespeare's play according to our three-point, recursive methodology. That robust, comparative adventure took a whole week but was well worth the effort.

As with any archive a scholar visits, knowledge of how and why it was created gives insight into what it holds. We have found it instructive, accordingly, to explain to students that *EEBO* has its roots in the traditional practice of compiling bibliographies. This archive reaches back to the 1920s cataloging efforts of A. W. Pollard and Gilbert R. Redgrave and the monumental microfilming project begun in the 1930s by Eugene Powers, which then began to be digitized in the 1990s. The company, now called Pro-Quest, estimates that this project will be completed in 2020, spanning almost ninety years! (On *EEBO*, see the essays by Shawn Martin and by Eveyln Tribble in this volume.)

Locating the quartos of *Richard II* in *EEBO* is straightforward: using Basic Search, enter "Shakespeare" as author keyword, "Richard II" as title keyword, and limit the search by a date (1597) or range of dates (1597–1634). The quartos are also available on microfilm, and reel numbers can be found by searching *WorldCat* or the *English Short Title Catalogue* (*ESTC*). Faculty members and students who do not have access to *EEBO* or the microfilm sets may use the British Library's Web site *Treasures in Full* instead, which allows side-by-side comparisons of all six editions and also provides in-depth information about Shakespeare's sources, early performances, and the complete publication history of *Richard II*.

Consulting the bibliographic information Forker includes, our students searched *EEBO* for sources to which Shakespeare might have had access before 1595, when the play was first performed: Holinshed's *Chronicles*, Hall's *The Vnion of the Two Noble and Illustrate Families*, Daniel's *The*

**Figure 1.** *Wordle* collage of deposition scene from *Richard II*

*First Fowre Bookes of the Ciuile Warres*, Marlowe's play *Edward the Second*, Berners's translation of Froissart's *Cronycles*, and *A Mirrour for Magistrates*. The anonymous play *Thomas of Woodstock* is not in *EEBO* because it existed only in manuscript, but the 1929 Malone Society text is available in print and online through Chadwyck-Healey's *English Drama*. In order to create our own archive of those source texts, students posted durable URL links to these works in the course wiki under the category "Shakespeare's Source Texts," where they also contributed their own annotations on each document.

The following steps raised our comparative classroom activities to an even more exciting level: students were asked to select one open-access e-text version of *Richard II*; to locate a key moment in the play; to copy and paste the language from that moment into *Wordle* (a word-cloud generator that gives prominence to words according to their frequency in a given section of text); then to create, edit, and publish their *Richard II* collages to the public *Wordle* platform. We used *Jing* to create .png files of our students' *Richard II* word clouds and gathered those into an open-access gallery in *Blackboard*. Students then visited the gallery and wrote one-hundred-word comments on the collages in reply to this question: "How and why does each word cloud teach you something new about close-reading the corresponding key moment from *Richard II*?" Figure 1 shows a collage that remixes a portion of the deposition scene (4.1.268–318). Through that sequence of activities, our students discovered and engaged critically with a variety of digital archives and electronic versions of Shakespeare's play; they took their first steps toward theorizing the dynamics of remediation involved in each of those resources; and they became cocreators of digital collages that led them to profound, new understandings about old-fashioned close reading, which has perhaps always been an exercise in remediation.

*Eikon Basilike* is Greek for "royal portrait," and, because the image of the king plays an important role in understanding the historical figures of Richard II and Charles I, our students examined portraits of both as well as the symbolism employed to illustrate their divine right. We considered the Wilton Diptych of Richard II (National Gallery, London) and the Westminster Abbey portrait of Richard II. A variety of freely available and subscription digital image collections provide access to these portraits. But there are still difficulties: image quality can be poor, and copyright law can restrain posting online. In *Google Images*, portraits of Richard II are available, but their origin and quality are sometimes questionable. *ARTstor*, a subscription database, includes the Wilton Diptych but not the Westminster portrait. To identify surviving portraits of historic British figures systematically, we recommend that one start by consulting the "Likenesses" section at the end of biographical sketches in the *Oxford Dictionary of National Biography*, then search for digital images in *Google Images*, *ARTstor*, and the Web sites for the institutions that own the objects.

The best image of the jewel-like Wilton Diptych is the high-quality digital copy located on the National Gallery Web site. This portable, private altarpiece, with two panels hinged together like a book (roughly 22" x 11.5" in size when closed), reveals inside a religious world, in which Richard on the left is presented by three saints to Mary, Jesus, and a host of angels on the right. On the exterior of the diptych are the symbols of Richard's secular world: his arms and a chained white hart with a crown about its neck. Although the image is not downloadable, the ability to zoom in on the religious scene allows a close analysis. Richard is the center of attention, surrounded by very personal symbolism: the livery of his father-in-law, Charles IV; the white hart from his mother; and the rosemary from Anne of Bohemia, his wife. The viewer can see the minutest detail, such as the carefully crafted badge of a hart, with pearls on its antlers and a crown about its neck, on Richard's chest. In contrast, the much larger (roughly 6' x 3.5') Westminster Abbey public portrait shows Richard sitting on a throne with the emphasis on his regalia. This painting symbolizes that kingship is inherited and holy. Students were unable to locate a digital copy of the Westminster Richard to equal the quality of the National Gallery's digital copy of the Wilton Diptych, so sometimes a book may prove to be the best resource.

Our archival investigation of *Eikon Basilike* centered on the cultivated role of Charles I as characterized in his last masque and the similar performative spectacle of his trial and execution. The printed text of *Salmacida Spolia*, surviving theatrical sketches, periodical accounts of the trial proceedings and execution, broadside ballads, scaffold speeches, and published memoirs served to illustrate how political events were reflected in and remediated by seventeenth-century high and popular culture.

First performed on 21 January 1639, *Salmacida Spolia* was the only masque in which both Charles and Henrietta Maria performed together and was the last masque of their court. Written by William D'Avenant, with scenes and inventions by Inigo Jones and music by Lewis Richard, *Salmacida Spolia* presents the king as Philogenes, lover of his people, who appears to the audience seated on the Throne of Honour. Although he maintains the divine attributes standard to the genre, Charles is specifically praised for his patience to "out last those stormes the peoples giddy fury rayse" (from the song "To the King, When He Appears" [st. 2]), and the masque is tempered by the political reality of the time. Students used the version in *EEBO* to draw parallels with the antimasque figures and contemporary civil unrest and to note how the staging and text work to create representations of the royal couple. Surviving stage designs and costume sketches by Jones contributed further to our students' understanding of how the masque served as a propaganda tool. Only a few sketches for *Salmacida Spolia* are available in *Google Images*, and no relevant images are found in *ARTstor*, so the best resource for Jones's sketches remains Stephen Orgel and Roy Strong's *Inigo Jones: The Theatre of the Stuart Court*. Having to rely on the printed book spurred class discussion about the online availability of archival materials, the nature of and access to private collections, and the decision to house this particular book in our library's special collections.

Seventeenth-century periodicals, especially those from the time of the civil wars, offer insight into the range of public opinion concerning contemporary events. (See Laura McGrane's essay in this volume.) After the Star Chamber was abolished in July 1641, the press was afforded greater liberty in publishing and promoting causes on both sides of the conflict. Scholars are fortunate that George Thomason, Charles Burney, and others had the foresight to understand the historical value of these ephemeral publications. Thomason's collection of civil war periodicals (1641–63) has been scanned from the microfilm and included in *EEBO*. The collections of Burney and John Nichols compose the subscription database *Seventeenth and Eighteenth Century Burney Collection Newspapers* (1603–1800), referred to as *Burney*, which is based on the microfilm collection *Early English Newspapers*, with additional contributions from the British Library's holdings. Students may use either database to review issues for commentary on specific events or to search across a date range for mention of relevant key terms. Although *EEBO* does not permit full-text searching of periodical contents, the periodicals sometimes are characterized by lengthy and descriptive titles, such as *The Armies Modest Intelligencer: Communicating to the Whole Kindom* [sic], *Certaine Passages in Parliament, the Full Proceeding upon the Kings Triall, Debates at the General Councell, vvith Varietie of Intelligence from Several Places in England, and Other Parts of Europe.* *Burney* offers the distinct advantage of full-text periodical contents searching.

In our classes, students consulted *EEBO* and *Burney* to assess contemporary reception to the trial and execution of Charles I. Since the trial and execution occurred in January 1648 (Julian) or 1649 (Gregorian), this discrepancy in historical dating provides an opportunity to discuss problems that may arise when one searches for accounts of events in archival materials, the role played by catalog records, and possible search strategies. Our students discovered that the news accounts present Charles in a range of roles, from sympathetic to tyrannical.

In addition to periodicals, our students investigated popular accounts of the trial and execution in contemporary broadside ballads. The freely available *Bodleian Library Broadside Ballads* collection features more than thirty thousand ballads, dating from the sixteenth through the twentieth century. Browsing the subject index for the heading "Charles I, King of England, 1600–1649" yields fourteen ballads, two of which specifically address the end of Charles's life: "The Manner of the King's Tryal at Westminster" and "England's Black Tribunal; or, King Charles's Martyrdom." The *English Broadside Ballad Archive* contains an additional ballad, "The Kings Last Speech at His Time of Execution," as well as a copy of "The Manner of the Kings Tryal at Westminster-Hall . . . with His / Speech Made upon the Scaffold before He Was Beheaded." (See the essay by Patricia Fumerton, Simone Chess, Tassie Gniady, and Kris McAbee in this volume.) These ballads enabled our students to explore differences in textual and visual representations of the king and also to note contextual information, such as the tune to which the ballad was sung (e.g., "Aim Not Too High, Gerheards Mistris").

Published accounts of Charles's speech on the scaffold are numerous in *EEBO*: printed as separate documents; included with other materials regarding the trial and execution; or sometimes collected with various scaffold speeches, as in the 180-page *England's Black Tribunal . . . together with His Majesties Speech on the Scaffold . . . together with . . . Several Dying Speeches from the Year 1642 to 1658.* Students may compare the king's scaffold speech with that of the earl of Strafford (or with those of other contemporaries) by searching keywords ("scaffold" or "last dying") and "speech*" (using the asterisk to truncate the term). They may also use subject headings in conjunction with desired date ranges: "Last words—England—Early works to 1800," "Last words—Early works to 1800," "Executions and executioners—England—17th century." Our students also read accounts of the events as related in the memoirs of Sir Thomas Herbert, who was an attendant to Charles I during his captivity. Herbert published *Threnodia Carolina* in 1678, which is not in *EEBO*, but we used *ECCO* to find his narrative published in 1702, *Memoirs of the Two Last Years of the Reign of That Unparallell'd Prince, . . . King Charles I*, which offers a moving description of Charles's final day.

## Remediating Renaissance Literature and Culture

These courses have been exciting and rewarding to teach, not only because of the new possibilities for research that digital technologies provide but also because those electronic resources and interpretive strategies resonate so strongly with the temper of the Renaissance, when the boundary between text and context was quite fluid. As Jay David Bolter and Diane Gromala observe, at least since the sixteenth century two competing epistemologies have been shaping the Western fields of knowledge and technological development: one concerned with permanence and transparency, the other with contingency and reflectivity (60–74). "Good Web design is both transparent and reflective. It reflects the user's needs and wants in all their complexity" (74). Digital archives, electronic texts, and interactively designed tools for research and teaching underscore the interinvolvement of both traditions. The six quartos of *Richard II* may be discovered and engaged through *Treasures in Full* as transcendent artifacts and as constitutive works of cultural remediation. Researchers and librarians, educators and their students, authors and publishers all thus share the heightened responsibility of working collaboratively in the active process of building and maintaining the archives, texts, and contexts that matter most for the fields of knowledge about early modern England.

## Notes

1. To remediate is to convey information through varying means of representation. See Bolter and Gromala.

2. The deposition scene (4.1.155–318) appears in four of the early editions of Shakespeare's play: the Fourth Quarto (1608), possibly based on a performance; the First Folio (1623); the Second Folio (1632); and the Sixth Quarto (1634),

which is derived from the 1632 Second Folio. The scene does not appear in Q1 (1597), Q2 (1598), Q3 (1598), or Q5 (1615). In 1649 alone, thirty-five editions of *Eikon Basilike* were published in England; twenty-five, elsewhere in Europe. Our students used *EEBO* to compare versions of *Eikon Basilike* against the Daems and Nelson edition, noting in particular the presence or absence of the controversial "Prayer in Time of Captivity" (first printed in William Duggard's March 1649 edition).

3. Our syllabus for Archives on Trial is available at http://mysite.du.edu /~showard/S07.3223.html; our research guide from Digital Archives is available at http://libguides.du.edu/engl2202. In the first class we used *PBwiki* (now *PBworks*) and in the second *Blackboard* to create various Web 2.0 interactive tools, including blogs, discussion boards, synchronous chat sessions, and wikis.

4. Our students used *EEBO* to compare printings of the engraved portraits of Charles I by William Marshall and Thomas Rawlins, which served as frontispieces for some of the seventeenth-century editions of *Eikon Basilike*.

## Works Cited

Bolter, Jay David, and Diane Gromala. *Windows and Mirrors: Interaction Design, Digital Art, and the Myth of Transparency*. Cambridge: MIT P, 2005. Print.

D'Avenant, William. Salmacida Spolia: *A Masque: Presented by the King and Queenes Majesties, at White-hall, on Tuesday the 21. Day of Ianuary 1639*. London, 1639 [1640]. *Early English Books Online*. Web. 25 Feb. 2010.

Eikon Basilike *with Selections from* Eikonoklastes. Ed. Jim Daems and Holly Faith Nelson. Peterborough: Broadview, 2006. Print.

Orgel, Stephen, and Roy Strong. *Inigo Jones: The Theatre of the Stuart Court . . . [from] the collection of the Duke of Devonshire*. Berkeley: U of California P, 1973. Print.

Shakespeare, William. *King Richard II*. Ed. Charles R. Forker. London: Thomson Learning, 2002. Print. Arden Shakespeare, 3rd ser.

**Angelica Duran**

# Not *Either-or* but Rather *Both-and*: Using Both Material and Electronic Resources

During the early modern period, a common image used to refer to educational institutions, texts, and scholars was *fons sapientia*, "font of wisdom or of knowledge." I was reminded of that term when reading Thomas Friedman's 2005 best-selling *The World Is Flat*. Friedman compares using the Internet at the beginning of the period he terms "Globalization 3.0," starting in 2000, to turning on a fire hydrant of information. He goes on to describe what it will take to become "untouchables." While Friedman's purview includes a broad swath of economic and social positions, the most germane meaning of his coy term for the graduate students I encounter is highly desirable world citizens who can siphon off and apply information constructively: they will possess "not only a new level of technical skills but also a certain mental flexibility, self-motivation, and psychological mobility" (278). His and others' arguments that place the ability to wield information among the set of the world's always urgent intellectual and practical needs echo those during that other period of information explosion, the early modern period, when similar skills were acquired by the untouchables we study today: the Queen Elizabeth Is, Francis Bacons, John Miltons, and Isaac Newtons.

As well as being the bread and butter of early modern scholarship, archival research is an activity that can help us as we strive to be untouchables and train our students to be so in whatever professional fields they enter. This essay describes an approach to training graduate students in archival research through material archive tours, electronic searching, and assignments in a way that promotes the complementary use of material and electronic archives, as well as human collaboration, so that students recognize and participate in the "plasticity" of libraries, a quality Jennifer Summit has cogently identified in old texts and new technologies (1, 234–39). Students are invited to recognize the subtle permutations and importance of archival organization: electronic catalogs, Dewey decimal allocation, physical placement in special collections. The differing attributions of authorship, disciplinary domains, and other identities in various archives have the power to shape reception and direct research down different paths. A clear example is that of the works of George Sandys (1577–1644): that he appears in anthologies and bibliographies with the designations "American literature" and "British literature" demonstrates the flexibility of national affiliation in the British-American colonial period (Elliott; Kermode and Smith; Shields). My job is to help frustrated graduate students see that, instead of impeding scholarship, inconsistencies like these can enhance it. I try to promote interest in the vastly underused archives housed at my university and, by extension, to prepare students for fellowships at libraries and cultural sites and for the academic and nonacademic careers they will eventually have.

## Groups A, B, and C: Access, Books, and Collaboration

A text called, in one of its guises, *A Manifesto of the Lord Protector . . . wherein Is Shewn the Reasonableness of the Cause of This Republic against the Depredations of the Spaniards* (1738) is a particularly wily British anti-Spanish propaganda piece, and its promiscuous history can be fully appreciated through the complementary use of material and electronic archives. It is great for classroom use because it is short, so it does not pressure always packed syllabi; its attribution to John Milton generally piques the interest of students, familiar with his epic *Paradise Lost*; and, finally, its availability at the Krannert School of Management's Special Collections at my home university (Purdue) enables me to avoid the necessity of an off-campus field trip and, instead, to demonstrate the resources made available to students by their tuition dollars. Instructors may know of similarly multitasking texts at their home institutions or can work with their special collections librarians to find one or more such texts.

I introduce students to *Manifesto* in a special collections tour. The librarian on hand shows the entries in our campus's electronic library catalog for this and the other texts we review, so that we can pause at categories that would otherwise be neglected, such as physical description. Having Milton's slim, homely, forty-page, twenty-one-centimeter tall *Manifesto* sitting next to the collection's handsome 1791 edition of Adam Smith's gilded 520-page, twenty-nine-centimeter tall *Wealth of Nations* (orig. 1776) helps students see why I have cautioned them to override any digital archive's tool that automatically levels all electronic texts to the same size to fit a viewing screen. Setting the scale to a hundred percent for at least a few seconds will give students some sense of the social meaning of the texts being reviewed. In early modern publishing, size mattered; large texts were often produced on high-quality paper and possess other characteristics that signify higher cost of production, characteristics that are imperceptible to casual users of electronic archives but that indicate the purpose and initial readership of a text. I also have on hand the heavy, gold-edged 1859 *Del pauperismo* ("On Pauperism"), by Manuel Pérez y de Molina. This book impresses on students that small or average size may not mean low quality and that electronic catalogs are incomplete: *WorldCat* does not list Purdue's copy in its list of "libraries worldwide that own item," yet we have the book in front of us.

To give students some sense of the research I did to present them with a tidy special collections tour, I set them on weeklong, out-of-class group assignments designed to show them how group work, an activity usually despised, can lead to a more nuanced understanding of the complex issues of authorial attribution, textual use, and textual recovery (see the appendix to this essay). My university's catalog is linked to other catalogs, such as *WorldCat*, as well as to electronic archives of primary texts for the period, including *Early English Books Online* (*EEBO*), *Eighteenth Century Collections Online* (*ECCO*), and *Sabin Americana, 1500–1926*. The assignments lead students to use a number of these resources.

The group that reads all the English editions of *Manifesto*, group A, may consider itself the luckiest, thinking that it can complete its task using the university's electronic archives, because there are only two editions and both are available through the university library's catalog: one by a link to *ECCO*, the other by a link to *Sabin*. But if the students of group A do not read carefully, they may miss the main difference between the first and second editions of 1738. On page 30 of 40, in the half page between the text and the poem "Britannia," one edition has a design and blank space, the other an advertisement for various works from the publishing house of Thomas Birch, including "A Compleat Collection of the . . . Works of John Milton . . . with the Addition of This Manifesto, in the Original Latin."

Group A students sometimes fail to use the material copy that our university possesses in its special collections. If they come to office hours or contact me through e-mail in preparation for the class presentation, I make sure to ask them if someone in the group has read it so that during their presentation the group can tell us which of the two English editions our university possesses and discuss differences between the electronic and material texts.

Group B's assignment, to find all Latin versions of *Manifesto*, alerts them to the plasticity of the text, that it exists in different languages and was printed at different times. Their work can be facilitated if they communicate with the students of group A, because "A Compleat Collection," mentioned in the Birch advertisement, contains a Latin version. Mental flexibility is required to overcome the difficulties that arise here. One difficulty is that searching under the keyword "Compleat," even in the Title tab, does not call up this text, because the data entry in our university catalog corrects the word to *complete*. Group B has always had trouble locating the original 1655 Latin edition electronically. Although there are many keywords they can use to find *Scriptum Dom: Protectoris . . . in quo hujus reipublic causa contra Hispanos justa esse demonstratur*, these students tend to search under "Milton" and "Manifesto," which yields them nothing because, as they later see from printing the title page of the original 1655 edition, Milton's name does not appear. I bring in volume 5 of the second edition of *The Complete Prose Works of John Milton*, the standard material resource that Miltonists and early modern scholars know to check. It provides the Latin title that group B could have keyed in, if only its students had checked with the Purdue resident Miltonist: me. *The Complete Prose* also tells them that Milton, in his role as secretary of foreign tongues (1649–59), penned many works for the Cromwellian government but that we do not know how much, if any, input he had in writing this text.

How and when, then, did this misattribution to Secretary Milton come about? *The Compleat Prose* notes that "A Compleat Collection" was the first to attribute the work to Milton "without a shred of clear evidence" (712). Students can turn to the electronic *Compleat Collection*, which tells them the basis for the publisher's attribution: "This piece, from the peculiar Elegance of the Stile, appears to have been drawn up in *Latin* by our Author [Milton], whose Province it was, as Secretary to *Cromwell* in that Language" (xxxiv). Luckily, our short-term collaborators need not read the 747-page work to find that explanation, because I already did that work. We discuss how this eighteenth-century misattribution hints at the political value of constructing the once-scorned Cromwellian supporter but now national epic author Milton as the author of this propaganda piece, presented as historical but newly minted. Having read the text, students know that the work first rallied national and international support for Cromwell's Western Design, the British plan for securing Spanish territories in the Caribbean in the mid-1650s. It then lay dormant until the renewed efforts of King George II (r. 1727–60) to wrest American holdings from Spain.

This use of Milton in the eighteenth century shows students the currency of his authority across disciplines, which they otherwise note only in terms of the placement of the material copy of *Manifesto* in the section of our special collections devoted to economics. We tease out the text's interdisciplinary dimension by incorporating the findings of group C about two other English editions: *The British Sailor's Discovery; or, The Spanish Pretensions Confuted* . . . (1739) and *A True Copy of Oliver Cromwell's Manifesto against Spain* (1741), both of which are published by T. Cooper and attribute *Manifesto* only to Cromwell. It is interesting that *True Copy* informs readers that "the *Latin* Copy" resides at the end of the second "volume of *Milton*'s works lately published" (v).

Students' interests dictate our use of the in-class projection of digital facsimiles of the texts. For example, if a student wishes to create a more inclusive literary history of mid-eighteenth-century England, we might click on the hyperlink to James Thomson, the hack writer of the appendixed poem "Britannia" in the 1738 editions of *Manifesto* to see that he is the author of more than two hundred eclectic publications readily available for research. The varied subject categories in the catalogs (*EEBO, ECCO, Sabin, WorldCat*) reflect textual anxiety about authorship and by extension about the role of literature and literary figures in other fields.

## Groups D and E: Developing and Expanding

Groups D and E extend the conversation to plurilingualism in electronic and material archives. Some research might stop at the English and Latin versions. After all, we all know that, although the vernacular was used more and more in the seventeenth century for national audiences, Latin was still used for international audiences. If Spaniards were interested in British justifications, they could look at the Latin. Also, the Yale edition of Milton's *Complete Prose* states that the original work "appeared in official Latin and English versions" (711).

I still wondered, though; and group D's assignment to find all Spanish versions of the text is the result of that wondering. Using the reports of groups B and C, group D gains some clues for a successful electronic search. They can find on *WorldCat*, but not on our university library catalog, a Spanish edition published in 1655, presumably unofficial: *Manifiesto del Protector de Inglaterra . . . declarando á fabor desta Republica, la justicia de su causa contra España*. I am interested in what group D presents as "anything else that the group believes is important," but I make sure that we cover the following three matters. First, we conduct a quick in-class search of all the available catalogs for their different holdings and attributions. We find that the Spanish edition's publishers, Henry Hills and John Field, were Londoners responsible for many publications related to Commonwealth and Protectorate documents. If we go a bit further by limiting the language to Spanish, we discover that *Manifiesto* is the only one of Hills and Field's 676 publications that was printed in Spanish. Second, *WorldCat* gives Cromwell and Milton as the authors. So does this work in Spanish, contemporary with the first Latin and English editions, provide textual evidence of Milton's authorship, which we, along with the Yale editors, believed to be unfounded? Or did *WorldCat* simply repeat the eighteenth-century misattribution? Students cannot find the answer easily because of the third piece of pertinent information: the Spanish edition is unavailable in electronic archives, listed as residing in only one library, the Newberry Library. I have reviewed the Newberry's copy and found it to be a faithful translation of the English of 1655; it provides no additional information about authorship.[1] My answers add to students' appreciation of the value of material special collections worldwide and the legwork, rather than fingerwork on keyboards, that scholars should still conduct. Moreover, this in-class research drives

home the importance of thoroughness in research and intellectual curiosity, since group D could have presented this or similar kinds of findings or
questions had it delved a little further.

Group E's assignment to identify differences among the English,
Latin, and Spanish versions is structured to be the least successful in terms
of direct answers but most successful in assembling and expanding many
of the ideas that have emerged from the other assignments. Students have
no easy access to the Spanish edition, so they are left with trying to assess
the differences between the Latin and the English. Sometimes they are
lucky enough to have a group member who knows Latin; sometimes they
come to me. It is curious that they have never asked one of our Latin
professors to help. The assignment clearly shows the students of group E
the limitations of monolingualism for a full appreciation of a text that is
relevant to literature, politics, government, and more, as the subject categories suggest.

In connection with group E's assignment I give a minilecture on
the fact that Spain and the Catholic Church lagged behind England and
Protestant countries in adopting the vernacular for publications, prefer-
ring (little c) catholic Latin for (big C) Catholic communication. Thus,
this Spanish version signals to all Spanish readers that it was not created
by Spanish or Catholic officials or for Spanish or Catholic purposes. Additionally, the seemingly modest text represents an affront, of sorts, to
Spanish and Catholic officials in its very promotion of the use of the vernacular, not just vernacular English within its borders but also vernacular
Spanish wherever the text might travel. Students' lack of Latin perpetuates
the suppression of the study of Spanish contributions to British conversations like the ones expressed in *Manifesto*.[2] I make the analogy to the
need for accessing all sides of international, multilingual, and multireli-
gious conversations today. The MLA's recent findings on the low level of
multilingualism of citizens of the United States (*Foreign Languages*) can
serve to precipitate discussion about scholars' roles as world citizens and
about such issues as the dedication of more money and energy to language
assessment and training by the United States Department of Homeland
Security and other agencies since 9/11 for the purposes of increasing general cultural awareness and global security.

Archival research can contribute to the mental flexibility, self-motivation,
and psychological mobility that are so important for students. Research
assignments like those described in this essay can go far in demonstrating
that, while material-only or electronic-only research may sometimes be

sufficient, there are many contexts in which neither is entirely responsible; in showing how multilingualism fosters constructive transcultural leadership; and in explaining how authors function as cultural capital. Developing research skills in the use of both material and electronic archives will equip students, if I may return to the image of the fire hydrant at the beginning of this essay, with the right tools to manage information effectively and thus to experience those exhilarating, steeped moments that some of us teachers have been fortunate enough to have in our research.

## Notes

I thank Jonathan Gil Harris for presiding at the panel Early Modern Research in the Digital Age, arranged by the Division on Literature of the English Renaissance, Excluding Shakespeare, at the 2007 MLA Annual Convention; my research was first presented on that panel. I also thank the Newberry Library's 2008 Lumsden-Kouvel Fellowship, which facilitated part of my work on this essay.

1. The long title says that the Spanish was "[t]ranslated from the English to Spanish" ("Traducido del Ingles a Español"), a detail that indicates the translation was done from one vernacular to another rather than from the Latin source.

2. For recent work to fill the gap in the study of these Spanish contributions, see Marotti; Corthell, Dolan, Highley, and Marotti.

## Works Cited

*The British Sailor's Discovery; or, The Spanish Pretensions Confuted.* London, 1739. Print.

Corthell, Ronald, Frances E. Dolan, Christopher Highley, and Arthur F. Marotti, eds. *Catholic Culture in Early Modern England.* Notre Dame: U of Notre Dame P, 2007. Print.

Cromwell, Oliver. *Manifiesto del Protector de Inglaterra . . . declarando á fabor desta Republica, la justicia de su causa contra España.* London, 1655. Print.

———. *A True Copy of Oliver Cromwell's Manifesto against Spain, Dated October 26, 1655.* London, 1741. Print.

Elliott, Emory, ed. *American Colonial Writers, 1606–1734.* Detroit: Gale, 1984. Print. Vol. 24 of *Dictionary of Literary Biography.*

*Foreign Languages and Higher Education: New Structures for a Changed World. Modern Language Association.* MLA, 2007. Web. 13 Mar. 2014.

Friedman, Thomas. *The World Is Flat: A Brief History of the Twenty-First Century: Further Updated and Expanded.* 2005. New York: Picador, 2007. Print.

Kermode, Frank, and A. J. Smith, eds. *The Oxford Anthology of English Literature.* New York: Oxford UP, 1973. Print.

Marotti, Arthur F. *Catholicism and Anti-Catholicism in Early Modern English Texts.* New York: St. Martin's, 1999. Print.

Milton, John. *A Compleat Collection of the Historical, Political, and Miscellaneous Works of John Milton.* Vol. 1. London, 1737. Print.

———. *The Complete Prose Works of John Milton.* Vol. 5. 2nd ed. Ed. Don Wolfe. New Haven: Yale UP, 1971. Print.

———. *A Manifesto of the Lord Protector . . . wherein Is Shewn the Reasonableness of the Cause of This Republic against the Depredations of the Spaniards.* 1738. Print.

Pérez y de Molina, Manuel. *Del pauperismo, según los principios de la economía política y social: Verdaderas causas que lo originan, y medios de disminuirlo en lo posible, en conformidad con las máximas de la moral católica.* Jerez Imp. de Guadalete: D. Tomas Bueno, 1859. Print.

Shields, David S. *American Poetry: The Seventeenth and Eighteenth Centuries.* New York: Lib. of Amer., 2007. Print.

Smith, Adam. *An Inquiry into the Nature and Causes of the Wealth of Nations.* Basil, 1791. Print.

Summit, Jennifer. *Memory's Library: Medieval Books in Early Modern England.* Chicago: U of Chicago P, 2008. Print.

## Appendix:
## Group Assignments That Follow the Special Collections Tour

You should use all electronic, material, and human resources (one another, the reference libraries, me, or any others) to complete the assignment.

During class session on [supply date], students will share findings and explain their research process. Each group will turn in an annotated bibliography of all resources used. The annotations should include the date of access for each, which group member used which resource, page numbers related to any particularly challenging and illuminating information found in each resource, other information as requested below, and anything else that the group believes is important.

> Group A: Read all the English editions of the text known as *Manifesto* and report to us the importance or significance of any differences.
>
> Group B: Find all the Latin versions of the text known as *Manifesto* and print out their title pages. Your annotated bibliography should indicate where the texts are referenced (i.e., which catalog lists them) and where they reside (i.e., which library has them).
>
> Group C: Find all English versions of the text known as *Manifesto*. Your annotated bibliography should indicate where the texts are referenced (i.e., which catalog lists them) and where they reside (i.e., which library has them).
>
> Group D: Find all Spanish versions of the text known as *Manifesto*. Your annotated bibliography should indicate where the texts are referenced (i.e., which catalog lists them) and where they reside (i.e., which library has them).
>
> Group E: Describe the importance of at least three differences among the English, Spanish, and Latin versions of the text known as *Manifesto*.

**Part IV**

---

# Beyond Literature

**Joseph M. Ortiz**

# Teaching the Early Modern Music Archive

Scholars wishing to learn what Shakespeare knew and thought about music have often begun by looking at Lorenzo's speech about music in *The Merchant of Venice*:

> Sit, Jessica. Look how the floor of heaven
> Is thick inlaid with patens of bright gold.
> There's not the smallest orb which thou behold'st
> But in his motion like an angel sings,
> Still choiring to the young-eyed cherubins.
> Such harmony is in immortal souls,
> But whilst this muddy vesture of decay
> Doth grossly close it in, we cannot hear it.
> (5.1.57–64)

As a number of critics have noted, the speech, which continues at some length, is a compendium of widely disseminated views about music in the Renaissance, all of which are commonly found in the standard speculative works on music that circulated in sixteenth-century England. As James Hutton demonstrated over sixty years ago, archival research on Renaissance music treatises shows that Lorenzo's speech closely follows the order of Gioseffo Zarlino's discussion of music in his *Institutioni Harmoniche* (1558), one of the most widely read academic treatises on musical theory. What this archival research does not immediately reveal, however, is the degree of skepticism that the play exhibits about such universalizing, Neo-platonic theories of music. Although John Hollander's landmark study of music in English Renaissance poetry claims that speculative works like Boethius's *De institutione musica* "remained an unquestioned authority on the music of Antiquity and on music in general for a thousand years after its composition" (25), recent studies by Marc Berley, by David Lindley, and by me have shown that there was in fact much questioning of orthodox music theory in early modern England, not least by Shakespeare himself. For this reason, any approach to teaching Renaissance literature that seeks to incorporate the rich store of early modern music archives can benefit from a historical and theoretical sensitivity to the various ways in which music was represented and understood.

In my literature classes that incorporate discussion of Renaissance musical thought, I often begin by asking students to reflect on their own experiences and assumptions about music. For example, in my standard Shakespeare class, I give the following writing assignment early in the semester, before students read plays like *The Merchant of Venice*, *Twelfth Night*, or *Othello*:

> Write a one-page paper describing a piece of music that you know. Any genre is fine. How does the music affect you? If there are words accompanying the music (e.g., if the music is a song), how does the music affect your understanding of the text? Would other listeners get the same meanings from the music as you? Would you be able to communicate—in words—the experience of hearing this music to someone who hadn't heard it before?

When I have my students discuss their responses in class, two things immediately become clear. First, many comment on the difficulty or impossibility of describing the experience of music in words—even as they produce lavish, metaphorically rich descriptions of pieces ranging from Beethoven's *Moonlight Sonata* to Tool's *Ten Thousand Days*. In this way, even the most florid prose stylists in my class come to see poetic treatments of music as a somewhat dishonest translation. Second, student responses demonstrate that the impulse to hear meaning in music in our culture is incredibly strong. At the same time, by writing about these meanings, my students are often compelled to acknowledge, without my prompting, the arbitrariness by which meanings accrue to music. This last point was illustrated more than once when two students unwittingly chose the same piece of music, only with dramatically different interpretations about its meaning.

I have found that such self-reflective exercises are useful because they generate questions that are pertinent to understanding the concerns and motives, often very different from our own, of people writing about and composing music in Renaissance England. For example, What assumptions about human psychology would someone need to make in order to call a particular piece of music sad? When would we say that music is not like a language? Are our reactions to music learned? Armed with a theoretical approach, even students with no musical training can make important observations about the representation of music in early sources.

This essay is divided into three sections, each focusing on a different area of the musical archive: texts, images, sounds. Each section provides information about some of the more recently available resources for early modern music, both traditional and online versions, along with some discussion of the various contexts associated with the production and dissemination of these sources in early modern England. My intention is to suggest starting points for the discussion of music in the classroom, particularly in Renaissance literature classes, rather than to provide a research guide for advanced musical study.

## Texts

Oliver Strunk's *Source Readings in Music History* (1950) and Joscelyn Godwin's *Music, Mysticism and Magic: A Sourcebook* (1986) remain two of the most convenient and efficiently organized compilations of writings on *musica speculativa*, the branch of medieval and early modern philosophy that deals with the nature and causes of music. Both anthologies contain excerpts of several works on music that were well known in Renaissance England, including Boethius's *De institutione musica* and Zarlino's *Istitutioni Harmoniche*. Their one notable omission, Macrobius's commentary on Cicero's *Dream of Scipio*, is glaring, since Macrobius's story of Pythagoras's discovery of the mathematical basis of musical harmony was adapted or reproduced in nearly every treatise on *musica speculativa* through the seventeenth century. Fortunately, William Harris Stahl's fine translation of the work is available online through the American Council of Learned Societies (ACLS) *Humanities E-book* Web site, a fully searchable digital collection. In my literature classes I have found Macrobius's narrative of

Pythagoras especially useful for illustrating the fact that in the Renaissance music was commonly considered a branch of mathematics—a fact that my students, most of them products of the American public school system, are always astonished to hear. It is important to note that the writings on *musica speculativa* constitute a closed set of educational texts, in other words one whose canonical authority had to be reinforced every time a new work was produced. Hence, for example, when John Taverner, a graduate of Oxford with little musical background, was hired as professor of music at Gresham College in 1610, he filled his lectures with quotations and summaries of most of the classical and early modern writers anthologized by Strunk and Godwin.

Recent developments in both traditional and online publishing have made more available a number of early modern texts on *musica practica*, the branch of music that deals with performance and composition. Kevin C. Carnes's edition of William Bathe's *A Briefe Introduction to the Skill of Song* (1596) is an exemplary work of editing and historical scholarship that offers much useful information about music publishing (and publishing in general) in early modern England. Along with Thomas Morley's *A Plaine and Easie Introduction to Practicall Musicke* (1597), Bathe's treatise is one of the earliest attempts in England to teach music performance through printed texts. The idea that one could learn how to sing by reading a book was by no means a foregone conclusion in sixteenth-century England; for this reason, Bathe's and Morley's treatises, both of which are available on *EEBO*, constitute fascinating case studies of the idea that a normally physical process, like singing or lute playing, could be transformed into a reading practice. Although Bathe and Morley include much technical detail in their treatises, little musical background is necessary to study their rhetorical and textual representation of music and learning. The diagrams in the original texts, such as Bathe's "Gladius Musicus," are themselves a sight to behold, remarkable for their ingenuity and elaborate presentation.

## Images

In my Shakespeare and Renaissance literature courses, I make frequent use of images to illustrate how music was taught and represented in early modern England. Penelope Gouk's "Gallery," part 2 in her recent book on music and science, is a treasure trove of images of instruments, scales and tablatures, harmonic diagrams, natural magic, and *musica speculativa*—most of them from editions of musical works that circulated in Renaissance England. Some of the images, like the illustrations of Pythagoras, are typical and demonstrate the enduring appeal of historical and philosophical approaches to music in the period. But Gouk's commentary makes clear that many of the elaborate diagrams of musical notation and tablature (tablature shows the location of musical notes on an actual instrument) attempt to find ways of representing musical sound through visual texts. These efforts had direct consequences for the development of early modern ideas about language: "As a highly developed symbolic system deploying numbers, letters and other graphic signs, musical notation provided an important model for anyone exploring new forms of language, including those intended for secret communication at a distance [i.e., cryptography]" (117).

The musical images produced by Robert Fludd and by Athanasius Kircher could in themselves provide material for a course, and I have often used them to generate questions about the relation between music and language. Like the emblems discussed by Erin Kelly in this volume, these images present both explicit and cryptic messages about music's meaning. For both Fludd and Kircher, music was central to the study of natural philosophy, and their pictures portrayed music alternately as writing, hieroglyphs, the human body, architecture, and machine. On more than one occasion I have spent a good twenty minutes in class on Fludd's remarkable "Temple of Music," prompting my students to pick out individual details and read them as bits of information about the nature of music or sound. Most of his illustrations, which first appeared in his *Utriusque Cosmi . . . Historia* (1617–21), are still available only in print sources, such as Godwin (*Robert Fludd*). By contrast, and for reasons I'm not sure I fully understand, there has been an explosion of Kircher resources on the Internet in recent years. Many of the musical images from his *Musurgia Universalis* (1650), for example, can be viewed online through the *Athanasius Kircher Project* at Stanford University and through a virtual exhibition of the *Musurgia* by the Special Collections Department of the University of Glasgow.

## Sounds

The possibilities for incorporating performances of early music in the literature classroom have grown immensely in the last few years, owing to the proliferation of recordings both on CD and online. In addition to the numerous compilations of Renaissance music available on CD (often under the Naxos, Harmonia Mundi, and Dorian Sono Luminus labels), many performances of individual works are online. Colleges and universities that subscribe to *Naxos Music Library* have access to a wide range of Renaissance music, from madrigals to lute songs. One free online source is Gavin Alexander's Web site *Sidneiana*, hosted by Cambridge University, which hosts a number of musical reconstructions of sonnets by Philip Sidney and Richard Sidney, in which sonnets originally designated as songs with possible tunes (e.g., "Sleep Baby Mine" to the tune of "Basciami Vita Mia") have been scored and performed by a consort of singers. The *Classical Music Archives* Web site contains several recordings of musical settings of early modern poems and psalms by John Dowland, William Byrd, Orlando Gibbons, Thomas Morley, and others. For popular music, the *English Broadside Ballad Archive* is an impressive, easy-to-use online resource that provides images and recordings of hundreds of early modern English ballads; Patricia Fumerton, Simone Chess, Tassie Gniady, and Kris McAbee discuss this resource at length elsewhere in this volume. Note that while early music compositions are in the public domain, performances of them are generally not, so students should be told that CD or online recordings of early music are subject to the same copyright laws as those that apply to today's music.

Ross Duffin's *Shakespeare's Songbook* is a resource for students and performers wishing to hear and sing the songs in Shakespeare's plays as the songs might have sounded. The product of many years of research, Duffin's book posits musical settings for the many songs quoted in the plays, including several quotations not previously recognized as songs (e.g., the First Gentleman's salutation "The news, Rogero?" as a brief quotation of a sixteenth-century ballad about jealousy [*WT* 5.2.18]). The CD recording of half the songs, attached at the back of the book, makes *Shakespeare's Songbook* an especially useful tool for classroom demonstrations. A caveat: the book's marketing blurbs give the impression that the book and CD re-create the songs as "actually heard" by Shakespeare's original audiences, a claim that is problematic for two reasons. First, a number of the musical settings proposed in the book are, as Duffin himself acknowledges, possible rather than probable tunes: in some cases, the tune is simply one that fits the ballad's versification and structure. Second, and more important, the idea of hearing a play or ballad with its original music carries much more weight today than it did with early modern audiences. As both Duffin and Lindley point out, the relation between a lyric text and a musical setting was almost never stable, and melodies were promiscuously attached and detached to different texts, regardless of their subject matter or sentiment. Thus a particular melodic or harmonic progression would not have been perceived as meaningful on the early modern stage in the same way that it would be perceived in, say, a passage in Verdi's *Aida*.

This caveat aside, sound recordings can be a marvelous classroom tool for exploring the ways in which Shakespeare complicates the relation between music and language. When I teach *Hamlet*, I play for my students Duffin's recording of "And Will He Not Come Again" as part of a discussion of the history of theatrical representations of Ophelia. This performance, exquisitely beautiful, comes across almost as a stand-alone set piece that accords with Romantic descriptions of Ophelia as existing outside the mucky world of the play. I then show a clip of a recent performance of Ophelia, either by Helena Bonham Carter or Kate Winslet, in which the songs are spoken, or even snarled, rather than sung. The point is not whether one performance is more authentic than another but how musical sound affects a listener's understanding of language. What difference, I will ask, does it make whether Ophelia sings or speaks the ballads? How might a particular musical setting reinforce our sense of her madness? What is it about the singing voice that might cause one to say that Ophelia's "speech is nothing" (4.5.7) or that her hearers "botch the words up fit to their own thoughts" (4.5.10)? Shakespeare was well aware of how music accommodates the different narratives imposed on it. Accordingly, I encourage my students to use the occasion of musical sound to complicate common assumptions about musical meaning—as Jessica does in *The Merchant of Venice*—rather than find tidy solutions for understanding music in a dramatic context.

## Note

Instructors and students interested in exploring further Shakespeare's songs should see Lindley; Winkler. On the connections between music and early modern science, see Gouk. The indispensable work on sound and language in early modern England is Smith.

## Works Cited

Bathe, William. *A Briefe Introduction to the Skill of Song.* 1596. Ed. Kevin C. Karnes. Aldershot: Ashgate, 2005. Print.

Berley, Marc. *After the Heavenly Tune: English Poetry and the Aspiration to Song.* Pittsburgh: Duquesne UP, 2000. Print.

Duffin, Ross W. *Shakespeare's Songbook*. New York: Norton, 2004. Print.

Godwin, Joscelyn, ed. *Music, Mysticism and Magic: A Sourcebook*. London: Routledge, 1986. Print.

———. *Robert Fludd: Hermetic Philosopher and Surveyor of Two Worlds*. Boulder: Shambhala, 1979. Print.

Gouk, Penelope. *Music, Science, and Natural Magic in Seventeenth-Century England*. New Haven: Yale UP, 1999. Print.

Hollander, John. *The Untuning of the Sky*. Princeton: Princeton UP, 1961. Print.

Hutton, James. "Some English Poems in Praise of Music." *English Miscellany* 2 (1950): 1–63. Print.

Lindley, David. *Shakespeare and Music*. London: Thomson, 2006. Print.

Macrobius, Ambrosius Aurelius Theodosius. *Commentary on the* Dream of Scipio. Trans. William Harris Stahl. *ACLS Humanties E-book*. Amer. Council of Learned Socs., n.d. Web. 17 May 2013.

Ortiz, Joseph M. *Broken Harmony: Shakespeare and the Politics of Music*. Ithaca: Cornell UP, 2011. Print.

Shakespeare, William. *The Norton Shakespeare*. Stephen Greenblatt, gen. ed. New York: Norton, 1997. Print.

Smith, Bruce R. *The Acoustic World of Early Modern England: Attending to the O-Factor*. Chicago: U of Chicago P, 1999. Print.

Strunk, Oliver, ed. *Source Readings in Music History from Classical Antiquity through the Romantic Era*. New York: Norton, 1950. Print.

Winkler, Amanda Eubanks. *O Let Us Howle Some Heavy Note: Music for Witches, the Melancholic, and the Mad on the Seventeenth-Century English Stage*. Bloomington: Indiana UP, 2006. Print.

**Phillip John Usher**

# Typefaces and Title Pages: Archives in Undergraduate Courses

When teaching early modern literature, one must ignite a spark of curiosity to encourage students to decipher unfamiliar orthography, investigate allusions to classical authors, and generally deal with unfamiliar world-views. The flame needs to burn even brighter when the texts are in a foreign tongue: sixteenth-century French (or Italian, or Spanish, etc.) is too similar to the language today to warrant a modern French translation yet strange enough to make reading a time-consuming challenge. This essay suggests that online archives of early modern texts are an important resource to meet this challenge. I focus my attention on how instructors in a classroom context can use extracts from materials available through online archives to draw student attention to typefaces and title pages, to prompt discussion, and to create excitement about the text at hand. I draw on my experiences in a French department, but the approach is of course not language-specific.

## Typefaces

It was not until the nineteenth century that the Renaissance as a historical period was born. Still, early modern authors and artists spoke often of

181

renewal: Lorenzo Valla spoke of the arts as again "coming to life" (4); Albrecht Dürer of the "Wiedererwachsung" ("growing up") of art (qtd. in Panofksy 201); François Rabelais of the "restitution des bonnes lettres" (Vie 67; "restoration of good literature" [my trans.]); and Giorgio Vasari of "la rinascita" (qtd. in Sankovitch; "rebirth") of art. Now let us imagine a French literature class, taught in French, in which students read Rabelais's *Pantagruel* (1532). Instead of a lecture, the first class period might seek to involve students with the very appearance of the letters on the sixteenth-century page, in order to approach both the text itself and its wider historical implications. More specifically, the goal would be to show how the change from Gothic to roman typeface that took place in 1530s France related to Rabelais's text as a work about (among other things) humanist education as well as to his contemporary French society. Before presenting a concrete class-room activity, I give a brief exordium on the legitimacy of this approach.

The switch from Gothic to roman typeface was, as Henri Zerner has noted, one of many symptoms of a "discontinuité" (11; "discontinuity"). For early modern readers, that a book was printed in Gothic or roman was an immediate clue both to when the book was printed and to what kind of book it was. Although some very early books published in France were in roman type, it was not until the 1530s that the practice became wide-spread and symptomatic of a wider cultural renewal, sponsored largely by Francis I, the "père des arts et des lettres" ("father of arts and letters") (Martin 180–209; Jacquart 303). The perceived modernity of the roman typeface can be traced back to fifteenth-century Italy and to the redis-covery of Roman handwriting in ancient manuscripts. Petrarch imitated that handwriting, as did his French counterparts, like Guillaume Budé (Martin and Chartier 206–07). The change in handwriting was followed by the change in typeface. After the publication in France, in roman type, of Paolo Emilio's *De rebus gestis Francorum libri IIII* ("The Four Books of the Deeds of French Kings"; 1517–18), Galliot du Pré began printing certain French-language works in roman type (Martin 192–93). Works imported from Italy, such as the *Hypnerotomachia Poliphili* (or *Le songe de Poliphile*; *Poliphilo's Dream about the Strife of Love*), were increasingly printed that way; in 1533, Marot republished Villon in roman type (Con-ley 42). That the trend quickly spread but did not become universal re-sulted in a coexistence of the two typefaces. Although a generalization, it is a fair rule of thumb that while French works related to the concerns and promotion of humanism were printed in roman, for decades the Gothic typeface was maintained for popular literature, such as romances.

The advent of various online archives makes it relatively easy to put students in contact with literary texts as they would have appeared to early modern readers. The Bibliothèque Nationale de France's *Gallica* archive and the University of Virginia's *The Renaissance in Print* project both provide many editions of Rabelais and his contemporaries. To enter into the debate about renewal portrayed in Rabelais's first works, one might begin by examining in class the typefaces used in the University of Virginia's 1542 edition of *Pantagruel* (in Gothic type; see fig. 1) and its 1552 edition of the *Tiers livre* ("Third Book") in roman type (see fig. 2). Asking students to read aloud both texts, in pairs or to the class, without explaining which edition is being used, yields immediate reactions: Gothic type is more difficult to read, roman more familiar. Although some of what is recited is similar, the two texts look very different. Every time I have done this exercise, students perceive the Gothic type as older, and some venture the term *medieval* to describe it.

With our discussion of the reading exercise still in mind and the images still on the table (or on the screen), attention might now be turned to the eighth chapter of Rabelais's *Pantagruel*, a letter sent to the book's hero by his father, Gargantua. Therein Gargantua explains that, although his father was devoted to providing him with a solid education and although he was a diligent student, the cultural and literary climate of his childhood was hardly propitious: "Les temps étaient encore ténébreux, se resentant du malheur et du désastre causés par les Goths, qui avaient mis à sac toute bonne littérature" (*Vie* 246; "[The] times were still dark, and mankind was perpetually reminded of the miseries and disasters wrought by those Goths who had destroyed all sound scholarship" [*Histories* 194]). This sentence may not seem that important to students, but Rabelais's opposition between the Goths and the restitution of literature will surely have a familiar echo now that students have experienced firsthand, in the typefaces, the change in Rabelais's world. The use of the term *Goths* never goes unnoticed, and it has always been exciting for them to learn that the earlier type was indeed Gothic.

In their reading for the second class, students might be encouraged to follow themes of change and development, and the shift in typefaces might be shown as paradigmatic of the giant's own development, which is connected to contemporary treatises on the education of Renaissance princes. It is easy to imagine a parallel class in which the instructor uses *Early English Books Online* (*EEBO*) to introduce students to the related history of English typography. Gothic type, also known as black letter or English

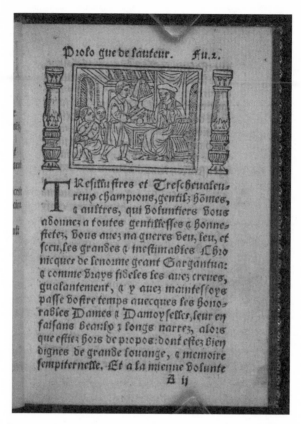

**Figure 1.** *Pantagruel*; Lyon: Francoys Juste, 1542. (Gordon Coll., Univ. of Virginia Lib.)

letter, was "the first dominant typeface in England"; the earliest extant use of roman in an English book dates to 1555 (Bland 93). A Renaissance survey course might then productively encourage students to contrast the black-letter editions of the printer Richard Tottel's miscellany *Songes and Sonnets* (1557–87) with the roman typography of Sidney's *Arcadia* and Spenser's *Faerie Queene*, both set in 1590, which defined "new conventions for the printing of poetry and prose" (107). After teasing out student responses to the varying typefaces, the instructor might lay out current scholarly debates over typographic evidence for readership and cultural status (e.g., Bland; Weiss; Lesser).

# &PROLOGVE

## DE. L'AVTHEVR M.

*François Rabelais pour le tiers li-*
*ure des faicts & dicts Heroïques*
*du bon Pantagruel.*

ONNE S gens, Beu-
ueurs trefilluftres, & vo⁹
Goutteux trefprecieux,
veiftez vous oncques
Diogenes le philofophe
Cynic ? Si l'auez veu,
vous n'auiez perdu la
veue: ou ie fuis vrayement foriffu d'intelligence, & de fens logical. C'eft belle cho-
fe veoir la clairté du (vin & efcuz) Soleil.
I'en demande a l'aueugle né tant renommé
par les treffacrés bibles : lequel ayant o-
ption de requerir tout ce qu'il vouldroit,
par le commandement de celluy qui eft
tout puiffant, & le dire duquel eft en vn

A iiij

Figure 2. *Le tiers livre*; Paris: Michel Fezandat, 1552. (Gordon Coll., Univ. of Virginia Lib.)

## Title Pages

Electronic archives also make title pages available to students and instructors. I discuss two ways of using title pages in the classroom. First, let us note that early modern title pages are very different from book covers today. One should not expect to find, on the title page of Ronsard's *Discours des misères de ce temps* ("Speeches on the Miseries of Our Present Times"; 1562), an engraving showing the brutality of the wars of religion. That a Renaissance title page is not a modern book cover could in itself be the subject of an enjoyable and useful classroom lesson. But there are many instances when the title page of a literary work can help open discussion about the work. The original edition of Agrippa d'Aubigné's *Tragiques* (1616), housed at the Bibliothèque Nationale and available for download through *Gallica*, is a case in point. Instead of beginning the first class on d'Aubigné's difficult text with a lecture on the wars of religion that were raging in France in the late sixteenth century, one might turn to the work's title page. Besides the bare title "Les tragiques," a simple printer's ornament, and the date of publication, the page also says that the text is "DONNEZ AU PUBLIC PAR le larcin de Promethee AU DEZERT PAR L. B. D. D." ("Given to the public by the theft of Prometheus in the desert by L. B. D. D.").

Asked to think about the page in terms of authorial identity, students would pick up on the fact that the book was stolen and produced only by L. B. D. D. Students could be asked, for example, to come up with possible meanings for the acronym, after which its actual meaning could be written on the blackboard—"Le bouc du désert" ("the desert goat")—and discussed. Why a goat? Why does it live in the desert? What does it mean to live in the desert? What does it mean to live in the desert in reality or as a metaphor? Lexical brainstorming around *bouc* ("billy goat") could involve consideration of the expressions "le bouc émissaire" ("scapegoat") and "sentir le bouc" ("to stink to high heaven"), which could lead to discussion about what it meant to be a Calvinist in sixteenth-century France: to fight with one's horns, to be a scapegoat for various problems, to be thought stinky by Catholics, and so forth. The author's hesitation to name himself on the cover of his book is surely a good point of entry into a work about religious violence, about the difficulty of being a Calvinist in France, and about the search for identity and freedom.

My own sampling of early modern French title pages suggests that the best use of them in the classroom involves introducing nonliterary texts alongside literary ones. It should be no surprise that the title pages that open works on cartography, mathematics, or medicine are generally more exciting than those accompanying literary texts. The connection of early modern literature to the history of science in general and to the science of anatomy in particular might, for example, be made visible to students reading Michel de Montaigne through observation of the title page of Andreas Vesalius's *De humani corporis fabrica* ("On the Fabric of the Human Body"; 1543), available through *Gallica*. Vesalius, born in Brussels, studied medicine at the University of Paris while developing his knowledge of anatomy by examining cadavers at the Cemetery of the Innocents. Later, having discovered that Galen's anatomies were based on animal bodies, he began work on what would become the *Fabrica*, a seven-volume epoch-making treatise on anatomy. Its impact was immediate. Many critics have commented on the important role of medicine and anatomy in Montaigne's *Essais* ("Essays"); the question here is how to facilitate and enrich students' reading of Montaigne. One approach would be to offer students a copy of the title page of *Fabrica* to be read alongside an essay by Montaigne (e.g., bk. 2, essay 6, "De l'exercitation" ["On Practice"]), in order to investigate the question of experience and (self-)scrutiny.[1] The crisp title page contains a wealth of visual clues as to the book's content (*Illustrations* 42–45). It depicts a public anatomy that Vesalius himself conducts, the traditional ostensors (dissection assistants) now forced under the anatomy table, where they quarrel with one another. Vesalius has his hand on the cadaver, whose skin he is holding open in order to make the organs visible. One can imagine classroom discussion noting the purpose of dissection, the public nature of the event (which takes place outside, not in a theater), the presence and use of the skeleton (drawing on students' own lab experience), the diversity of the assembled crowd (men and women, young and old), and so on. The body is despiritualized; the theoretical underpinning of the practice is that experimentation leads to knowledge.

Turning to "De l'exercitation," we come to the close encounter with death when Montaigne was thrown from his horse. The account and his comments on why he tells the story can be likened to Vesalius's emphasis on experimentation as knowledge of the self. Montaigne presents a detailed account of his loss of consciousness, interpreted as an apprenticeship of death. For two hours, having fallen from his horse, he was "tenu pour trespassé" ("taken for dead"); later he began "à reprendre un peu de vie" (353; "to get a bit of life back into [him]" [*Essays* 419]); and later still he "vin[t] à revivre" (357; "came back to life" [423]). The experience of losing consciousness was of mind being separated from body without the sensation of pain.

The point of telling the story, says Montaigne, was "instruction que j'en ay tiree pour moy" ("instruction I drew from it for my own purpose"); but, more generally, "chacun est à soy-mesmes une très-bonne discipline, pourveu qu'il ait la suffisance de s'espier de près" (357; "each man is an excellent instruction unto himself provided he has the capacity to spy on himself from close quarters" [424]). The anatomical and dissective aspect of Montaigne's valorization of experience is the occasion for reflection on his writing of the essays.

When I invite students to consider the connections between Vesalius's actual anatomy and Montaigne's literary project of self-scrutiny, discussion has always been lively. Students often notice Montaigne's mention of the difficulty of penetrating "les profondeurs opaques [des] replis internes [de nostre esprit]" (358; "[the] dark depths and [the] inner foldings [of our mind]" [424]), which, as Nicholas Paige has suggested, is likely a hint at the cranial folds of the brain depicted by Vesalius (38). Students usually understand the idea of the essays as body: "Je m'estalle entier: c'est un *skeletos* où, d'une veuë, les veines, les muscles, les tendons paroissent, chaque piece en son siege" (359; "I am *all* on display, like a [skeleton] on which at a glance you can see the veins, the muscles, and the tendons, each in its place" [426]). The experimentation and scrutiny associated with the anatomist's knife thus mesh with the experience of death when Montaigne fell from his horse and, finally, with the essays as a whole. Language itself appears dissective, almost eviscerating. One might pursue a similar approach to John Donne's lyric poetry and devotional essays, guiding students to read his obsession with anatomy and self-scrutiny through his autobiographical account in *Devotions upon Emergent Occasions* (1624) of nearly dying and through contemporary anatomical treatises.

Approaching authors such as Rabelais, d'Aubigné, and Montaigne, whose language is dense and difficult even for undergraduates with a good grasp of modern French, requires the instructor to be imaginative. Online archives provide one resource for using students' visual intuition and natural curiosity to begin dialogues with texts. The examples adduced here are from French literature, but analogous online material can be adapted for other languages. Many other creative ways of using typefaces and title pages as part of student-centered pedagogy suggest themselves, from a relatively simple exercise (having students transcribe a short passage from Gothic script, in an attempt to focus attention on each word, its different spelling, and so forth) to group projects (relating the history of the book to the history of ideas). While online archives might be too labyrinthine for the uninitiated undergraduate, careful use of extracts in my classroom has proved to be most enriching.

## Notes

Unless otherwise indicated, all translations are mine.

1. Other Montaigne essays suggest themselves for such pairing and discussion: book 1, essay 26, "De l'institution des enfants" ("On Educating Children"); book 2, essay 8, "De l'affection des peres aux enfans" ("On the Affection of Fathers for Their Children"); and book 3, essay 13, "De l'experience" ("On Experience").

## Works Cited

Bland, Mark. "The Appearance of the Text in Early Modern England." *Text* 11 (1998): 91–154. Print.

Conley, Tom. *The Graphic Unconscious in Early Modern French Writing.* Cambridge: Cambridge UP, 1992. Print.

*The Illustrations from the Works of Andreas Vesalius of Brussels: With Annotations and Translations, a Discussion of the Plates and Their Background, Authorship and Influence, and a Biographical Sketch of Vesalius.* Ed. J. B. de C. M. Saunders and Charles D. O'Malley. Cleveland: World, 1950. *Gallica.* Web. 24 Aug. 2014.

Jacquart, Jean. *François 1er.* Paris: Fayard, 1981. Print.

Lesser, Zachary. "Typographic Nostalgia: Popularity and the Meaning of Black Letter." *New Ways of Looking at Old Texts.* Vol. 4. Ed. Michael Denbo. Tempe: Arizona Center for Medieval and Renaissance Studies–Renaissance English Text Soc., 2008. 279–93. Print.

Martin, Henri-Jean. *La naissance du livre moderne.* Paris: Cercle de la Librairie, 2000. Print.

Martin, Henri-Jean, and Roger Chartier. *Histoire de l'édition française.* Vol. 1. Paris: Promodis, 1982. Print.

Montaigne, Michel de. *The Essays.* Trans. M. A. Screech. London: Penguin, 1991. Print.

———. *Œuvres complètes.* Ed. Maurice Rat and Albert Thibaudet. Paris: Bibliothèque de la Pléiade, 1962. Print.

Paige, Nicholas D. *Being Interior: Autobiography and the Contradictions of Modernity in Seventeenth-Century France.* Philadelphia: U of Pennsylvania P, 2001. Print.

Panofsky, Erwin. "Erasmus and the Visual Arts." *Journal of the Warburg and Courtauld Institutes* 32 (1969): 200–27. Print.

Rabelais, François de. *The Histories of Gargantua and Pantagruel.* Trans. J. M. Cohen. London: Penguin, 1955. Print.

————. *La vie très horrificque du grand Gargantua père de Pantagruel. Œuvres complètes.* Ed. Guy Demerson. 33–353. Paris: Seuil, 1973. Print.

Sankovitch, Anne-Marie. "The Myth of the 'Myth of the Medieval': Gothic Architecture in Vasari's Rinascita and Panofsky's Renaissance." *RES: Anthropology and Aesthetics* 40 (2001): 29–50. Print.

Valla, Lorenzo. *Opera Omnia.* Ed. Eugenio Garin. Vol. 1. Turin: Erasmo, 1962. Print.

Vesalius, Andreas. *De humani corporis fabrica.* Basiliae, 1543. *Gallica.* Web. 13 Mar. 2014.

Weiss, Adrian. "Casting Compositors, Foul Cases, and Skeletons: Printing in Middleton's Age." *Thomas Middleton and Early Modern Textual Culture.* Ed. Gary Taylor and John Lavagnino. Oxford: Oxford UP, 2007. 195–225. Print.

Zerner, Henri. *L'art de la Renaissance en France: L'invention du classicisme.* Paris: Flammarion, 2002. Print.

**Erin E. Kelly**

# Online Emblems in the Classroom

Emblems are strange. Emblem books confront readers with images of hands extending from clouds, birds making themselves bleed, and women consorting with wheels. Above these visions float cryptic Latin phrases or unfamiliar names. Below appear enigmatic verses surrounded by French, Latin, Greek, or Italian glosses. Such elements make students looking at emblems for the first time recognize that the past is a foreign country, one for which they may not have the language skills or cultural contexts necessary to travel with ease.

It is this strangeness that I believe makes emblems exceptionally useful primary texts to bring into undergraduate classes, even those composed of students without much interest in early modern literature, and arguably even into K–12 classrooms. This essay recounts how I have introduced emblems to my undergraduate Shakespeare classes, but I assume that teachers will be able to extrapolate my ideas to other texts and in other educational settings. The following brief introduction to emblem literature and emblem studies suggests that there is a variety of ways that time spent with emblems can facilitate students' engagement with Renaissance literature.

Critical studies have long argued for the importance of emblems and emblem books to sixteenth- and seventeenth-century literary culture.[1]

While the commonplace ideas regularly conveyed by emblems appear in visual and verbal art before and after the early modern period, emblem books are a Renaissance form. Andrea Alciato's *Emblematum liber* ("Book of Emblems"), considered by many the first true emblem book, was first published in 1531. By 1600 there were at least five hundred emblem books in print on the Continent and in England, according to Huston Diehl's conservative estimate ("Protestant Emblem Books" 49).

Admittedly, it is difficult to count the number of unique emblem books because woodcuts from one book were used in others and sometimes accompanied by newly written text. Later emblem books copied images from other works in print, making small or significant changes to their visual and verbal elements. Furthermore, printed emblem books are a small subset of a staggering number of emblematic objects and texts, ranging from printed title pages to printers' colophons to inn signs and including painted wall hangings, embroidered tapestries, and masque or tournament apparel. Elizabeth Traux has convincingly argued that emblems were the visual environment in which both educated and illiterate, elite and everyday people lived. William B. Ashworth associates the early modern period with an "emblematic world view," implying that people analyzed anything they observed in ways that fit it into the structure and moralizing purpose of an emblem.

Emblem scholarship has given rise to digital editions that make important emblem books widely available. The Web site *Emblematica Online*, also called the *Open Emblem Portal*, hosted by the University of Illinois, provides links to emblem projects from Denmark, England, Germany, Scotland, and other countries in addition to providing controlled vocabularies for indexing and searching iconographic images. Penn State University Libraries digitized their collection as *The English Emblem Book Project*; this Web site offers high-quality photographic facsimiles of nine books, including significant texts by Geffrey Whitney and Claude Paradin. The *Minerva Britanna Project* not only digitized Henry Peacham's 1612 emblem book but also offers helpful introductory essays written by Middlebury College students. Since 1995, Memorial University has hosted a Web edition in English and Latin of the 1612 version of Alciato's *Book of Emblems*.[2]

Although these digitized emblem books are accessible on the Internet, they can be difficult for the nonexpert to use. *Open Emblem Portal*'s indexical link headings assume a level of familiarity with the history and terminology of emblem studies that one can't expect undergraduates to have. *The English Emblem Book Project* lists the headings for individual emblems in separate tables of contents for each emblem book. Unfortunately, since the site doesn't translate the headings that take the form of Latin mottoes, much less expand those that cryptically declare their subject to be "THE Sixth Emblem Illustrated" or "EMBELEME 13," looking at each emblem is often the only way to understand a book's focus. Even the *Minerva Britanna Project*, a site created with an undergraduate class, doesn't translate Latin or French glosses and presents commentary only for select emblems.

The absence of metatextual apparatus for those new to emblem studies is a problem because print scholarship in the field is so hard to survey. Critics generally agree that most emblems in printed emblem books, like the quintessential models offered by Alciato, have three parts—a motto, or *inscriptio*; an image, or *pictura*; and a prose or verse text, or *subscriptio*—that work harmoniously to reinforce one another. The impresa is distinguished from the emblem by having only two parts, a motto and a symbolic image.[3] Out of this set of definitions, irresolvable debates emerge about what texts should and should not be labeled emblems. Is it appropriate to consider only documents featuring the three-part structure emblems, or might one call George Herbert's shape poetry, masque sets and costumes, and scenes from coronation processions emblems? What are the interrelations among the terms *emblem, emblematic, icon,* and *iconographic* when it comes to discussions of Renaissance visual and literary artifacts? Does contemporary advertising, with its use of trademarked visual and verbal logos, exemplify the formal and conceptual features of the early modern emblem? My sense is that some scholars, including Peter Daly and Michael Bath, would answer yes to this last question. Others, such as Rosemary Freeman, would probably say no.[4]

Because it has been difficult for those who study emblems to agree what constitutes an example of the genre, debates about whether a particular literary text should be deemed emblematic are complex. Monographs by Daly (*Literature*) and Bath and essays by numerous others (e.g., Mehl) explore ways in which the emblem tradition was in conversation with Renaissance poetry and drama, and all describe cases when the term *emblematic* has been applied too broadly to cases more properly termed iconographic, symbolic, or simply metaphoric. Emblem scholars do not concur about when a scene, speech, or character in a play should be considered a reference to or an original example of an emblem. Those wishing to introduce students to emblem literature will need to be aware of these arguments before they can guide students through independent research related to this topic.

That being said, as someone who works with emblems in her courses but does not hope to turn students into emblem scholars, I have familiarized myself with these debates but chosen to leave such questions about terminology outside the classroom. Instead, my primary goal has been to make emblems more accessible to undergraduates encountering Renaissance literature for the first time. Instructors do not have to be experts in emblem scholarship to employ online emblem books to introduce classes to the challenges and opportunities of working with these archival materials. During several years of teaching with emblems, I have developed assignments in which students read, write about, and discuss them. These assignments can be modified for students working at a wide range of educational levels.

Emblems and emblem books were regularly used as part of early modern grammar school curricula to encourage rhetorical skills. Those who wrote emblems both developed existing proverbs and common topics and attempted to turn their own observations of the world into *sententiae*. Because educated people were taught to recognize and compose emblems, emblem-like moments appear frequently in literary texts (Bath 31–48).

I began to use emblems in my Shakespeare classes by identifying such moments and having students discuss them in relation to an emblem expressing a related idea. For example, in a class on *Comedy of Errors*, I begin by asking students to consider Antipholus's wife, Adriana, in relation to the emblem "*Vxoriae virtutes*" in Whitney's *A Choice of Emblemes* (1586), which "representes the vertues of a wife" as a woman who perches on a tortoise and keeps her tongue still with her own fingers (sig. M3r). When Luciana responds to her sister's complaint about her absent husband, "Why should their liberty than ours be more?" by declaring, "Because their business still lies out o' door" (2.1.10–11), she parrots advice found in Whitney's emblem. Familiarity with the emblem prepares a class to recognize how Adriana violates expectations that early modern women be chaste, silent, and obedient when she confronts her husband on the street (2.2.109–210) and when she admits to the abbess that she regularly scolds her wayward mate (5.1.38–91). But it also leads them to recognize that the play's attitudes toward such prescriptions are ambivalent. The lines that most resemble Whitney's standards for evaluating a wife's virtue are uttered by an unmarried sister and a nun. Adriana's speeches, in contrast, express her sense of being emotionally wounded and morally wronged.

The complexity of Shakespeare's plays becomes apparent to students when they compare his works to the moralistic images and texts found in emblem books and thus discover the many different relations that can exist between and among early modern texts. Students readily debate whether Maria's reference to Malvolio in *Twelfth Night* as "a kind of Puritan" (2.3.130) echoes, expands on, inverts, or parodies the representation of Puritans as hypocritical, ambitious, and rebellious found in Peacham's "*Sanctitas simulata*" ("simulated or feigned sanctity"), from his *Minerva Britanna* (171), an emblem based on a passage in *Basilicon Doron* (1599). This emblem shows a crown peeking out from under a Puritan hat and condemns a member of that "sect" as so proud he "presumes to overlooke his King" and disregard royal authority under the pretext of reforming the church. Excellent essays have been produced by students who have brought emblems into conversation with Shakespeare's plays, especially students who have considered how Peacham's emblems most flattering to King James (e.g., his representation of the concept of the divine right of kings in "*Nisi desuper*" ["nothing except from above"; 1]) differ from plays regularly discussed as appealing to or being written to suit a monarch's interests (e.g., *Macbeth* or *Henry V*).

Surveying emblem literature provides students with background knowledge about early modern English culture. Emblem books are appropriate for this sort of classroom use because they are so often didactic, intended to communicate to their readers hegemonic social and religious ideals. By dividing the emblems in an emblem book among members of a class (with two or three assigned to each student) and asking students to present informally what they've noticed, I can help acquaint students in one class period with what educated sixteenth-century English readers would be expected to know (including the Bible, classical literature and mythology, and English history) and to articulate what those readers might be expected to value (hierarchical order in religion, government, society, and the household). (For a sample assignment, see the appendix.) One could provide students with such information through a lecture or by requiring them to read a chapter in a textbook, but in my experience they are more likely to think critically about what they have established on their own. It is a rich moment for me in a class discussion when, for example, a student mentions that "her emblem" from the beginning of the semester seems relevant to some aspect of the play we have just read.

Admittedly, using online versions of emblem book materials requires work on the part of an instructor. Most digital archives housing emblems offer photographic facsimiles with little additional apparatus. The ones that include introductions and contextual materials may not translate foreign languages or modernize spelling. All emblems require students to gloss allusions and to look up unfamiliar vocabulary. Yet these very difficulties help students understand what it means to work with archival materials, if only through a Web site. Students tend to ask more questions about emblem books than they do about Shakespeare's plays. My classes ask who made these emblem books, how many copies were produced, how much the books cost, and who read them. Such queries have motivated me to bring some classes to campus or area libraries that house sixteenth- and seventeenth-century books (and that have archivists willing to show undergraduates their collections). Applying similar questions to other early modern texts, including Shakespeare's plays, makes students aware how much scholarly intervention goes into creating a textbook, and with this awareness they become more savvy users of student editions.

My most unexpected realization about the place emblems might have in classrooms came from students at Nazareth College in Teaching Shakespeare, an upper-level course for English majors pursuing education certification, who remarked to me that emblems would be appropriate for primary- and secondary-school language arts classes. University faculty members who research early modern literature might think of emblem books as primary sources, but future and current schoolteachers recognize them as examples of sixteenth- and seventeenth-century visual culture. Visual materials are of great interest to K–12 teachers, who have been trained to design classes that will reach students with a range of different learning styles, including those who are visual learners. Education scholarship stresses the need for students to develop multiple literacies so they can thrive in a culture that bombards them with images, multimedia presentations, and film (Moje and O'Brien). Moreover, the official learning goals for many secondary-level English language arts classes across Canada and the United States require that students graduate able to analyze and create effective visual texts.

My students admitted that they tended to think of every period before our own as less visually and more textually oriented. This impression is reinforced when the only visual materials used to teach Shakespeare's plays or other early modern literary texts are videos or film adaptations of play performances. Eager to try other options, some in the class designed and carried out assignments that required groups to create their own emblems based on a passage from a play as a way of analyzing its imagery. For example, emblems based on key lines from the balcony scene in *Romeo and Juliet* (2.2) helped students track references to light and darkness, the sun and the moon. These future educators convinced me that even very young students could participate in this exercise after being introduced to emblems. This sort of exercise enables a class not only to encounter the habits of mind of the early modern period but also to think critically about the emblematic vocabulary of its own visual culture, ranging from corporate logos to television advertisements to representations of superheroes in comic books.

Having used online emblem books in my classes and having seen my students experiment with emblems, I am certain that what makes emblem literature a valuable addition to a Shakespeare course involves the visual, verbal, and archival aspects of emblems. Another reason to introduce undergraduate students to online emblems is that they are available for free to anyone with an Internet connection.

Undergraduate English majors I have taught at different institutions seem inspired by archival materials. Their work with primary sources accessed through databases like *Early English Books Online* (*EEBO*) has led to fine presentations and essays. But those who hope someday to step into K–12 classrooms have expressed frustration that many of these documents will not be available to them after they graduate. It is still only at large research universities and wealthy private colleges that libraries can provide subscriptions for a digitized archive like *EEBO*, for example. Also, small public schools don't have extensive libraries, and it is difficult to transport a high school class to a university library, much less a rare-books archive, from a rural area. Online emblem books, because they are available without subscription, are a resource my students can use now and, as K–12 teachers, in the future. Their response to that resource indicates the importance of creating and maintaining high-quality, free digital archives. It also suggests that such projects should consider offering pedagogy sections that include teachers' guides, lesson plans, and samples of student work. This essay, like others in this volume, asserts that encounters with early modern archives can lead students to engage seriously and enthusiastically with early modern literature. I hope it has also demonstrated that, when we introduce emblems or other archival materials to our classes, we need to think about how such documents will be used by those who eventually walk into their own classrooms.

## Notes

Special thanks are owed to Pablo Alvarez, curator of rare books at the University of Rochester's River Campus Libraries, and to Anne Meyers, bibliographic coordinator for rare books at the University of Georgia's Hargrett Rare Book and Manuscript Library.

1. For sample discussions of emblems in relation to other early modern texts, see the work of Freeman; Daly (esp. *Literature in Light of the Emblem*); and Bath. *Emblems and Drama*, a special issue of *Comparative Drama*, offers essays about emblems in relation to non-Shakespearean plays.

2. Feltham and Barker thoughtfully consider the difficulties and opportunities of preparing Alciato's book for an Internet edition.

3. For a clear overview of this terminology, see Daly, "Emblems."

4. Freeman defines emblems most narrowly, counting only those that feature a three-part structure as examples of the form. Diehl's catalog of English emblems (*Index*) follows Freeman's definition. Daly analyzes advertisements and logos as emblems in "*Nachleben* of the Emblem." Bath's monograph, *Speaking Pictures*, and the volume of essays he edited with Daniel Russell take an inclusive view of what counts as an emblem.

## Works Cited

Alciato, Andrea. *Alciato's* Book of Emblems: *The Memorial Web Edition in Latin and English*. Ed. William Barker and Mark Feltham. Trans. Barker and Jean Guthrie. Memorial U, 1995–2002. Web. 15 May 2010.

Ashworth, William B. "Natural History and the Emblematic World View." *Reappraisals of the Scientific Revolution*. Ed. David C. Lindberg and Robert S. Westman. Cambridge: Cambridge UP, 1990. 303–32. Print.

Bath, Michael. *Speaking Pictures: English Emblem Books and Renaissance Culture*. London: Longman, 1994. Print.

Bath, Michael, and Daniel Russell, eds. *Deviceful Settings: The English Renaissance Emblem and Its Contexts*. New York: AMS, 1999. Print.

Daly, Peter M., ed. *A Companion to Emblem Studies*. New York: AMS, 2008. Print. AMS Studies in the Emblem 20.

———. "Emblems: An Introduction." Daly, *Companion* 1–24.

———. *Literature in Light of the Emblem*. Toronto: U of Toronto P, 1979. Print.

———. "The *Nachleben* of the Emblem in Some Modern Logos, Advertisements, and Propaganda." Daly, *Companion* 489–517.

Diehl, Huston. *An Index of Icons in English Emblem Books, 1500–1700*. Norman: U of Oklahoma P, 1986. Print.

———. "Protestant Emblem Books in England." *Renaissance Quarterly* 39.1 (1986): 49–66. Print.

*Emblems and Drama*. Spec. issue of *Comparative Drama* 29.1 (1995): 1–182. Print.

Feltham, Mark, and William Barker. "The Web and the Book: The Memorial Electronic Edition of Andrea Alciato's *Book of Emblems*." *EMLS* 5.3 (2000): 43 pars. Web. 15 May 2010.

Freeman, Rosemary. *English Emblem Books.* London: Chatto, 1948. Print.

Mehl, Dieter. "Emblems in English Renaissance Drama." *Renaissance Drama* ns 2 (1969): 39–57. Print.

Moje, Elizabeth B., and David G. O'Brien, eds. *Constructions of Literacy: Studies of Teaching and Learning in and out of Secondary Schools.* Mahwah: Erlbaum, 2001. Print.

Paradin, Claude. *The Heroicall Devises of M. Claudius Paradin.* Trans. William Kearney. London, 1591. *English Emblem Book Project.* Penn State U Libs., 2004. Web. 15 May 2010. STC 19183.

Peacham, Henry. *Minerva Britanna.* London, 1612. *The Minerva Britanna Project at Middlebury College.* Ed. Timothy Billings et al. Middlebury Coll. 2001. Web. 15 May 2010. STC 19511.

Shakespeare, William. *The Complete Pelican Shakespeare.* Ed. Stephen Orgel and A. R. Braunmuller. New York: Penguin, 2002. Print.

Traux, Elizabeth. "Emblematic Pictures for the Less Privileged in Shakespeare's England." *Comparative Drama* 29.1 (1995): 147–67. Print.

Whitney, Geffrey. *A Choice of Emblemes, and Other Devises.* Leyden, 1586. *English Emblem Book Project.* Penn State U Libs., 2004. Web. 15 May 2010. STC 25438.

## Appendix:
## Emblem Analysis Assignment

In an article on early modern understandings of science, William B. Ashworth characterizes sixteenth- and seventeenth-century European society as having "an emblematic world view." What he means is that early modern society had a tendency to see objects and events in the natural world as representations of complex moral and social lessons for those who could read them correctly. Many common morals were codified in texts called emblem books, works that combined a visual element (the *pictura*) with a prose or poetic text to illuminate the meaning of a wise saying.

Looking at English emblem books gives us a sense of what notions might have seemed correct (or at least officially correct) to early modern English people. Additionally, emblems bring us into contact with some commonplace references, such as popular proverbs and characters from classical mythology, with which Shakespeare and his audiences would have been familiar. While I would not argue that emblems offer an accurate or complete sense of what E. M. W. Tillyard once described as an "Elizabethan world picture," they can introduce us to an important set of ideas in Elizabethan and Jacobean culture. Having a better understanding of these ideas can only enrich your reading of plays.

To prepare for our class meeting on [date], I ask that you do the following:

1. For each of the three emblems you have been asked to examine, be able to
   - describe the main point of the emblem;
   - explain the relation between the visual material and the moral lesson;
   - identify whether the emblem is making reference to another type of text (such as the Bible or classical mythology) or to another type of source (such as folklore, proverbs, or "common sense" thinking).

2. Then pick one of these emblems to present to the rest of the class. Be sure to explain
   - why you selected this emblem
   - what aspect of this emblem seems in some way relevant to [title of play most recently read for class], Shakespeare's plays more generally, or what you know of early modern English literature and culture.

3. Finally, look for trends among all the emblems you examined and answer the following questions as you prepare to discuss these observations in class:
   - What do all the emblems you looked at have in common?
   - What do all the lessons of the emblems you examined seem to have in common?
   - Do you notice any inconsistencies or contradictions in the emblems you examined?
   - Did anything surprise or confuse you about these emblems?
   - Why might the emblem have been seen as an effective way to convey moral lessons to readers?

You will be expected to offer a brief (three-minute) presentation of one of your emblems and then to participate in a fifteen-minute general discussion, but our consideration of these documents will help shape our discussions of key characters and scenes in plays throughout the term.

**Marjorie Rubright**

# Charting New Worlds: The Early Modern World Atlas and Electronic Archives

Perusing a world atlas in the seventeenth century may have been as close an approximation to surfing the World Wide Web as early modern subjects experienced. Readers of European atlases, like surfers of the Web, traveled across a world charted on the descriptive and pictorial pages of ever-expanding volumes, without ever leaving home. For today's undergraduate student who enjoys access to a library that holds even one early modern atlas, the experience with its pages is likely limited. In special collections exhibits, early modern printed books are often museumized: displayed behind glass and held open in book cradles that show just one of the many pages illustrated within. Because reproductions of early modern world atlases are not yet published in affordable editions for classroom teaching, for most students access to the pages of those atlases requires a passport into the world of electronic archives.

Engagement with electronic archives introduces students to a broad range of texts that shape scholarship in the field of early modern literature and culture. In the wake of the spatial turn across the humanities, for instance, scholarship on constructions of race, ethnicity, nationhood, and gender has brought renewed focus to atlases and chorographies and the map-mindedness of early modern English culture. Having access to these texts in our literature classrooms opens the possibility for exciting and so-phisticated engagements around questions of cultural identity and alterity in the period. This essay charts one voyage through the rewards and chal-lenges of working with both electronic and special collections archives in the undergraduate classroom.

In my Imagined Communities of Early Modern England, 1500–1700, an upper-level course I have designed for English majors, students explore the epistemologies of race circulating in and across plays and at-lases, two forms of cultural representation that were actively producing "geographies of difference" in the Renaissance.[1] Throughout the semes-ter, students probe the conceptual proximity between the stage and atlas and learn about London's Globe Theater and cartographic and descriptive theaters that claimed to display the world and its inhabitants before the readers' eyes.[2] Atlases presented English readers not only with maps but also, like the dramatic representation of foreign characters on the stage, with studies of types of people from around the globe and in doing so traf-ficked in shared cultural tropes and commonplaces. The major European atlases translated into English during this period contained both maps of various regions of the world and descriptions that cataloged in rich detail the habits, fashions, history, and languages of their peoples. In a semester-long research project, students elect to research a real or imagined figure that appears in both drama and atlases (e.g., Englishman, Jew, Muslim, Venetian, Turk, Indian, Amazon, anthropophagus, Gypsy); a geographic location (Istanbul, Egypt, Rome, Ireland, Java, Morocco, Bermuda, the Antipodes); or a trope of race thinking (ablution, civility, barbarism).[3]

Our reading of *Othello*, early in the term, provides a shared textual touchstone throughout the semester. As we read the play, I introduce the electronic resources that will be useful as the class embarks on its research project. Together, we focus on the word *Moor* as our topic of inquiry. I make this particular choice because a significant body of critical work has attended to the semiotic range of *Moor* in Renaissance literature. Be-coming familiar with the secondary criticism, students learn the broad contours of the debates regarding the category of race in early modern studies. Also, in a class that grapples with the complexities of race thinking across visual and discursive fields, I want students to delve beneath episte-mologies by which notions of race today have been constructed in North America. The category of the Moor, with all its religious and geographic indeterminacy, helps students do just that.[4] A nuanced study of the figure of the Moor requires that students acknowledge the interconnection of somatic, religious, and geographic influences that were shaping ideas about race in the period.[5]

To introduce students to early modern cartography, I invite them to tour two online exhibitions. The first is the Folger Shakespeare Library's *Mapping Early Modern Worlds*, which poses engaging questions about how mapping shaped both inner and outer worlds. It is organized by conventional cartographic categories, such as "Orbis Terrarum" and "City and Road Maps," and by conceptual engagements, such as "Mapping the Other" and "Mapping the Body and Embodying the Map." Students are introduced to digitized color images of single pages drawn from a variety of influential atlases and maps. The second online exhibition, *Envisioning the World: The First Printed Maps, 1472–1700*, features The Wendt Collection at Princeton University. It is organized diachronically, offering the viewer an introductory overview of important changes and continuities in representation across more than two hundred years of European cartographic history. I supplement these virtual tours with color slides and printed secondary sources (Harley and Woodward; Wolter and Grim; Blaeu).

The most immediate challenge to working with early modern atlases is the dearth of complete online editions in English. While a wealth of digitized images of individual illustrated pages is available, there is not, to my knowledge, a single portal through which students might access complete digitized editions of a broad range of seventeenth-century atlases printed in English. However, the Folger Shakespeare Library's *Online Digital Image Collection* (luna.folger.edu) offers a rich and growing collection of high-quality digitized images of some of the most influential atlases of this period. I have found that English-language editions of atlases are less widely available through electronic archives than are their Latin, Dutch, and French counterparts. For instructors interested in compiling a list of links to specific images or atlases, I recommend starting with Rhonda Lemke Sanford's article, which provides online cartographic resources and helpful descriptions of their content. Another starting point is *Map History / History of Cartography: The Gateway to the Subject* (Campbell), a site that describes various online resources for the study of early modern atlases.[6] Both the *Gateway* site and Sanford's article are addressed to scholars and therefore include links to journal articles and discussion forums about cartography, Continental sources in foreign languages, and portolan and celestial charts.[7] As a result of the wealth of material provided, the *Gateway* site and Sanford's article tend to produce hyperlink fatigue among most undergraduates, who are better served by being directed to a culled, preselected list of resources.

The scope of students' searches is helpfully narrowed to English-language resources by *Early English Books Online* (*EEBO*). I provide students with a list of atlases whose descriptive material is available for viewing on *EEBO*, selecting editions with the best image quality for ease of reading; when possible, I direct them to editions that have been transcribed, which greatly improves searchability (e.g., Mercator, *Historia*; Ortelius [1606]; Speed, *Prospect* and *Theatre*). Unlike many online resources that feature only images of the maps in atlases, *EEBO* displays both the descriptive and cartographic pages. A diachronic study across editions of a single atlas or a synchronic study across two atlases reveals that this information about people and place was regularly recycled, even duplicated verbatim, from edition to edition and from atlas to atlas. For instance, that Gerhard Mercator's *Historia Mundi* ("History of the World"; 1635) and Abraham Ortelius's *Theatrum Orbis Terrarum* ("Theater of the World"; 1608) both launch their descriptions of America with a record of its discovery in 1492 suggests to students just how prevalent the trope of discovery was in framing the ideological context of Europe's encounter with the New World.

Learning that ideas about Italian, Dutch, English, and French cultural habits are similarly recycled prompts students to question the truth claims of these purported descriptions and generates conversation regarding the production of cultural stereotypes. Furthermore, it sparks questions of literary interpretation central to an upper-level English course. Having discovered that atlases market material from previous editions as new and that the material in atlas descriptions sometimes reaches back to classical sources, such as Herodotus, for its content, students consider whether Othello's story of his encounter with the mythic anthropophagi, for instance, exposes more about his audience's taste for the exotic than about his experience.[8] Students wonder, In what way is Othello's story a recycled description of Africa? Where might Othello have learned these tales? Such questions have the effect of recasting our investigation of race thinking in the direction of the play's audience. If, as J. B. Harley has argued, "maps are preeminently a language of power, not of protest," a close study of early modern atlases sheds light on the role they played in repeating and ossifying the conceptual categories by which peoples and places were organized (79).

What *EEBO* does not provide is color images. This lack is more than an aesthetic loss, because color can be a constitutive part of the semiotics of race on many early modern maps and their frontispieces. For instance, display *EEBO*'s image of the black-and-white engraved frontispiece of the Mercator-Hondius *Atlas* (1637), which features the mythological Atlas framed by allegorical figures representing Europe, Asia, Africa, and America, and students are immediately impressed with how color shaped ideas of the self, civilization, and home in relation to ideas of what is other, strange, and exotic.

As we expand our survey of atlases to compare black-and-white *EEBO* images with digital color copies and to examine rare books themselves, new questions arise about the relation of electronic to traditional archives. I invite students to compare the black-and-white *EEBO* image of the hand-colored frontispiece of Ortelius's *Theatrum Orbis Terrarum* with a color digital photograph of the same frontispiece ("History"). They are struck by how both shading and color were mobilized to draw distinctions among the four allegorical figures of the continents. I display a digitized color image of the hand-colored frontispiece of Joan Blaeu's *Atlas Maior*, which features an allegorical figure of a richly adorned pale-faced female raised onto a lion-drawn chariot alongside which half-naked tawny and brown figures stroll (www.loc.gov/rr/geogmap/guide/gm013001.jpg), and students are struck by what they interpret as unapologetic imperialist iconography that is moving ever closer, in their estimation, to forging links between skin color and race. Indeed, color of skin and costume register differences that matter if students are to engage in nuanced interpretation of how such images are both like and unlike current epistemologies of race.[9]

To supplement the use of *EEBO*, I show slide images and direct students to online high-resolution digital images of a number of important seventeenth-century world atlases. However, restoring color to the atlas page does not entirely remedy issues raised by the use of electronic archives. For early modern readers of maps, as well as for our students, what one sees and how one sees are integrally linked. Many sites that provide color images from early modern atlases overdetermine how a viewer might wish to engage with the map's imagery. A notable exception is *Rare Book Room* (www.rarebookroom.org/), which offers a complete edition of digitized color images of Mercator's *Atlas sive Cosmographicae* (1595; *Mercator's Atlas*). Viewers can page through the text, enlarging or reducing details as they go. This site's agile zoom feature allows for a fluid movement of the eye across the maps. The interaction with the text facilitates intensely focused looking, as zooming in on details does not obscure or occlude the clarity of imagery surrounding the point of interest. In comparison, the British Library's online exhibition *Magnificent Maps* mobilizes a zoom feature that isolates and frames particular details on a map as stable snapshots (www.bl.uk/magnificentmaps/). This technical choice frustrates the comparative and cross-referential way of looking that early modern maps encourage, even as it enables educational information to be attached to particular details on a map. The Charles E. Young Research Library at the University of California, Los Angeles, publishes digitized images from volume 1 of the Latin edition of Willem Janszoon and Joan Blaeu's *Theatrum Orbis Terrarum* (1645). Helpfully, the atlas contents are searchable by three different indexes: Latin names, English translation of the Latin names, and a list based on modern country equivalents of the Latin place names (http://unitproj.library.ucla.edu/cris/blaeu/). The site does not include, however, the descriptive material in the atlas, and it presents its maps as individual thumbnails, thus abstracting the book's cartographic imagery from its textual content.[10] The Folger Shakespeare Library's Digital *Image* Collection includes a complete copy of Ortelius's *The Theatre of the Whole World*, which students can browse cover to cover (luna.folger.edu). Individual pages are easily enlarged and may be added to a workspace or downloaded for study and presentation purposes. The high resolution of the digital images on this site renders visible even the smallest details.

As students stand before early modern books, their questions differ from those raised by digital reproductions that appear on computer screens. The difference is due in part to what students see for the first time when they look at a text unmediated by photographic or digital reproduction and by the computer interface. Visiting the University of Toronto's Thomas Fisher Rare Book Room, they instantly respond to the difference in scale between early modern playbooks and atlases. Asked to characterize the difference, they describe playbooks as small, portable, thin, even fragile and unadorned when viewed alongside the large, heavy, substantial, impressive, and colorful Latin edition of Mercator's *Atlas sive Cosmographicae* or Ortelius's *Theatrum Orbis Terrarum*. Looking at examples of both playbooks and atlases, students want to know how much an early modern atlas cost compared with a playbook, why some atlases were hand-colored while others were not, whether people used atlases while traveling, if readers preferred individually bound plays to a folio edition of collected works, or if books were ever just for show.

As we linger over the books on display, I invite the class to consider how working with an electronic archive might differ from working with an early printed book. One difference that students always identify regards distortions of scale produced by digital reproduction and the computer interface. Quarto and folio pages may appear identical in scale on a computer screen, but when they are set side by side, the difference is immediately apparent. Even an impressionistic response to the variation in size among early printed books alerts students to questions of the conditions of production and consumption, to the social and commercial economies of booksellers and consumers, and to readers' experiences with early printed books. Students wonder whether a groundling attending Shakespeare's *Othello* would have had access to the descriptive content of early modern atlases? In terms of our course's focus on constructions of race in the period, students question how ideas travel across the socioeconomic boundaries implied by the great difference in cost among a quarto playbook, admission to a stage play, and a multivolume folio atlas. Questions about the book as object can help transform a student into a budding researcher.

Less obvious than distortions of scale is the photographic overexposure of an image in electronic collections that use microfilm as their source. On *EEBO*, for instance, important tonal details can be lost and colors literally blanched. By placing *EEBO* images alongside the same pages in a rare book, students begin to notice differences that are minor but can radically alter their interpretation of a text or image. For instance, when I taught this course in 2012, *EEBO* provided students with four images of the frontispiece to Mercator's *Historia Mundi*: the editions held by the Folger Library (printed in 1635), Cambridge University Library (1635), the New York Public Library (1637), and the Huntington Library (1637; see fig. 1).

When comparing a digital photograph of the Huntington Library frontispiece with a copy of the same Huntington edition on *EEBO*, students discover that on *EEBO* the person sitting in the bottom left corner labeled "Africa" appears to have nearly the same tonal quality as the other persons on the page. When looking at the book itself, the viewer registers distinct differences in shading between the person of Africa and those of America, Europa, and Asia (these differences are somewhat reduced even by the digital reproduction of the Huntington Library copy, which has been copied yet again for print here). Students who search multiple images of this text's frontispiece on *EEBO* will find that in many cases, Africa appears much like the other three persons on the corners of the page. Conversely, in some of the other *EEBO* images of this frontispiece, the shading of all four figures appears either so dark or so faint as to obscure both physiognomy and ethnographic detail, such as the flora and fauna surrounding each figure. Students tracing metaphors of darkness and light or the trope of "washing the Ethiope" might easily overlook Mercator's frontispiece as pertinent to their analysis, if their research was limited to *EEBO*.[11]

Fine-grained details are also sometimes obscured. Compare, for instance, the *EEBO* copy of the figure of America to the digital photography

**Figure 1.** *Above, EEBO* copy of the lower section of the frontispiece of the Huntington Library edition (STC 17825); *below,* a digital photograph of the Huntington Library edition (reprinted by permission of the Huntington Library). Differences between them show how research that depends exclusively on *EEBO* may affect the conclusions that students draw.

of that same book in the Huntington Library (see fig. 1). On *EEBO*, the body burning on a pyre behind the person of America cannot be made out. A student tracing themes of cannibalism to the New World would therefore remain unaware of the scene of cooking bodies that sets America into relief on Mercator's *Historia Mundi* frontispiece. Further, the *EEBO* image captures that there are animals flanking Africa and America, but precisely what kind of animals these are is lost because of the overexposure of the image. Details such as these played an important part in forging racial epistemologies that linked ideas about bodies, habits, and the natural world to particular geographies in early modern world atlases. Reading these details sometimes requires a return to the early modern printed book. A visit to one's special collections library—even ordering a high-resolution digital photograph from a research library—can help restore to our view the fainter details of the printed page.

Students experience the relation of electronic archives to the rare-book room as circular rather than one-directional. Indeed, it has been my experience as a teacher and researcher that there is a feedback loop between traditional and electronic archives. To characterize the early modern text as the source and electronic archives as merely resource is to obscure an important part of what electronic archives enable in our classrooms. The various modes of searching made possible by electronic archives (word searches as well as metadata searches, for instance) open up traditional archives in a unique way. Electronic archives point back to the source texts on which they draw, but the searches enabled by them also point across a diverse body of texts, fostering thematic, conceptual, and diachronic connections that traditional card catalogs (organized by subject, author, title) do not. For our twenty-first-century students, having a passport to the world of electronic archives not only expands access to and encounters with early modern literatures, it also alters the shape of the journey. Discoveries in the electronic archives lead to discoveries in rare-book rooms, which in turn send us back to the electronic databases that are helping to chart new paths into the study of early modern literature in undergraduate classrooms.

## Notes

1. I borrow this phrase from Gillies.

2. Ortelius's *Theatrum Orbis Terrarum* ("Theater of the World"), printed in Antwerp in 1570, is considered the first systematically compiled printed atlas.

3. Students begin by mining Loomba and Burton, which offers a wide array of selections from early modern poetry, prose, and visual and emblematic works. Further, it provides a useful index organized conceptually by geography and ethnicity as well as topically by categories such as diet, lineage, lust, and barbarism.

4. For an insightful and teachable exposition on the "notorious indeterminacy" of the Moor in early modern drama, see Bartels 1–20.

5. In conjunction with *Othello*, students read a selection of essays that summarize the critical debates regarding race in early modern England. They then generate a working definition of early modern race thinking as a flexible intersection between two or more of the following ideas: kinship, household, gender, nation, rank, religion, language, and imagined community (for instance, students have in mind the mythic geography of the Antipodes and stories of Amazons or monstrous races). This broad definition emboldens students to explore a range of figures and tropes that arise in the drama of the period and lays the groundwork for sensitive engagement with the factors that shaped racial epistemologies in the period.

6. Both Sanford and Campbell draw on what is among the most comprehensive sites on maps and map libraries, *Odden's Bookmarks* (oddens.geog.uu.nl/). Invaluable for the researcher, the comprehensiveness of *Odden's Bookmarks* tends

to overwhelm the undergraduate who has difficulty distinguishing between scholarly sites and those published by map aficionados.

7. Some of the links lead to error messages. Often one can recover the resource by typing its name into a search engine. The links may be outdated, but many of the resources remain in use.

8. For more on this topic, see Relaño.

9. That consumers of early modern atlases could elect for the maps within to be colored by hand or not introduced a high degree of variability into even the same edition of an atlas. Because skin and costuming were colored differently for different consumers, color was a less stable signifier than students first think.

10. My students find useful Taschen's (2005) folio-sized, multivolume edition of Blaeu. Its size, color reproductions, introductory material, and index provide a good starting point for students interested in understanding the scope and scale of Blaeu's monumental work. But this multivolume edition is prohibitively expensive for them. In many libraries these volumes are in restricted circulation, available for use only on the premises. In short, high-quality, artfully produced, expensive editions like Taschen's can introduce students to a likeness of the original, but students often return to the electronic archive for sustained engagement with particular sections of the text.

11. On this trope, see Hall 106–15.

## Works Cited

Bartels, Emily. *Speaking of the Moor: From Alcazar to Othello.* Philadelphia: U of Pennsylvania P, 2008. Print.

Blaeu, Joan. *Atlas Maior of 1665.* Köln: Taschen, 2005. Print.

Campbell, Tony, ed. *Map History / History of Cartography: The Gateway to the Subject.* N.p., 24 Aug. Web. 2014.

*Envisioning the World: The First Printed Maps, 1472–1700.* Princeton U, n.d. Web. 24 Aug. 2014. <http://libweb5.princeton.edu/visual_materials/maps/websites /wendt-world-maps/old-site/index.html>.

Gillies, John. *Shakespeare and the Geography of Difference.* Cambridge: Cambridge UP, 1994. Print.

Hall, Kim. *Things of Darkness: Economies of Race and Gender in Early Modern England.* Ithaca: Cornell UP, 1995. Print.

Harley, J. B. "Maps, Knowledge, and Power." *The New Nature of Maps: Essays in the History of Cartography.* By Harley. Ed. Paul Laxton. Baltimore: Johns Hopkins UP, 2001. 51–82. Print.

Harley, J. B., and David Woodward, eds. *History of Cartography.* Chicago: U of Chicago P, 1987. Print.

"History, #95." *Jewels in Her Crown: Treasures of Columbia University Libraries Special Collections.* Columbia U Libs., 2004. Web. 15 July 2010.

Loomba, Ania, and Jonathan Burton, eds. *Race in Early Modern England: A Documentary Companion.* New York: Palgrave, 2007. Print.

*Mapping Early Modern Worlds. Folger Shakespeare Library.* Folger Shakespear Lib., n.d. Web. 15 July 2010. <http://www.folger.edu/Content/Whats-On/Folger -Exhibitions/Past-Exhibitions/Mapping-Early-Modern-Worlds/>.

Mercator, Gerhard. *Atlas sive Cosmographicae Meditationes de Fabrica et Fabricati Figura*. Duisburg, 1595. Print.

———. *Historia Mundi: or, Mercator's Atlas Containing His Cosmographicall Description of the Fabricke and Figure of the World*. London, 1635. *Early English Books Online*. ProQuest. Web. 15 July 2010.

Ortelius, Abraham. *Theatrum Orbis Terrarum*. Antwerp, 1570. Print.

———. *Theatrum orbis terrarum = The Theatre of the Whole World*. London, 1606 [1608]. *Early English Books Online*. ProQuest. Web. 15 July 2010.

Relaño, Francesc. *The Shaping of Africa: Cosmographic Discourse and Cartographic Science in Late Medieval and Early Modern Europe*. Burlington: Ashgate, 2002. Print.

Sanford, Rhonda Lemke. "Early Modern Cartographic Resources on the World Wide Web." *Early Modern Literary Studies* 4.2 (1998): n. pag. Web. 15 July 2010.

Speed, John. *A Prospect of the Most Famous Parts of the World*. London, 1646. *EEBO*. ProQuest. Web. 15 July 2010.

———. *The Theatre of the Empire of Great Britaine Presenting an Exact Geography of the Kingdomes of England, Scotland, Ireland, and the Iles Adioyning*. London, 1612. *Early English Books Online*. ProQuest. Web. 15 July 2010.

Wolter, John A., and Ronald E. Grim, eds. *Images of the World: The Atlas through History*. Washington: Lib. of Congress, 1997. Print.

**Laura McGrane**

# News and Material Culture in Early Modern and Restoration England: Using and Making Digital Archives

Humanists at four-year liberal arts colleges bring specialized scholarship into the undergraduate classroom on a regular basis. My institution has a strong rare-books collection from which students sample etchings and early editions. My own research and pedagogical projects, however, engage a broad swath of material culture that lies outside the parameters of these wonderful resources. I want students to interact with early print materials, including newspapers, political pamphlets, and almanacs, regularly and in the classroom, as scholars and amateur archivists in their own right. These aims translate for me into a professional interest in the role that historical digital archives can play in generating undergraduate research. My students get at the materiality of early modern Britain even before they travel to museums and libraries in London or Oxford, and we work together to understand the perils and promise of the databases that grant them this access.

In teaching students the tools of the trade for digital materials, I am learning firsthand about the economic and curricular factors that both limit and enhance the participation of liberal arts colleges in complex conversations about such resources. When a library makes decisions about which databases to acquire, faculty members at a smaller college can have a difficult time demonstrating to even the most sympathetic administrator the need for a digital collection that might be used by only a handful of professors. As we partner with students and like institutions to study how archives and the media shifts they represent affect acts of close reading and interpretation, we demonstrate the centrality of digital archives to our pedagogical mission. The benefit for undergraduates is (at least) twofold: a more nuanced understanding of the minutiae of early modern popular culture and a sense of what is involved in using, producing, and presenting archival materials in various media.

A devotee of realia (rare books, paintings, prints, eclectic miscellany, auditory phenomena, ephemera), I recognized early in my career that one way to share objects and performances with my students and to teach the practices of original research on a regular basis was through the use of first microfilm and microfiche and now databases: *Early English Books Online* (*EEBO*), *Eighteenth Century Collections Online* (*ECCO*), the *Seventeenth and Eighteenth Century Burney Collection Newspapers, ARTstor, Early American Imprints, Early American Periodicals,* and other specialized resources. My courses draw on these facsimile collections to introduce students to the material culture of early modern life—gardens, poultry, gallows, maps, and fashion plates—and to connect these dots to larger literary issues, both formal and generic. In these encounters, students' fresh work on popular texts of the period anchors secondary and theoretical criticism on consumption, capital, fashion, and public spaces—the things of everyday life.

I have designed the assignments I describe in this essay to travel across different early modern and Restoration courses, such as Spectacle and Spectatorship in Restoration London and Anatomies of Transatlantic Exchange. My latest course, New(s) Media and Print Culture in Early Modern and Restoration London, is an upper-division seminar for English majors on the development of news in the popular, performance, and print cultures of the period. Students read works by John Donne, Andrew Marvell, John Milton, Aphra Behn, William Congreve, John Dunton, and Jonathan Swift; histories of print and media theory; and many, many newspapers. How did writers detail the grit of a city street in various news forms? the visual excess of a theatrical performance? the grisly violence of a public execution? the death counts of plagues and other disasters? In the social space of the city, where power often resided with those who could read postures and ploys, the signs, streets, and behaviors of London as reported in such publications mattered. The rise of periodicals and newsprint in the seventeenth century tells us much about the history of print culture, but these papers also inscribe novel encounters with materiality through news items, advertisements, literary samplings, and dialogic exchanges.

Studies of early news culture and its readers by Joad Raymond, Joseph Frank, Robert DeMaria, and Adrian Johns contextualize for students the various archives that they will encounter over the semester. The main resource for the class is the recently digitized *Seventeenth and Eighteenth Century Burney Collection Newspapers*, the most comprehensive compilation of the period's newspapers in one (virtual) space. Digitized by the British Library in partnership with Gale, the collection is now available free to all institutions of higher education in the United Kingdom and offered by subscription internationally. (My institution, for example, in the United States would pay about $6,000 for the database, less if we were to access it as part of a consortium.) For decades a key resource for researchers who had access to the actual collection or its microfilm format, the digitized *Burney* now offers crucial material to undergraduates as well. To combat the sheer scope of the collection, I first provide students with a short list of papers published in mid- to late-seventeenth-century London. These texts introduce them to generic distinctions among the news book, newspaper, and periodical (and their many hybrid forms); familiarize them with fonts and formats, search tools, and orthography; and give them some basic historical events. The current list includes, chronologically, the following papers:

> *Kingdomes Intelligencer* (1660–63)
> *London Gazette* (1666–1792)
> *City Mercury* (1675–94)
> *Domestick Intelligence; or, News from Both City and Country* (1679–81)
> *Observator in Dialogue* (1681–84)
> *Post Boy* (1695–1728)
> *Flying Post* (1695–1731)
> *London Post with Intelligence Foreign and Domestick* (1699–1792)

Each has an extended run and can demonstrate for students the unique character, political inclinations, and agendas of editors and advertisers.

Before we discuss these papers, I assign two preparatory exercises to encourage familiarity with the database, print history, and editorial knowledge of specific titles and to facilitate immersion in the period:

The genesis and history of a particular publication are given, with examples of its format from one issue. Students are invited to spend time with an issue or number of a newspaper or serial. Questions asked: In what format is content offered? How would students describe the style of writing: esoteric, colloquial, or a mix? How do politics come into play? How often was the periodical printed? Who might the intended readership have been?

Accounts of a particular event, poem, or play in three to five different publications are compared. Examples are the Great Fire of London, the Great Plague of London, Halley's comet, a Congreve production, and the use of oil lamps. Students are asked to offer a brief rhetorical analysis of the accounts.

In a third assignment, I invite students to draw on the entire *Burney* database, along with *EEBO* and *ECCO* (and, for those interested in transatlantic publications, *Early American Imprints*). This task is more complex, because students must figure out how to search different databases to compile materials around a commodity, street, piece of apparel, or historical figure. (They have traced patches, wigs, ribbons, anatomy theaters, and pickpockets, to give a few examples.) Students often begin with an idea prompted by the reading of a theoretical or primary text—one of Behn's fops or Swift's enthusiasts—and narrow their search from there.

The project raises awareness about the question of extensive versus intensive reading and of mere dabbling versus serious engagement. Students quickly realize that they have to do some homework even before they begin. If, for example, one types "wig" into the advanced search function of the *Burney* database, 28,141 hits will register. Many of them are fuzzy, misread words like "will" and "was." But if "periwig" is entered instead, students will find fewer than four hundred source pages and can then think about how they want to limit the project by gender, date, class, or location. It is important to know that "ribbons" are also "ribbands" and that the London fire of 1666 was not always referred to as great. The discoveries made and frustrations experienced in these assignments reveal to students the vast scope of cultural production in the period and the diversity of research projects they might undertake later in their studies of early modern culture, in scholarship framed in literary and historical fields. Some students have continued with honors-level thesis work on—for example, garden architecture and the pastoral or sewing and costuming on the Restoration stage.

The second stage of our work focuses on the archives themselves as productions of knowledge. Methodological readings are followed by a sustained archival project of the students' own. Before students embark on their projects, I spend some time alerting them to the debates about and challenges of these resources. Otherwise, set loose in undisciplined fashion, students who use data mining, term searches, title scanning, and grouped catalogs too soon in their research lives can mistake accumulation for argumentation. Moreover, databases can promote a shallowness of historical and generic sensibility. For example, a function that allows one to explore *ECCO* and *EEBO* simultaneously makes possible more expedient searches but may blur the temporal and historical categories that have traditionally marked off specific collections. A trenchant analysis of the *Burney* database describes the challenges of using this particular tool and discusses the problems related to search technologies as well as the field perspectives that retain the often marginalized role of newspapers more broadly in curricular approaches to the period (Marshall and Hume).

Such appraisals can guide the technical engineers who revise databases and the scholars who must understand both the software glitches in cataloging and search engines and the political debates about canons. They also act as wonderful case studies for undergraduates apt to assume that digital archives contain everything in compendious and frictionless bytes. To launch a metaconversation about the archive as search tool, creator of order, and producer of knowledge, I use the Ashley Marshall and Rob Hume piece alongside two recent critical articles about *ECCO* and *EEBO* (resp., May; Gadd) and a 1936 *PMLA* piece about Restoration Drama advertisements and the Burney newspaper collection (Rosenfeld). Michel Foucault's well-trodden "Of Other Spaces" and chapters from books by Roger Chartier and by Elizabeth Eisenstein expand on this historiography of the archive.

Students must make a cognitive shift, must recognize the archive as tool and argument as they begin their experiment of producing and presenting cultural work in minidigital formulations. Since all archives and collections, whether in museums, zoos, libraries, virtual catalogs, or bound vellum, are produced in history and by specific groups of people, these acts of construction reflect the attitudes and social practices of the people and institutions that perform them. Students look to current examples—various Norton anthologies, iTunes new releases, the Web site *Boing Boing*—to recognize that embedded in every act of compilation and grouping is an argument, a political enterprise, a scholarly idea, that juxtaposition and collection are always already a kind of shaping of the materials at hand. An effective if obvious way to exemplify this principle is to take students to a local museum or gallery to discuss what aesthetic, political, or rhetorical statements are made in how objects are grouped or displayed and how they are listed in exhibition catalogs.

These methodological discussions lead into the final phase of the course project, the construction of a digital archive. Most undergraduates lack both the IT resources and the know-how to create a sophisticated digitized collection of their own. And I am not interested in devoting an entire course (at least not yet) to teaching students the digital and biblio-graphic skills necessary to create such a collection, though many of them come to literature courses with advanced social media and technological experience. (As a contrast, Janelle Jenstad's students assisted in creating *The Map of Early Modern London*. See her essay in this volume describ-ing it.) Rather, the goal is to use relatively simple software and interface models to create an archival argument that can be made in the classroom and public sphere both, through conference presentations, Web sites, and blogs. Although users cannot search these collections, different models of-fer degrees of flexibility in moving through the student archive or gallery. *PowerPoint*, for example, now has multidirectional functionality, and the most recent *HyperStudio* and *WordPress* software allows greater freedom of movement and architecture in setup.

I base the course's final archival assignment on John Dunton's popular *Athenian Mercury* (1691–97), best known for its role in popularizing the question-and-answer paper. First printed as a newspaper and later as re-dacted compilations of questions and answers retitled *The Athenian Oracle* (1704, first printing), Dunton's publication invites students to collate ma-terials in archival form to interrogate both their relation to knowledge and the oracular tendencies of electronic information today. In small groups, students either choose one of the questions posed by Dunton or create their own based on them. Topics from the papers have varied greatly. The literally thousands of questions give students a sense of the myriad aspects of culture—religion, love, science, law, and philosophy—that interested readers of the period. From a single node—the genesis of a sneeze, the rules of courtship, castration, debt repayment—students develop a constellation of responses through literary essays, poems, plays, pamphlets, and news items.

Basic decisions like what to include and what to exclude, how to organize the materials and in what electronic form to put them, and how to construct the user interface and navigation all become part of the archival production. Students are welcome to collect materials from whatever genres apply, but they have to give reasons for their choices. Those who conduct some preliminary research on, say, debtors' prisons will have a much better sense of which publications to approach than those who simply type terms into search engines. Those who choose specific years associated with a literary text or natural phenomenon or who follow a particular line of inquiry (e.g., the demonic sneeze) will find that the project begins to cohere more quickly. Some will focus on a primary text from the course, like John Milton's *Areopagitica* (1644) or Jonathan Swift's *A Tale of a Tub* (1704), to situate the archive around a literary work. Others will incorporate passages from the theoretical essays on print culture that frame many of our conversations. Students have also integrated modern materials on such topics as plastic surgery, divorce, animal rights, or séances to think about early modern attitudes toward beauty, marriage, bestiality, and the supernatural.

The two guiding principles amid this diversity are that students will engage some aspect of news and materiality and that they will collect and arrange texts with the goal of creating an archival argument. Students use flash drives and receive instruction in the basics of the software options available to them. They are also invited to suggest their own virtual models. Some have used formats and tools like *Pachyderm* and blog software to create a space for more active and public user engagement. They save source materials from various databases as PDF files, JPGs, or videos, and they must document all sources in an index card (*HyperStudio*), slide (*PowerPoint*), or hypertext footnotes.

Though the look, content, and functionality of the students' digital archives vary widely, the key goals are the same, as the outcomes should be, for all projects:

> To familiarize students with cultural materials of the period not encompassed in canonical, easily available trade texts. To allow them to share these materials with one another and a broader public sphere in new media forms. To give them a basic understanding of literary-historical research that will inform future research projects across disciplines.

To encourage students to recognize the importance of textual production and framing materials in the reading of texts and production of archives. How, for example, does the framing of a text with news items or advertisements affect how the text signifies? How do practices of juxtaposition, organization, caption, highlight, font size, and directional instructions affect how we read and interpret groups of texts?

To demand a greater engagement with the political and advertising cultures surrounding a text than one may find in certain edited and compiled editions that are the product of a more static approach to literary history. Such localized awareness might translate into increased sophistication about editions and syllabus production itself: how courses are constructed, how texts are introduced and commented on, how chosen editions differently open up and limit our epistemological practices.

To recognize that an archive is always an action, an argument, a statement, and an endeavor shaped both by the archivist and by the reader and that the very shape, media form, and order of an archive become part of its content. This understanding of the archive, in turn, demands of students that they recognize and take responsibility for their use of materials as they turn to more extensive scholarly engagement in their senior thesis projects—some of which will become conference papers and published essays.

To build research and analytic skills in the archives and encourage a desire to engage historical culture, in order to motivate more extended research projects at both an undergraduate and graduate level; to demand a basic literacy that will inform students' reading practices regardless of their chosen professions after college.

Even though I am still in the early stages of mentoring these projects (not all of which are wholly successful by the standards outlined above), students have already created rich and original archives. Their uses of captions, juxtaposition, dialogue, advertisements, voice recordings, and prints are always imaginative and often illuminating. At the end of the course, they present the materials to the class and are now beginning to experiment with public engagements as well, including a national undergraduate digital humanities conference. Students also write an eight-page analysis of their project in an essay that demands more complex argumentation around primary, secondary, and theoretical materials than can be made explicit in the archive itself. This analysis presents the project's goals but also a practical commentary on students' choices in putting together a digital archive.

Student responses have generally confirmed my sense that the creation of digital archives enables students to practice serious scholarship even as it sensitizes them to the means by which archives as tools frame their source materials. In acting the parts of amateur archivist and scholar while using digital databases, they become more sophisticated readers of these materials. In bringing primary sources that they have selected and organized to the set readings of the course syllabus, they engage early modern London at least partially on their own terms instead of simply adopting mine. And in using news books, newspapers, and periodicals as the starting point for their encounters, they discern the relation between these fascinating subgenres and those plays, novels, poetry, and philosophical essays that have traditionally been considered the more obvious fare of undergraduate literary study.

## Works Cited

Chartier, Roger. *The Order of Books: Readers, Authors, and Libraries in Europe between the Fourteenth and Eighteenth Centuries.* Stanford: Stanford UP, 1994. Print.

DeMaria, Robert. "Periodical Literature." *New Cambridge History of English Literature.* Ed. John Richetti. Cambridge: Cambridge UP, 2005. 527–48. Print.

Eisenstein, Elizabeth. *The Printing Revolution in Early Modern Europe.* Cambridge: Cambridge UP, 2005. Print.

Foucault, Michel. "Of Other Spaces." *Diacritics* 16 (1986): 22–27. Print.

Frank, Joseph. *The Beginnings of the English Newspaper, 1620–1660.* Cambridge: Harvard UP, 1961. Print.

Gadd, Ian. "The Use and Misuse of *Early English Books Online.*" *Literature Compass* 6.3 (2009): 680–92. Print.

Johns, Adrian. *The Nature of the Book: Print and Knowledge in the Making.* Chicago: Chicago UP, 1998. Print.

Marshall, Ashley, and Rob Hume. "The Joys, Possibilities, and Perils of the British Library's Digital Burney Newspapers Collection." *Papers of the Bibliographic Society of America* 104 (2010): 5–52. Print.

May, James. "Some Problems in *ECCO* (and *ESTC*)." *Eighteenth-Century Intelligencer* 23.1 (2009): 20–30. Print.

Raymond, Joad. "The Newspaper, Public Opinion, and the Public Sphere in the Seventeenth Century." *News, Newspapers, and Society in Early Modern Britain.* Ed. Raymond. London: Cass, 1999. 109–40. Print.

Rosenfeld, Sybil. "Dramatic Advertisements in the *Burney Newspapers*, 1660–1700." *PMLA* 51.1 (1936): 123–52. Print.

**Georgianna Ziegler**

# Historical Resources for Students of Early English Literature

What was the political situation in England when Milton wrote much of his poetry? What were the actual physical aspects of the country houses that hosted theatrical performances outside London and that inspired country house poetry? What is the evidence about foreigners in London in the sixteenth century that might help us read literature of the period? Many literary scholars today have been using historical resources to investigate these and a host of other topics. But most of us have not been formally trained in doing historical research.

What follows is a brief introduction to some of the major sources consulted by historians, many of which have now been made available wholly or partially online. The *Hathi Trust* (*HT*) archives are better organized and easier to use than *Google Books* (*GB*). *British History Online* (*BHO*) is a major resource of the Institute of Historical Research and the History of Parliament Trust.

## General Historical Resources

### Bibliography

The basic bibliography for resources in British history is the Royal Historical Society's *Bibliography of British and Irish History* (www.history.ac.uk
/projects/bbih?rhs.ac.uk). This subscription site covers publications since
1900 and currently references 756 journals as well as thousands of books.
It is possible to search for a bibliographic item or to search by subject,
limiting by date. When you search a person's name as a subject, you are
thrown into an index that references the form of the name used in the
bibliography. For example, a search on "Sidney, Mary" will give the correct heading, "Herbert, Mary, countess of Pembroke, 1561–1621," and
immediately register the number of relevant items in the bibliography.
Results can be exported in various formats.

### Calendars

A calendar, according to the *Oxford English Dictionary*, is "a list or register of documents arranged chronologically with a short summary of the
contents of each, so as to serve as an index to the documents of a given
period" ("Calendar"). Many British historical societies and groups have
compiled calendars of their papers over the years. The Royal Historical Society provides *Guide to Record Societies and Their Publications (Texts and
Calendars)* (www.royalhistoricalsociety.org/textandcalendars.php). Some
of the societies covered on this Web site are the Catholic Record, Church
of England Record, Early English Text, Hakluyt, and the Historical Manuscripts Commission. During the Victorian period, the Royal Commission
on Historical Manuscripts (aka HMC) undertook the enormous project of
inventorying the archives of corporate bodies and private collections. The
reports are quite detailed and often provide summaries of the documents
inventoried (www.royalhistoricalsociety.org/histmanscommission.pdf). As
an example, if you are working on the Sidney family and want to see what
papers might be at Penshurst in Kent, a search of "de l'Isle," the family
name of the owner, or "Penshurst" will send you to item 77 in the series,
representing six volumes surveying the collection. You then must go to
the volumes themselves in a library to look at the indexes and contents.
(The *HT* site has about sixty of these volumes; a few HMC volumes are
on *GB*, and seven are searchable on *BHO*.) You can also do a search in the

Royal Historical Society bibliography on, say, "Sidney family (of Penshurst Place)" as a subject.

For students of English history, some of the most important calendars are of the State Papers. Beginning in the nineteenth century, these were published in series covering State Papers Domestic (SPD) and Foreign and those relating to Ireland, Scotland, Milan, Spain, the Vatican, and Venice. Some of the volumes are now being reedited. They tend to be well indexed and give excerpts from the actual papers, most of which are housed in the National Archives or in the various foreign archives. In addition, 264 volumes of the calendars of State Papers are now available through *BHO* (go to http://www.british-history.ac.uk/statepapers.aspx for a list). The calendars of State Papers are searchable, but for full-text access a modest subscription to *BHO* is required. The full text of the calendars, with links to images of the manuscripts, is available through the subscription database *State Papers Online* from Gale (http://gale.cengage.co.uk/state-papers -online-15091714.aspx). The documents themselves from the State Papers Domestic series and some of the foreign are also available on microfilm.

The State Papers Ireland from Henry VIII to George III (1509–1782) is a major source of information on the fraught relations between England and Ireland during this period. These have been indexed in the printed volumes of the *Calendars of State Papers Ireland* (1509–1670) and then in the regular *Calendars of State Papers Domestic* to 1704, held by many libraries. Eight volumes of the *Calendars of State Papers Domestic* (1586–1601) are searchable on *BHO*, but subscription is needed for full-text access. Microfilms of the papers themselves are at the Folger Library in Washington, DC, and at the National Archives in London. For a more comprehensive introduction to their contents, see the research guide of the National Archives (www.nationalarchives.gov.uk/catalogue/RdLeaflet .asp?sLeafletID=231).

Other important calendars are those for the treasury, for documents relating to the City of London, and for the Cecil Papers at Hatfield House. The papers belonging to the earl of Salisbury are some of the most interesting for English history. Many of them are records left by William Cecil, Lord Burghley, Elizabeth I's chief minister, and his son, Robert Cecil, earl of Salisbury, secretary of state to James I. The twenty-four printed volumes have been digitized and are full-text searchable through *BHO* (www.british -history.ac.uk/subject.aspx?subject&gid=144). The documents are also on microfilm at the Folger Library and the British Library. A subscription site from ProQuest provides full access to digitized images of the papers and to the calendar (http://cecilpapers.chadwyck.com/home.do?instit1=stand rew&instit2=standrews).

## Archives

Most State Papers and the papers of many private families are found at the National Archives at Kew (formerly the Public Record Office [PRO]). Papers relating to local jurisdictions and to families in those areas are often found in county record offices. The British Library has a large collection of both royal and family papers. Holdings in the National Archives may be searched at www.nationalarchives.gov.uk/catalogue/default.asp?j=1.

County record offices of England and Wales can be searched for documents at www.nationalarchives.gov.uk/a2a/advanced-search.aspx?tab=1.

British Library manuscripts are searchable at http://searcharchives.bl .uk/primo_library/libweb/action/search.do?vid=IAMS.VU2.

A ten-volume printed *Index of Manuscripts in the British Library* is also available in many research libraries. Sometimes it is useful to find a heading in the printed catalog before searching online. This is particularly true for headings for women. As an example, Elizabeth, daughter of James I, is listed as "Elizabeth, Daughter of James I of England" and "Elizabeth, Q. of Bohemia," but she is also found under "England, Sovereigns of, James I," "Rhine, Electors Palatine of the, Frederick V," "Rhine, Princes Palatine of the, Frederic V," and "Frederic V"! Different manuscripts will be indexed under these various headings. It is possible to find the headings by doing an index search on "Elizabeth" as name and "daughter" as descriptive adjunct in the online catalog.

Many important historical documents have been published by the Camden Society, beginning in 1838 and subsequently merging with the Royal Historical Society. Lists of contents of the early volumes are given at www.royalhistoricalsociety.org/camden.htm. A number of research libraries have sets of the Camden Society volumes, and over a hundred volumes are available online through *HT*, while some may be accessed through *BHO* or *GB*.

Beginning in the late eighteenth century, John Nichols, an antiquarian printer, brought out two important collections of historical documents: *Progresses and Public Processions of Queen Elizabeth . . . Now First Printed from Original MSS of the Times* (1788, 1823) and *Progresses, Processions, and Magnificent Festivities, of King James the First* (1828). These have been invaluable sources for the texts of items such as Queen Elizabeth's New Year's gift rolls and royal civic and private house entertainments. Larger research libraries have these volumes, as do *HT* and *GB*. The John Nichols Project at the University of Warwick is working on a modern edition.

## Legal Documents

Acts of Parliament are an important resource for historical research. The standard reference work for them is *Statutes of the Realm*, a set of ten folio volumes reproducing statutes dating from the Magna Carta (1225) through the reign of Queen Anne (1714). They include alphabetical and chronological indexes. Several of these volumes, covering 1608–1701, are available and searchable at *British History Online* (www.british-history.ac .uk/subject.aspx?subject=6&gid=83). Some libraries also have the whole series on microform. A related resource is English Reports, a large collection of cases from various English courts, dating from 1220 to 1873. They have been made available online by the Commonwealth Legal Information Institute (www.commonlii.org/uk/cases/EngR/) and can be searched by date, name, or phrase (e.g., "femme sole").

Acts of the Privy Council are another important resource. The Privy Council, made up of advisers closest to the ruler, developed during the reign of Henry VIII and lasted until the later Stuarts. The acts work much like a calendar, recording the various kinds of business taken up by the council, which considered appeals from all over the country. A random selection from the volume for 1596–97 contains many petitions, several from women such as Joan Pitt of Weymouth, who asked for compensation for the loss of her husband and his ship, which was carrying grain on Her Majesty's business. There are also pleas for those in prison, information on musters for the army, regulation of the corn trade, much Irish business, news about ships and merchants from other lands, and plays stopped because of the plague in Middlesex. The Colonial Series of the Acts of the Privy Council (1613–1783) deals with matters relating to English colonies abroad, such as Virginia, the Barbados, Massachusetts Bay, Maryland, and Pennsylvania. Larger libraries will have these two series, but the Colonial Series is also available on microform, and some of the volumes of the regular series may be purchased as e-books or on CD-ROM (see www .tannerritchie.com/books/apc.php).

## Local History

For centuries the British have had a keen interest in their own local history. Many societies were formed around the country to record interesting genealogical, architectural, and other facts, and their publications contain much valuable information. Bristol, Durham, East Yorkshire, Lincolnshire, and Warwickshire are only some of the areas that produce publications. One of the most prominent is the Surtees Society, founded in 1834 and focused on the north of England. The society has now published over two hundred volumes—a list of those can be found at http://surteessociety.org .uk/ (many of the older volumes are on *HT*). The *English Local History Handlist* (1965), published for the Historical Association of Great Britain, provides a bibliography and guide to doing research in local history. See also W. B. Stephens's *Sources for English Local History* (1972).

The Victoria County History (VCH) project was founded in 1899 near the end of the reign of Queen Victoria and was dedicated to her. Its aim was to provide detailed descriptions of the archaeology, geographic features, towns, great houses, churches, sports, and more for every county in England. Most counties are now represented by at least one volume, and the process continues as the original volumes are put on the Web. They are being made accessible at www.british-history.ac.uk/subject.aspx ?subject=5. The volumes are extensively indexed, and the online version may be searched electronically, making it possible, for example, to look up families who would have been active in a certain county. The volumes also provide extremely detailed information on the history of many of the great houses in England. If you are interested in Hatfield House, for example, where the children of Henry VIII lived, you will find in one of the Hertford volumes a history of the house from the thirteenth to the nineteenth century and a detailed description of its architecture, from the remains of the old building through the changes made in the seventeenth century and later, and the décor of the interior.

In addition to the VCH volumes, there are independent county histories, such as William Dugdale's seventeenth-century histories of counties like Derbyshire, Warwickshire, and Yorkshire; James Raine's *History and Antiquities of North Durham* (1852); and John Cussan's three-volume *History of Hertfordshire* (1870–81). Many local histories are now on *GB*.

## Resources on London

If you are working on London, or more specifically the cities of London and Westminster as well as their outlying boroughs, much information is available in printed books and online. *BHO* has gathered many of these resources for easy searching. For example, it now has a section on pre-1800 maps and plans of London, as well as John Stow's important *Survey of London* (1603); the diary of Machyn, merchant-tailor of London (1550–63); and records from various companies in the city—livery, scriveners, merchant-tailors, and carpenters. The University of Michigan has a new online edition of Machyn's diary (http://quod.lib.umich.edu/m/machyn), and the eighteenth-century expanded edition of Stow, John Strype's *Survey of the Cities of London and Westminster*, is online at www.hrionline.ac.uk /strype/. The Strype survey provides many images of important buildings in the city and a map of Elizabethan London. Machyn is especially good at witnessing the troubled times around the succession first of Lady Jane Grey, then of Queen Mary, followed by that of Elizabeth I. He describes food and clothing and street parades. When Queen Mary rode through Cheapside and Smithfield on 13 March 1551, "fifty knights and gentlemen in velvet coats and chains of gold" went before her, and she was followed by "fourscore gentlemen and ladies, everyone having a pair of beads of black." Machyn makes a point of noting the "beads of black" (i.e., rosaries) carried by followers of the new Catholic queen, who succeeded her Protestant brother, Edward (*London Provisioner's Chronicle*).

Finding aids for some of the archives of London companies and other institutions are available online at *AIM25: Archives in London and the M25 Area* (www.aim25.ac.uk/index.stm). A number of these institutions are modern, but there are earlier ones, such as the carpenters', drapers', and goldsmiths' companies and the Royal Society. The *Records of the Worshipful Company of Stationers* has been microfilmed and is available at larger research libraries. The *Records of the Worshipful Company of Carpenters* for the sixteenth and seventeenth centuries was published in seven volumes (1913–68), and volume 1 (1654–94) is searchable on *BHO*.

Excellent background on living conditions in early modern London can be found on two sites: *People in Place: Families, Households and Housing in London, 1550–1720* (www.history.ac.uk/cmh/pip/) and *Housing Environments and Health in Early Modern London* (www.geog.cam .ac.uk/research/projects/earlymodernlondon/).

Much information about crime and the lower classes from 1674 on may be culled from the *Proceedings of the Old Bailey* (www.oldbaileyonline.org/). The Old Bailey was London's chief criminal court, and the proceedings of its trials are searchable by type of crime, punishment, dates, and more. Here we meet characters such as Mall Floyd, who in July 1674 kidnapped a little girl, stole some of her clothes, then "lost" her in the churchyard of Saint Giles. The child was found and safely returned to her mother, who the next day saw the clothes for sale in Holbourn. Mall was sentenced to transportation "to some of the Plantations beyond the Seas" ("Mall").

## Biographical Resources

### General

The *Dictionary of National Biography* (*DNB*), now the *Oxford Dictionary of National Biography* (*ODNB*), has been completely redone by Oxford University Press and is available in a hard-copy sixty-volume edition and an online subscription that is periodically updated. This resource is the first stop when you look for any British person or any person who operated in Britain and had any claim to fame. You can search by the person's name or, in the online version, over all records. This all-record function is particularly useful for finding women, for although more women are now included in their own right, some are still listed only under their fathers or husbands.

Much information may be gleaned from these records. At the end of each is a listing of the available archives, other biographical sources, and portraits. Many of the online entries feature photographs of portraits from the National Portrait Gallery in London.

A useful contemporary source is Thomas Fuller's *Worthies of England*, published in 1684 as *Anglorum Speculum; or, The Worthies of England in Church and State*. Modern editions are available, and the 1684 edition is in *HT* and *GB*. For information on people who emigrated to North America in the seventeenth century, see Charles Knowles Bolton's *The Founders: Portraits of Persons Born Abroad Who Came to the Colonies in North America before the Year 1701* (1919–26). Volumes 1 and 2 are in *HT*.

### Oxford and Cambridge

If you are looking for an Englishman who may or may not appear in the *DNB*, the biographical dictionaries for Oxford and Cambridge are a second important source. The Reverend Joseph Foster's magisterial volumes, *Alumni Oxonienses*, cover the periods 1500–1714 and 1715–1886. They were published in the late nineteenth century but are available in a modern Kraus reprint (1968). The earlier five-volume work by Anthony à Wood, *Athenae Oxonienses* (1813–20), is also available in a 1969 facsimile edition and contains some longer biographies. The Oxford records were updated by A. B. Emden in *Biographical Register of the University of Oxford* (1957–59, 1974). The first volume covers the period to 1500 and the second extends to 1540. Emden also compiled the *Biographical Register of the University of Cambridge to 1500* (1963). Other important sources for Cambridge are *Alumni Cantabrigiensis: A Biographical List of All Known Students, Graduates and Holders of Office . . . from the Earliest Times to 1900*, compiled by J. and J. A. Venn (1922–54), and *Athenae Cantabrigienses*, compiled by C. H. and T. Cooper (1858–1913). All three volumes of *Athenae Cantabrigienses* are at *HT*.

## The Peerage

George E. Cokayne's *The Complete Peerage of England, Scotland, Ireland, Great Britain and the United Kingdom*, in fourteen volumes, is a major resource for tracing British families of title. It is full of biographical details, including useful information about women. For example, we learn that when Henry, Baron Stafford, died unmarried in 1637, he left his sister as heir; she inherited the family estates and was created baroness and then countess of Stafford. Cokayne is good about giving manuscripts or printed books as his sources. The older *Peerage of England*, by Arthur Collins, may also be useful (all nine volumes of the 1812 augmented edition are available at *HT*). Sir Bernard Burke's *Genealogical History of the Dormant, Abeyant, Forfeited, and Extinct Peerages of the British Empire* (London, 1883) was reprinted in 1962 and is also now available in an updated version on the Web in two formats. Some libraries subscribe to the full service, which includes more than one million names in over 15,000 records covering the United Kingdom and including "historical families of Ireland" and "the royal families of Europe." Free but limited access is available at http://www.burkespeerage.com/. A useful primary source is William Dugdale's *Antient Usage in Bearing of . . . Arms: With a Catalogue of the Present Nobility . . . of England* (1682), republished in the nineteenth century.

## The Church

### General Resources

*BHO* has a subsection on ecclesiastical and religious history, providing links to a number of sources, biographical, administrative, and historical (www.british-history.ac.uk/subject.aspx?subject=2). Among these sources are records of several church parishes in London; the history of Greyfriars, the Franciscan convent; and a whole collection of documents relating to Saint Paul's Cathedral in London.

Catholic books published for the English market are listed in *Contemporary Printed Literature of the English Counter-Reformation between 1558 and 1640*, by Anthony F. Allison and D. M. Rogers (1989–94), and *English Catholic Books, 1641–1700*, by T. H. Clancy (1996). A good source on Catholics in early modern England is the *Records of the English Province of the Society of Jesus: . . . in the Sixteenth and Seventeenth Centuries*, by Henry Foley (7 vols., 1877–83). The biographic information includes "catalogues of assumed and of real names," an important resource since many of the Catholics in this period worked underground. This set is in research libraries, and all volumes are available online at *HT*. Cokayne's *Peerage* also identifies Catholics.

"Fast Sermons," that is, Protestant sermons preached before Parliament on religious fast days from 1640 to 1653, have been reprinted in thirty-four facsimile volumes with notes by Robin Jeffs (1970–71). Important early Quaker texts are available online from Quaker Heritage Press (www.qhpress.org/texts/index.html).

### Biography

A basic source recording English clergy is John Le Neve's *Fasti Ecclesiae Anglicanae*. First published in the eighteenth century and currently being updated by the Institute of Historical Research, it covers the period from 1066 to 1857. The books are available in libraries and also in *British History Online*, and the indexes for its three parts (1066–1300, 1300–1541, and 1541–1857) are accessible at http://www.british-history.ac.uk/catalogue.aspx?gid=157.

Walter Wilson's four-volume *The History and Antiquities of Dissenting Churches . . . Including the Lives of Their Ministers* (1808–14) is a handy source for clergy outside the established church (*HT*). For Catholics in England, see Joseph Gillow's *Literary and Biographical History . . . of the*

*English Catholics . . . 1534 to the Present Time* (1885–1902); volumes 2–4 of this work are available at *HT*.

## Church Court Records

Records of the early modern church provide insight not only into ecclesiastical affairs and matters of faith but also into marriage, birth, illegitimacy, wills, and general moral (or immoral) behavior. Two rather full sets of records from the dioceses of Ely and Chichester, dating from circa 1400 to circa 1660, are available on microfilm at university libraries. The contents of these sets may be viewed online for Ely (http://microformguides.gale.com /BrowseGuide.asp?colldocid=3250000&Page=1) and Chichester (http:// microformguides.gale.com/BrowseGuide.asp?colldocid=3251000&Page=1). For Kent, see *Church Life in Kent: Being Church Court Records of the Canterbury Diocese, 1559–1565* (1975), compiled by Arthur J. Willis.

Many early English bishops' registers and cathedral registers are also available in the microfilm set *Church Authority and Power in Medieval and Early Modern England: The Episcopal Registers: Parts 1–8*. A guide to this work is at http://microformguides.gale.com/BrowseGuide.asp?colldocid =3174000&Item=&Page=1.

## Other Ecclesiastical Records

Records of births, marriages, and deaths of people from nonconformist churches such as Baptists, Congregationalists, Methodists, Presbyterians, Protestant Dissenters, Quakers, and Unitarians may be searched online at the *BMD Registers Site* of the National Archives (www.bmdregisters .co.uk/).

Records pertaining to the French Huguenots in England may be found in the publications of the Huguenot Society. A list of the publications and their availability in print or on CD is provided by the society's Web site (www.huguenotsociety.org.uk/publications/quarto.html).

The Catholic Record Society (British) has published many volumes of records from the early modern period, including biographical information. The general contents to these are available at www.catholic-history .org.uk/crs/records.htm#01. The volumes themselves will be found in larger libraries.

*The Calendar of Entries in the Papal Registers Relating to Great Britain and Ireland* gives information on papers in the Vatican archives. This ongoing series began in 1893. See the article by Jane Sayers, "The Vatican Archives, the Papal Registers and Great Britain and Ireland: The Foundations of Historical Research," in *The Foundations of Medieval English Ecclesiastical History* (ed. Philippa M. Hoskin et al., 2005).

## Wills and Inventories

Wills provide important information about family wealth and relationships. In the early modern period, they were mostly used by those with some tangible property to endow. Many of these wills were registered in the Prerogative Court of Canterbury (PCC), and you can view them at www.nationalarchives.gov.uk/documentsonline/wills.asp. Indexes to many wills, including those in the PCC, were published by the British Record Society (15 vols. in *HT*). For the county court in London, called "husting," the reference work is *Calendar of Wills Proved and Enrolled in the Court of Husting, London: Preserved . . . at the Guildhall* (ed. Reginald Sharpe, 1889–90). This calendar is available online at *BHO*, as is *London Consistory Court Wills, 1492–1547*. In a consistory court will made for Annys Borde, 20 May 1544, she bequeathed a "fether bed with a bolster" to two male friends, and the rest of her goods to "Adam Gardener, cetezen and habardayscher." The inventory gives a good idea of the clothing and other goods in the possession of a middle-class woman; she had two gowns of "browne blew," two "kertells" red and scarlet, and several petticoats and chests (Darlington). In other parts of the country, local historical record societies may also be sources for wills. For example, the Bedfordshire Historical Record Society has published several volumes of wills; these are listed at www.bedfordshirehrs.org.uk/volumes.aspx. The Record Society of Lancashire and Cheshire has published seven volumes indexing wills and inventories from 1545 to 1760, preserved in the Court of Probate at Chester.

Other wills and inventories are published separately. For example, several inventories of collections belonging to Queen Anne, wife of James I, have been published in *Archaeologia* (1991) and *Journal of the History of Collections* (2001), while Janet Arnold published several wardrobe inventories in *Queen Elizabeth's Wardrobe Unlock'd* (1988). John Nichols, the great gatherer, published *Collection of All the Wills, Now Known to be Ex-*

*tant, of the Kings and Queens of England . . . and Every Branch of the Blood Royal, from the Reign of William the Conqueror, to That of Henry the Seventh* (1780 [available at *HT*], rpt. 1999). See also *An Index of the Names of the Royalists Whose Estates Were Confiscated during the Commonwealth* (ed. Mabel G. W. Peacock, 1879) and John Weever's *Antient Funeral Monuments* (1767), both in *GB*.

## Travel, Exploration, and Maps

The Hakluyt Society publications are the major source for information on early modern exploration. The society was formed in 1849 with the intent to publish "scholarly editions of primary records of voyages [and] travels." It was named after Richard Hakluyt (1551–1616), compiler of *Principal Navigations, Voyages, Traffiques and Discoveries of the English Nation* (1598) and publisher of other travel narratives. Many libraries have collections of the Hakluyt Society volumes, and many earlier ones are on *HT*. In its list of publications (www.hakluyt.com/hak-soc-bibliography .htm) are a few of the most important for early modern England, such as Walter Raleigh's *Discovery of the . . . Empire of Guiana*, William Strachey's *Historie of Travaile into Virginia Britannia*, the 1598 voyage of Richard Hawkins to the South Seas, and a couple of accounts of Francis Drake's voyages. Raleigh's *Discovery* and many other early modern texts related to exploration can be found at www.fordham.edu/halsall/mod/mods book03.asp.

The early modern period produced many atlases and maps for Britain, Europe, and beyond. Many of these were published in facsimile in the 1960s and 1970s by Theatrum Orbis Terrarum and should be available in larger libraries. The Web site *Map History / History of Cartography* organizes, updates, and provides links to the many online sites that reproduce maps (www.maphistory.info/index.html). The site is maintained by Tony Campbell, the former map librarian at the British Library. It includes links to such gems as the complete digitized six volumes of Joan Blaeu's 1659 *New Atlas* and the world atlas site at the Jewish National and University Library that contains atlases by Benedetto Bordone (1528), Peter Apian (1575), and Hugo Favolius (1585). There are other links to atlases and maps, by Sebastian Munster, Abraham Ortelius, Frederick de Wit, and many more. The site also offers a good bibliography on early maps (www .maphistory.info/litgen.html). (See also Rubright's essay, in this volume.)

## Images

The British Museum's Web site allows searching among thousands of the items in their collection at http://www.britishmuseum.org/research /collection_online/search.aspx. The Web site *British Printed Images to 1700* (www.bpi1700.org.uk/about/about.html) provides several thousand high-resolution prints and book illustrations from early modern England. It is based primarily on the collections of the British Museum and the Victoria and Albert Museum. There is a searchable subject index.

The *Folger Shakespeare Library Digital Image Collection* site (http://luna.folger.edu/luna/servlet) now contains over seventy-five thousand images from the Folger's collections, including the early quartos of Shakespeare's plays, several copies of the First Folio, engravings and maps from books, and hundreds of manuscripts. In addition, a linked database is focused on rare bindings at the Folger Library.

The National Portrait Gallery in London is a huge repository of portraits of the famous and infamous from British history up to the present. Its site (www.npg.org.uk) features a search engine for finding portraits by "sitter" and a mechanism for ordering copies. Sometimes the searching can be quirky, especially for female sitters. For example, Mary Sidney will not be found under "Sidney" but under "Mary Herbert, Countess of Pembroke." Queen Elizabeth II owns the most important private art collection in the world. Hundreds of images are searchable at http://www.royal collection.org.uk/collection.

The Victoria and Albert Museum is a museum of design and the repository for objects from Britain, such as jewelry, textiles, furnishings, musical instruments, coins, and paintings. It is possible to search its site by doing an advanced search on a date range (e.g., 1500–1700) and a place (England). Over six hundred images are shown of objects ranging from an embroidered casket, miniatures, and an early spinet to seventeenth-century goblets, gloves, playing cards, candlestick, ring, and chairs (http://collections.vam.ac.uk/). For more on the museum's collections of objects from British daily life, see its publication *Design and the Decorative Arts: Britain, 1500–1900* (2001).

Wenceslaus Hollar (1607–77) was one of the most important engravers working in England and on the Continent in the seventeenth century. His works document daily life, historical events, and city views, among other subjects. The site *Wenceslaus Hollar Digital Collection*, from the University of Toronto, offers excellent reproductions of hundreds of his images (http://link.library.utoronto.ca/hollar/).

## Works Cited

"Calendar." *Oxford English Dictionary*. Oxford UP, n.d. Web. 28 June 2103.

Darlington, Ida, ed. *London Consistory Court Wills, 1492–1547: London Record Society 3*. N.p.: n.p., 1967. *British History Online*. Web. 14 Mar. 2014. <http://www.british-history.ac.uk/report.aspx?compid=64538&strquery=annys%20bo rde>.

*A London Provisioner's Chronicle, 1550–1563, by Henry Machyn*. Michigan Pub.–U of Michigan Lib., n.d. Web. 15 Nov. 2013.

"Mall. Floyd, Theft." *Proceedings of the Old Bailey*. Old Bailey Proceedings Online, 2003–13. Web. 15 Nov. 2013.

## Part V

---

# Resources

**Heidi Brayman Hackel and Ian Frederick Moulton**

# Finding Archives Online

## Major Archives and Research Libraries

*United Kingdom*

Bodleian Library, Oxford
(www.bodleian.ox.ac.uk/bodley)
> In this core library of Oxford University, catalogs of books and manuscripts are available online, along with many other resources.

British Library, London
(www.bl.uk/)
> The main site for the library that holds 14 million books, 920,000 journal and newspaper titles, 58 million patents, and 3 million sound recordings. Online catalogs and lots of other materials are available.

Cambridge University Library, Cambridge
(www.lib.cam.ac.uk/)
> The main site for the library offers online catalogs and more. It includes links to the College and Department Libraries.

College of Arms, London
(www.college-of-arms.gov.uk/)
    This site is the official repository of the coats of arms and pedigrees of
    English, Welsh, Northern Irish, and Commonwealth families and their
    descendants.

Guildhall Library, London, now merged with the London Metropolitan
    Archives (www.history.ac.uk/gh/)
    Links accessing various materials, most of which are now housed at Lon-
    don Metropolitan Archives, include City of London Parish records and
    Livery Company membership guides.

Historical Manuscripts Commission, Archon Directory of Regional Record
    Offices and Repositories (www.nationalarchives.gov.uk/archon/)
    The directory includes contact details for record repositories in the United
    Kingdom and elsewhere that have substantial collections of manuscripts
    noted under the indexes to the National Register of Archives.

Hunterian Collection, Glasgow University (www.gla.ac.uk/services
    /specialcollections/collectionsa-z/hunteriancollection/#d.en.119689)
    Assembled by Dr. William Hunter (1718–83), the collection holds 400
    medieval and early modern manuscripts as well as 500 incunabula and
    2,300 sixteenth-century printed books. The site includes a catalog, images
    from manuscripts, and links to other resources.

Inner Temple Library, London
(www.innertemplelibrary.org.uk/welcome.htm)
    This main library of the Inns of Court, the professional organizations of
    English barristers, holds legal texts but also many historical and some liter-
    ary manuscripts.

Lambeth Palace Library, London
(www.lambethpalacelibrary.org/)
    The site for the library and record office of the archbishops of Canterbury
    and the principal repository of the documentary history of the Church of
    England has an online catalog as well as selected images from documents.

London Metropolitan Archives (http://www.cityoflondon.gov.uk/lma)
    In this archive repository of many London-based organizations, including
    civic government, religious, public, business, and local authorities, materi-
    als range from the medieval period to the present day.

National Archives, Kew, formerly Public Record Office
    (www.nationalarchives.gov.uk)
    The catalog of the United Kingdom government's official archive contains
    11 million government and public records and provides links to online re-
    sources, digital texts, and images. Access to Archives (www.a2a.org.uk/),
    the English and Welsh strands of this network, has citations for items from
    418 record offices and other repositories, searchable by keyword, date,

repository, and region. For tutorials and help with Latin, paleography, and currency conversion, see "Reading Old Documents" at http://national archives.gov.uk/records/reading-old-documents.htm. Early modern wills registered in the Prerogative Court of Canterbury can be accessed at www .nationalarchives.gov.uk/records/wills.htm.

National Art Library, Victoria and Albert Museum
(www.vam.ac.uk/nal/catalogues/index.html)
The site of the Victoria and Albert Museum's curatorial department for the art, craft, and design of the book and a major public reference library has extensive holdings of documentary material concerning the fine and decorative arts of many countries and periods. It also has an online catalog. Housed in the library are the Dyce and Forster collections of rare books and manuscripts. The Dyce collection has strong early modern holdings, the Forster many texts from the period of the English Civil War.

National Library of Scotland, Edinburgh
(www.nls.uk/collections/manuscripts/index.html)
This site has an online catalog.

National Library of Wales, Aberystwyth
(www.llgc.org.uk/)
This main site for the library has an online catalog.

National Maritime Museum, Greenwich
(http://www.rmg.co.uk/national-maritime-museum)
Collections range over every aspect of maritime history, including emigration, navigation, piracy, astronomy, shipping companies, shipwrecks, biographies, horology, and the merchant and royal navy, including 8,000 rare books dating from 1474 to 1850. The site features an online catalog and links to various resources. Over 1,500 charts and maps are available on the Collections Online site.

Oxford College and Department Libraries, Oxford
(www.ox.ac.uk/research/libraries)
Links to the various libraries at Oxford University include the College and Department Libraries.

Society of Antiquaries, London
(www.sal.org.uk/library/)
This major archaeological research library in the United Kingdom holds an outstanding collection of British county histories as well as a collection of eighteenth- and nineteenth-century books on the antiquities of Britain and other countries. The site includes online catalogs.

Trinity College Dublin Library
(www.tcd.ie/Library/)
This library, the largest in Ireland, has extensive holdings of early modern books and manuscripts, and the site includes online catalogs.

Wellcome Library, London
(wellcomelibrary.org)
> A major resource for the study of medical history. The site includes an
> online catalog and links to resources, including a few electronic texts.

Dr. Williams's Library, London, affiliated with the Hellenic Institute, Royal
Holloway, University of London (www.dwlib.co.uk)
> This library focuses on theology, religion, ecclesiastical history, philoso-
> phy, history, and literature. Its holdings of pre-nineteenth-century books
> and manuscripts relating to English Nonconformity are considerable. The
> online catalog is limited.

## United States and Canada

Beinecke Rare Books and Manuscript Library, Yale University
(www.library.yale.edu/beinecke/)
> Yale University's principal repository for literary papers, early manuscripts,
> and rare books in the fields of literature, theology, history, and the natural
> sciences includes the Osborn collection of English manuscripts and offers
> finding aids.

Butler Library, Columbia University
(http://library.columbia.edu/indiv/butler.html)
> The main library of Columbia University holds over 2 million volumes,
> primarily in the humanities and social sciences. Online resources include
> Arber's and Eyre's transcripts of the Stationers' Register (see http://
> cliobeta.cul.columbia.edu).

William Andrews Clark Memorial Library
(www.clarklibrary.ucla.edu)
> A major library at the University of California, Los Angeles, for rare books
> and manuscripts, with particular strengths in English literature and his-
> tory, 1641–1800. The site provides links to resources and to the university
> library online catalog, in which the Clark's holdings are listed.

Folger Shakespeare Library
(www.folger.edu)
> The world's largest collection of Shakespeare materials as well as major
> collections of other rare early modern books, manuscripts, and works of
> art. The site has links to online catalogs and other resources. The catalog
> (*Hamnet*) provides copy-specific notes on books and is available at http://
> shakespeare.folger.edu/.

Furness Library, University of Pennsylvania
(http://sceti.library.upenn.edu/sceti/furness/index.cfm?nav=furness)

The site's primary and secondary sources, including both texts and images, illuminate the theater, literature, history of Shakespeare, Shakespearean texts, theatrical production, and criticism. The site has an online catalog.

Harry Ransom Center, University of Texas, Austin
(www.hrc.utexas.edu/)
This center holds the Pforzheimer Library of Early English Literature.

Houghton Library, Harvard University
(http://hcl.harvard.edu/libraries/houghton/)
This primary repository for rare books and manuscripts at Harvard has an online catalog and provides access to the *Digital Medieval Manuscripts at Houghton* project.

Huntington Library, Art Collections, and Botanical Gardens, San Marino
(www.huntington.org/)
This library, one of the largest research libraries in the United States in the fields of British and American literature and history, holds substantial collections of early modern books and manuscripts. Its site has an online catalog.

Library of Congress
(www.loc.gov)
This research arm of Congress is the world's largest library, holding more than 35 million books and other print materials; more than 68 million manuscripts; the largest rare-book collection in North America; and the world's largest collection of legal materials, films, maps, sheet music, and sound recordings. Its site has an online catalog and links to other resources.

National Union Catalog of Manuscript Collections
(www.loc.gov/coll/nucmc/repositorieslist.html)
This list of participating American manuscript repositories is organized by state and is therefore useful for identifying lesser known archives near one's home institution.

Newberry Library, Chicago
(www.newberry.org/)
This independent humanities research library has especially strong collections in early modern English and Italian books. Its site has an online catalog and provides links to resources.

New York Public Library
(www.nypl.org/)
The main site for the system provides access to the library's catalogs, online collections, and subscription databases. The *NYPL Digital Gallery* provides open access to 700,000 images from the library's collections, including illuminated manuscripts and historical maps.

Thomas Fisher Rare Book Library, University of Toronto
(http://fisher.library.utoronto.ca/news/sidney-fisher-collection-2)
This collection houses rare early modern books in the University of Toronto library. Online resources include a catalog and digital collections.

## Digital Facsimiles of Early Modern Printed Texts

### General

*Early English Books Online (EEBO)*. ProQuest
(http://eebo.chadwyck.com)
*EEBO* contains digital images of microfilm copies of over 125,000 titles published in England or in English listed in Pollard and Redgrave's *Short Title Catalogue* (1475–1640) and Wing's *Short Title Catalogue* (1641–1700). Subscription is required; access to *EEBO* is also available to members of the Renaissance Society of America.

*Eighteenth Century Collections Online (ECCO)*. Gale, Cengage Learning
(www.gale.cengage.com/DigitalCollections/products/ecco/index.htm)
*ECCO* provides access to searchable digital images of more than 200,000 books published in the eighteenth century—works of history, literature, religion, law, fine arts, science, and more. Subscription is required, but *TCP* offers public access to searchable transcriptions.

*Folger Digital Image Collection*
(www.folger.edu/template.cfm?cid=3077)
This collection holds images of a growing number of items from the Folger's print, manuscript, and art collections.

*Rare Book Room*
(www.rarebookroom.org)
A collection of over 400 digitized rare books, reproduced in high-quality facsimile, including early editions of Shakespeare and Mercator's *Atlas sive Cosmographicae* (1595).

*Schoenberg Center for Electronic Text and Image (SCETI)*
(http://sceti.library.upenn.edu)
The site has over 2,000,000 images from various collections of rare books, manuscripts, papyri, photographs, and sheet music, including the Furness Shakespeare Library and *The English Renaissance in Context (ERIC)*.

### Specialized

*Bodleian Library Broadside Ballads (BLBB)*
(www.bodley.ox.ac.uk/ballads/)

*BLBB* has digital copies of the 30,000 sixteenth- to twentieth-century sheets and ballads held in the Bodleian Library. A few sound files are also available.

*Defining Gender, 1450–1910.* Adam Matthew Digital
(http://www.amdigital.co.uk/m-collections/collection/defining-gender
-1450-1910/)
This site has approximately 50,000 images of original manuscript and printed material, with a core of documents from the Bodleian Library. Includes ephemeral material such as ballads, cartoons, and pamphlets as well as diaries, advice literature, medical journals, conduct books, and periodicals. Subscription is required.

*English Broadside Ballad Archive* (*EBBA*)
(http://ebba.english.ucsb.edu)
*EBBA* contains high-quality digital facsimiles and transcriptions of surviving early ballads printed in English, especially black-letter broadsides of the seventeenth century, including the 1,800 ballads in the *Pepys Ballad Archive*. The site also provides background essays and sung versions of ballads.

*Shakespeare Quartos Archive*
(www.quartos.org/)
This archive expands *Treasures in Full* into an online collection reproducing at least one copy of every edition of Shakespeare's plays printed in quarto before the theaters closed in 1642.

*Treasures in Full: Shakespeare in Quarto*
(www.bl.uk/treasures/shakespeare/homepage.html)
This site of the British Library has full-color digital images of 107 copies of the twenty-one plays by Shakespeare printed in quarto before the 1642 theater closures. The interface facilitates comparison between volumes.

## Manuscripts

### General

*British History Online*
(www.british-history.ac.uk/Default.aspx)
This digital library, created by the Institute for Historical Research and the History of Parliament Trust, contains some of the core primary and secondary sources for medieval and modern history of the British Isles.

*British Library Manuscript Catalog*
(http://searcharchives.bl.uk)
> This online catalog of manuscripts in Western languages in the British Library gives some descriptions of early modern manuscripts not currently available online.

*Discovery* (http://discovery.nationalarchives.gov.uk/SearchUI/Home /OnlineCollections)
> This site provides digital images and transcriptions of selected documents in the United Kingdom National Archives.

*Harry Ransom Center*
(www.hrc.utexas.edu/)
> This site, from the University of Texas, Austin, has digital images of some of the center's 215 medieval and early modern manuscripts.

*Literary Manuscripts: Seventeenth and Eighteenth Century Poetry from the Brotherton Library, University of Leeds.* Adam Matthew Digital. (http://www.amdigital.co.uk/m-collections/collection/literary -manuscripts-leeds)
> The digitized microfilm and original color images of 190 manuscripts, with essays and biographies, on this site are searchable by author, title, first line, verse form, manuscript genre, and shelfmark. Subscription is required.

*University of Pennsylvania: Manuscripts to 1800*
(http://dla.library.upenn.edu/dla/medren/index.html)
> Digital images of a handful of early modern English manuscripts can be reached by narrowing the search to "English" + "facsimile" + "16ᵗʰ and 17ᵗʰ century."

## Specialized Collections (See also "Spenser, Milton, and Sidney.")

*Anglo-American Legal Tradition: Documents from Medieval and Early Modern England from the National Archives in London* (http://aalt .law.uh.edu/)
> This site has thousands of images of documents from King's Bench, Court of Common Pleas, Exchequer, Chancery, Court of Requests, Duchy of Lancaster, and the courts of the Palatinate of Chester. Paleography assistance is given.

*Constructing Elizabeth Isham*
(www2.warwick.ac.uk/fac/arts/ren/projects/isham/)
> This site provides both a Web edition of two manuscript diaries written by Elizabeth Isham (1609–54) and a collection of essays on self-construction in life writing by women in the early modern period.

*Henslowe-Alleyn Digitisation Project*
(www.henslowe-alleyn.org.uk/essays/digitalessays.html)
>Hundreds of manuscript images from Dulwich College's extensive archive on professional theater in early modern England are available, as well as supporting material.

*Holinshed Project*
(www.cems.ox.ac.uk/holinshed/)
>This project from Oxford University offers parallel digital texts of the 1577 and 1587 editions of Holinshed's *Chronicles* as well as a bibliography and catalogs of Holinshed's sources.

*Henry Machyn's Diary*
(http://quod.lib.umich.edu/m/machyn/)
>In this edition of the diary of Henry Machyn, Merchant Taylor of London (1550–63), Machyn provides details of daily life, including food, clothing, and parades, in mid-sixteenth-century London.

*Perdita Manuscripts, 1500–1700*. Adam Matthew Digital
(http://www.amdigital.co.uk/m-collections/collection/perdita-manuscripts
-1500–1700/)
>This compilation of digitized microfilm images of over 230 manuscripts by early modern British women is supported with detailed indexing, biographical and bibliographic information, and contextual essays. Subscription is required.

*Receipt Books from the Folger Shakespeare Library, ca. 1575–1800*. Adam
Matthew Digital (www.ampltd.co.uk/collections
_az/Receipt-Books/contents-of-reels.aspx)
>Among these digital images of eighty-nine sixteenth-to-eighteenth-century manuscripts containing recipes from the Folger Shakespeare Library are commonplace books, notebooks, and cookbooks. Subscription is required.

*Scriptorium: Medieval and Early Modern Manuscripts Online*
(http://scriptorium.english.cam.ac.uk/manuscripts/)
>These images and valuable detailed descriptions of twenty miscellanies and commonplace books are sponsored by Cambridge University.

*State Papers Online*
(http://gale.cengage.co.uk/state-papers-online-15091714.aspx)
>These digitized microfilm and original color images of state papers from the National Archives and the British Library, as well as calendars and transcriptions of the Cecil Papers at Hatfield House, are searchable through calendar entries and index points and are supplemented with essays. Subscription is required.

*Virginia Company Archives*
(http://www.amdigital.co.uk/m-collections/collection/virginia-company
-archives/)
    These digitized microfilm images, some transcriptions, and contextual
    material relating to the Ferrar Papers (1590–1790) are from Magdalene
    College, Cambridge. Subscription is required.

*Wellcome Library Recipe Manuscripts Online*
(http://library.wellcome.ac.uk/node9300909.html)
    This site contains images of seventy-five early modern manuscript recipe
    books.


## Paleography Tutorials and Related Sites

Beinecke's *English Paleography* and *The Osborn Collection* (http://beinecke
    .library.yale.edu/collections/highlights/english-paleography, http://
    beinecke.library.yale.edu/collections/highlights/osborn-collection)
    These sites provide digitized examples of English handwriting and search-
    able databases of early modern English manuscripts.

*Early Modern Paleography: A Daily Paleographical Gallery from the Beinecke
    Library's Osborn Collection* (http://earlymodernpaleography
    .wordpress.com/)
    This site posts digital images of pages from early modern manuscripts in
    the Beinecke Library.

*English Handwriting, 1500–1700: An Online Course*
(http://scriptorium.english.cam.ac.uk/handwriting)
    This online course is provided by Cambridge University.

*Letters of William Herle Project Transcription Tutorial*
(www.livesandletters.ac.uk/herle/index.html)
    These thirteen interactive transcription exercises are supported by the
    AHRC Centre for Editing Lives and Letters.

*Medieval and Early Modern Paleography Online Seminar Series*
(http://paleo.anglo-norman.org/palindex.html)
    This seminar is run by David Postle of the University of Leicester.

*Online Tuition in the Palaeography of Scottish Documents, 1500–1750*
(www.scottishhandwriting.com/)
    This tutorial is hosted by the Scottish Archive Network.

*Palaeography: Reading Old Handwriting, 1500–1800: A Practical Online*
    Tutorial (www.nationalarchives.gov.uk/palaeography/)
    This tutorial is hosted by the United Kingdom National Archives at Kew.

## Ink and Paper

*Handmade Paper*
(www.twinrocker.com)
 An American site selling eighteenth-century paper made from cotton rag.

*Iron Gall Ink Website*
(http://ink-corrosion.org/)
 This site tells you everything you ever wanted to know about iron-gall ink.

*Quill Pens*
(www.dennisruud.com/quills.html)
 This American site sells hand-cut goose quills.

*Scribblers*
(www.scribblers.co.uk/acatalog/Iron_Gall_Ink.html)
 This United Kingdom calligraphy site sells iron-gall ink and other supplies.

## Continental Books and Manuscripts, Digitized and Transcribed

*ARTFL Project*
(http://artfl-project.uchicago.edu/)
 This site provides searchable versions of 2,900 French texts spanning the twelfth to twentieth century. In addition to subscription databases, public databases include searchable transcriptions of multilingual Bibles, Montaigne, and sixteenth- and seventeenth-century French chapbooks (under Bibliothèque Bleue de Troyes).

*Digitale Bibliotheek voor de Nederlandse Letteren* ("The Digital Library of Dutch Literature") (www.dbnl.org)
 This site is a collection of primary and secondary information on Dutch language and culture.

*Early European Books*
 Over thirty thousand rare books and incunabula are digitized on this subscription-only site, and additional resources are added regularly. The site aims to include all European printed works as well as items printed outside Europe that are written in European languages.

*Gallica*
(http://gallica.bnf.fr/)
 This digital library of the French National Library contains tens of thousands of scanned volumes and images, plus maps and sound recordings. An English-language interface is included.

*Renaissance in Print*
(www2.lib.virginia.edu/exhibits/gordon/mainmenu.html)
This site of the University of Virginia offers selected digital facsimiles of some of the sixteenth-century French printed books in the Douglas H. Gordon Collection as well as links to online resources on the French Renaissance.

## Transcriptions of Early Modern Texts

*Chadwyck-Healey Literature Collections*
(http://collections.chadwyck.com/infoCentre/list_of_all.jsp)
This educational database of anglophone literary texts includes early modern drama, poetry, and narrative fiction as well as the King James Bible. Subscription is required.

*Emory Women Writers Resource Project (EWWRP)*
(http://womenwriters.library.emory.edu/)
This digital collection of over three hundred female-authored and female-centered texts contains recipe collections, travelogues, novels, romances, broadsides, plays, prophecies, and pamphlets, from the sixteenth century to the early twentieth.

*Luminarium: Anthology of English Literature*
(www.luminarium.org/)
This independent site has links to editions of works by canonical authors from the early modern period and after. It offers biographies, critical essays, and links to other sources.

*Renascence Editions*
(www.luminarium.org/renascence-editions/ren.htm)
This site, sponsored by the University of Oregon, has editions of English literary texts from the period 1477–1799.

*Stationers' Register. A Transcript of the Registers of the Company of Stationers of London, 1554–1640.* Ed. Edward Arber (http://www.columbia.edu /cu/lweb/digital/collections/cul/texts/ldpd_6177070_002/). *A Transcript of the Registers of the Worshipful Company of Stationers from 1640–1708.* Ed. G. E. Briscoe Eyre and Charles Robert Rivington (http://www.columbia.edu/cu/lweb/digital/collections/cul/texts /ldpd_6177199_001)
This searchable version of Arber's and Eyre's transcriptions of the *Stationers' Register* is hosted by Columbia University.

*Text Creation Partnership (TCP)*
(www.textcreationpartnership.org)
> *TCP* supports the creation of accurately keyboarded and encoded editions of thousands of works from *Early English Books Online (EEBO)*, *Eighteenth Century Collections Online (ECCO)*, and the *Evans Early American Imprints* collection. *ECCO-TCP* and *Evans-TCP* are now available to the public. Phase 1 of *EEBO-TCP* will be available in January 2015.

*Text Encoding Initiative Guidelines*
(www.tei-c.org/Guidelines/)
> The Text Encoding Initiative (TEI) "Guidelines for Electronic Text Encoding and Interchange" defines and documents a markup language for representing the structural, renditional, and conceptual features of texts. The focus is on the encoding of documents in the humanities and social sciences, in particular on the representation of primary source materials for research and analysis.

*Women Writers Online, Women Writers Project*
(www.wwp.northeastern.edu/wwo)
> Established at Brown University and based since 2013 at Northeastern University, this growing (178+ entries), full-text database of lesser-known early modern texts written by women is a searchable collection culled from original texts at twenty-six major research collections. Subscription is required.

## Finding Aids

### Bibliographies, Calendars, Indexes

*AIM25: Archives in London and the M25 Area*
(www.aim25.ac.uk/index.stm)
> This site provides finding aids for some of the archives of London companies and other institutions, including the Carpenters', Drapers', and Goldsmiths' Companies and the Royal Society.

*ArchiveGrid*
(http://archivegrid.org)
> This service of the Research Libraries Group contains nearly a million descriptions of historical documents, personal papers, and family histories held by thousands of libraries, museums, and archives worldwide. Subscription is required.

*Bibliography of British and Irish History*
(www.history.ac.uk/projects/bbih)

> The Royal Historical Society Bibliography lists thousands of sources on the history of the British isles. The site incorporates the *London's Past Online* database, containing about 40,000 records referring to books, articles, theses, and conference papers. Subscription is required.

*Bibliography of English Women Writers (1500–1640)*
(www.itergateway.org/resources)

> This site lists works by and about over seven hundred women writers. Subscription is required through *Iter*.

*BMD*
(www.bmdregisters.co.uk/ )

> This registers site of the National Archives contains records of births, marriages, and deaths from Nonconformist churches such as Baptists, Congregationalists, Methodists, Presbyterians, Protestant Dissenters, Quakers, and Unitarians. Registration and payment are required for access to full images.

*British History Online. Calendars of State Papers* (www.british-history.ac.uk /catalogue.aspx?type=3). *Calendars of State Papers Ireland (1586–1601)* (. . . gid=94)

> *Calendars of State Papers* contains two hundred volumes of the calendars of state papers. Subscription is required. Links to biographical, administrative, and historical sources, including records of three church parishes in London; the history of Greyfriars, the Franciscan convent; and a collection of documents relating to Saint Paul's cathedral in London can be found at the main site (www.british-history.ac.uk/subject.aspx). The Victoria County History project, comprising detailed descriptions of the archaeology, geographic features, towns, great houses, churches, and sports for various English counties, can be found at www.british-history.ac.uk /subject.aspx?subject=5.

*Camden Society / Royal Historical Society*
(www.royalhistoricalsociety.org/camden.htm)

> The Camden Society began publishing important historical documents in 1838. Lists of contents of the early volumes are available.

*Catalogue of English Literary Manuscripts, 1450–1700*
(http://celm.cch.kcl.ac.uk/)

> This greatly enlarged and updated version of Peter Beal's printed *Index of English Literary Manuscripts* is arranged by author and includes valuable introductions and descriptions of all known manuscripts associated with each.

*Catholic Record Society* (British)
(www.catholic-history.org.uk/crs/records.htm#01)

This site gives the general contents of volumes of records from the early modern period published by the society.

*Clergy of the Church of England Database, 1540–1835*
(http://theclergydatabase.org.uk/)
This relational database draws on material from over fifty archives in England, Wales, and overseas to reconstruct "career narratives" of nearly 150,000 clergy members. The database is searchable by name, date, diocese, and location.

*Database of Early English Playbooks*
(http://deep.sas.upenn.edu)
This search engine for every playbook produced in England, Scotland, and Ireland from the beginning of printing through 1660 provides information on original playbooks, title pages, paratextual matter, advertising features, bibliographic details, and theatrical backgrounds.

*English Short Title Catalogue (ESTC)*
(http://estc.bl.uk/)
This site lists over 460,000 surviving items published between 1473 and 1800, mainly in English and published mainly in the British Isles and North America.

Hakluyt Society
(www.hakluyt.com/hak-soc-bibliography.htm)
This complete bibliography of books, provided by the Hakluyt Society, was founded in 1846 to publish "scholarly editions of primary records of voyages [and] travels."

Historical Manuscripts Commission (HMC)
(www.nationalarchive.gov.uk/archives=sector/hmc.htm )
An inventory of the archives of corporate bodies and private collections. A list of these reports is available online as a searchable PDF file.

Huguenot Society
(www.huguenotsociety.org.uk/publications/quarto.html)
This site provides records pertaining to the Huguenots in England. A list of the publications and their availability in print or on CD is included.

*Map History / History of Cartography*
(www.maphistory.info/litgen.html)
This site has a good bibliography of early maps.

*Royal Historical Society Bibliography: Guide to Record Societies and Their Publications (Texts and Calendars)* (www.royalhistoricalsociety.org /textandcalendars.php)
Societies covered include the Catholic Record, Church of England Record, Early English Text, Hakluyt, Jewish Historical, Parliamentary History, Royal Historical, Scottish History, and the Royal Commission on Historical Manuscripts.

Surtees Society
(www.surteessociety.org.uk/)
> This local history society, founded in 1834 and focused on the north of
> England, has published over two hundred volumes; a list of those still in
> print is on the site.

*Union First Line Index of English Verse*
(http://firstlines.folger.edu)
> This database of the first lines of manuscript verse from a range of reposi-
> tories (in addition to verse from books printed in England, 1641–1700),
> is searchable by first line, last line (in some cases), author, title, shelf mark,
> author's gender, and repository.

## Dictionaries

*LEME: Lexicons of Early Modern English*
(http://leme.library.utoronto.ca)
> This historical database of sixteenth- and seventeenth-century monolin-
> gual, bilingual, and polyglot dictionaries, lexical encyclopedias, hard-word
> glossaries, spelling lists, and lexically valuable treatises in print or manu-
> script is available in public-access and subscription versions.

*Oxford English Dictionary (OED)*
(www.oed.com/)
> The *OED*, regarded as the most authoritative and comprehensive English-
> language dictionary, contains information on the English language, its
> history, and the social, cultural, and political influences that have shaped it.
> Subscription is required.

## Topics

### Shakespeare and Theater History

*English Renaissance in Context (ERIC)*
(http://sceti.library.upenn.edu/sceti/furness/eric/index.cfm)
> Hosted by University of Pennsylvania, *ERIC* comprises two separate but
> integrated units: a set of tutorials on some of Shakespeare's plays and on
> the making and selling of books during the early modern period; a data-
> base of scanned texts.

*Foul Whisperings, Strange Matters: A Multimedia* Macbeth *Installation*
(http://virtualworlds.nmc.org/2008/10/08/macbeth/)
> This site provides a fictional simulation in *Second Life*, based on
> *Macbeth*.

*Hamlet on the Ramparts*
(http://shea.mit.edu/ramparts/)
   This site contains texts, images, and film relevant to Hamlet's first encounter with the Ghost.

*Internet Shakespeare Editions*
(http://internetshakespeare.uvic.ca/index.html)
   This site offers scholarly, fully annotated texts of Shakespeare's plays;
   multimedia explorations of the context of his life and works; and records
   of his plays in performance. Side-by-side comparison of different facsimile
   editions is allowed.

*Learning Objects: Shakespeare's Globe Theater*
(http://learningobjects.wesleyan.edu/globe/)
   This virtual model of the Globe has 3-D line drawings and simple cylinder
   figures that can be moved around for blocking exercises.

*Open Source Shakespeare: An Experiment in Literary Technology*
(www.opensourceshakespeare.org)
   Based on the 1864 Globe edition of Shakespeare, this site provides fully
   searchable complete works with a concordance.

*Records of Early English Drama (REED)*
(reed.utoronto.ca/index.html)
   This international scholarly project attempts to locate, transcribe, and
   edit all surviving documentary evidence of drama, minstrelsy, and public
   ceremony in England before 1642. Much of its data, including genealogies and maps, is publicly available at its "Patrons and Performances" site:
   http://link.library.utoronto.ca/reed/.

*Shakespeare Searched*
(http://shakespeare.yippy.com)
   This site features a search engine allowing quick access to passages from
   Shakespeare.

*TextArc*
(www.textarc.org)
   This experimental site offers visual representations of texts, including
   *Hamlet*.

*Theatron[3]*
(http://cms.cch.kcl.ac.uk/theatron/index.php?id=88/)
   This site provides 3-D theater models in the *Second Life* environment,
   supplemented with interpretative content and interactive tools, scenarios,
   and automated tutorials. It incorporates actors, props, sound effects,
   lighting and scenic technologies, streaming video, and scripts that enable
   individual and group movement-choreography.

## Spenser, Milton, and Sidney

*Hap Hazard*
(www.english.cam.ac.uk/ceres/haphazard/about.html)
> Sponsored by Cambridge University, this site promotes the study of Edmund Spenser and of manuscript materials relating to his writings.

*John Milton Reading Room*
(www.dartmouth.edu/~milton/reading_room/contents/index.shtml)
> This site contains all Milton's poetry, in English, Italian, Latin, and Greek, as well as selections of his prose, much of it annotated. Selected digitized images are included.

*Sidneiana*
(www.english.cam.ac.uk/ceres/sidneiana/)
> This multimedia archive of projects and materials relating to the Sidney family is sponsored by Cambridge University.

## Women's History and Writing

*As One Phoenix: Four Seventeenth-Century Women Poets*
(www.usask.ca/english/phoenix/homepage3.htm)
> This site, built by Ron Cooley and his students at the University of Saskatchewan, has biography, bibliography, and transcriptions of poems by Margaret Cavendish, Aemilia Lanyer, Katherine Phillips, and Mary Wroth.

*Witches in Early Modern England: A Digital Humanities Project for Unveiling Witchcraft Narratives* (http://witching.org/)
> This humanities project, led by Kirsten C. Uszkalo of Simon Fraser University, uses various digital tools for searching and pattern finding in texts about early modern English witchcraft. Features include mapping, a time line, and various techniques of data mining, and there is a tutorial.

## Biography and Lives

*Bedfordshire Historical Record Society*
(www.bedfordshirehrs.org.uk)
> This site lists several volumes of early modern wills published by the society.

*International Genealogy Index*
(www.familysearch.org/eng/)
> This search engine for international birth, marriage, death, census, church, and other records is sponsored by the Church of Jesus Christ of Latter-Day Saints.

*Oxford Dictionary of National Biography (ODNB)*
(www.odnb.com)
> This site provides the online version of the authoritative source for British biography.

*Peerage*
(www.burkespeerage.com)
> This site offers free but limited access to the definitive guide to the genealogical history of the major royal, aristocratic, and historical families of the United Kingdom, Ireland, and the United States of America.

*People in Place: Families, Households and Housing in London, 1550–1720*
(www.history.ac.uk/cmh/pip/)
> This site introduces the methods and findings of a research project funded by the United Kingdom's Arts and Humanities Research Council and focused on family and household in London in the sixteenth and seventeenth centuries.

*Records of the English Province of the Society of Jesus: . . . in the Sixteenth and Seventeenth Centuries*, by Henry Foley, 7 vols. (1877–83) (http://openlibrary.org/b/OL7104739M)
> Vol. 2, series 2–4, of *Records* has been made available online by *Open Library*. The biographical information includes "catalogues of assumed and of real names," an important resource, since many Catholics in this period worked underground.

## London

*Housing, Environment and Health in Early Modern London*
(www.geog.cam.ac.uk/research/projects/heahlondon/)
> This project of the Cambridge Group for the History of Population and Social Structure explores the extent to which environmental factors and the social characteristics of individual, family, and locality determined the disease and mortality profile of London in the period 1550–1750.

*London's Past Online*
(www.history.ac.uk/cmh/lpol/index.html)
> This site contains about 40,000 records referring to books, articles, theses and conference papers. Subscription is required.

*Proceedings of the Old Bailey*
(www.oldbaileyonline.org/)
> This site provides information about crime and the lower classes from 1674 to 1913, containing records of 197,745 criminal trials held at London's central criminal court.

## Maps

*Blaeu Atlas*
(www.library.ucla.edu/yrl/reference/maps/blaeu)
  This site offers digitized images from volume 1 of the Latin edition of
  Willem Janszoon and Joan Blaeu's 1645 atlas *Theatrum Orbis Terrarum*.
  It is hosted by the University of California, Los Angeles.

*John Carter Brown Library*
(www.brown.edu/Facilities/John_Carter_Brown_Library/)
  This library at Brown University has one of the world's leading collections
  of books, maps, and manuscripts relating to the colonial period of the
  Americas, 1492–1825. The site gives links to online resources.

*Magnificent Maps: Power, Propaganda, and Art*
(www.bl.uk/magnificentmaps)
  This site presents a 2010 exhibit of maps at the British Library, including digitized images of three maps from the medieval and early modern
  period.

*Map History / History of Cartography: The Gateway to the Subject*
(www.maphistory.info/imageworld.html#atlas)
  This site organizes, updates, and provides links to the many online sites
  that reproduce maps. It includes links to the complete digitized six
  volumes of Blaeu's 1659 *New Atlas*, the world atlas site at the Jewish
  National and University Library, and links to atlases and maps by Münster,
  Ortelius, de Wit, and many more.

*Map of Early Modern London*
(http://mapoflondon.uvic.ca/map.php)
  This interactive map is based on the Agas map of early modern London
  and has a wealth of information on the streets, sites, and significant boundaries of late-sixteenth-century and early-seventeenth-century London.

*Mapping Early Modern Worlds*
(www.folger.edu/template.cfm?cid=1681)
  The site is for a 1998 Folger Library exhibit on early modern maps and
  cartography. It offers some images of maps and general information.

*Maps and Geospacial Information Center*
(http://library.princeton.edu/collections/pumagic/collections)
  Princeton University houses one of the largest academic collections of
  maps, including Henry Wendt's collection, which has been featured on
  the now defunct site envisioningtheworld.com. This site includes an online catalog and digitized versions of many maps.

*A Survey of the Cities of London and Westminster*, by John Strype
(www.hrionline.ac.uk/strype/)

Strype's survey is the eighteenth-century expanded edition of Stowe's *Survey of London* and includes a number of images of important buildings in the city and a map of Elizabethan London.

## Visual Arts

*ARTstor*
(www.artstor.org/)
> This site is a not-for-profit digital library of more than one million images in the arts, architecture, humanities, and social sciences. It has a suite of software tools to view, present, and manage images for research and peda-gogical purposes. Subscription is required.

*British Museum Collection Online* (www.britishmuseum.org/research/search _the_collection_database/advanced_search.aspx)
> This large collection of early modern prints and engravings is searchable by individual, topic, and date.

*National Portrait Gallery*
(www.npg.org.uk)
> This site of 160,000 portraits of famous British men and women from the sixteenth century to the present day features a search engine for finding portraits by sitter and a mechanism for ordering copies.

*Printers' and Publishers' Devices in England and Scotland, 1485–1640*, by Ronald B. McKerrow (London: Bibliographical Soc., 1913) (http:// base.kb.dk/manus_pub/cv/manus/ManusIntro.xsql?nnoc=manus _pub&p_ManusId=213&p_Lang=main)
> This site provides a digitized version of McKerrow's indispensable catalog of printers' devices.

*Victoria and Albert Museum*
(www.vam.ac.uk/collections/index.html)
> On this site for one of the world's leading museums of art and design, an advanced search on the date range "1500–1700" and place "England" retrieves images of various items, ranging from an embroidered casket, miniatures, and an early spinet to seventeenth-century goblets, gloves, playing cards, candlestick, ring, and chairs.

## Sound and Music

*Classical Music Archives*
(www.classicalarchives.com)

This commercial site offers downloads and streams classical music. Over 600,000 files are available, plus supporting material (e.g., biographies, reviews, forums). Among participating labels are DG, Decca, Philips, EMI, Virgin, Sony, Columbia, BMG, and RCA.

*Grove Music Online*
(www.oxfordmusiconline.com/)
This online compendium of the Grove music dictionaries contains over 50,000 articles and 30,000 biograpies, many including musical examples. Subscription is required.

*National Music Museum*
(http://orgs.usd.edu/nmm/index.html)
This site for the museum at the University of South Dakota holds over 15,000 European, American, and non-Western instruments, the most inclusive collection of its kind in the world. The site offers virtual tours of the museum as well as images of instruments, which are indexed by maker and kind.

*Sidneiana* (See also "Manuscripts, Specialized Collections.")
Includes settings of Sidney's songs.

## Church History

Church Court Records from the Dioceses of Ely and Chichester (http://microformguides.gale.com/BrowseGuide.asp?colldocid=3250000&Page=1, http://microformguides.gale.com/BrowseGuide.asp?colldocid=3251000&Page=1)
The contents of two sets of records from the dioceses of Ely and Chichester, dating from c. 1400 to c. 1660, are provided, as well as information on ecclesiastical affairs and matters of faith, marriage, birth, illegitimacy, wills, and general moral (or immoral) behavior.

*Project Canterbury*
(http://anglicanhistory.org/)
This archive is for out-of-print texts relating to the Anglican Church.

## Law and Government

*English Reports*
(www.commonlii.org/uk/cases/EngR/)
This large collection of cases from various English courts, dating from 1220 to 1873 and searchable by date or name, comes from the Commonwealth Legal Information Institute.

*Statutes of the Realm*
(www.british-history.ac.uk/catalogue.aspx?gid=83)
    This site contains acts of Parliament from the period 1628–1701. More
    volumes should be available in the future.

## Newspapers and Periodicals

*Index to English Literary Periodicals, 1681 to 1914*
(www.comp-index.com/english/)
    This site is a finding aid for subjects covered in 233 titles published begin-
    ning in the seventeenth century and primarily literary in focus. Subscrip-
    tion is required.

*Seventeenth and Eighteenth Century Burney Collection Newspapers* (http://gdc
    .gale.com/products/17th-and-18th-century-burney-collection
    -newspapers/)
    This full-text, searchable digital archive of nearly 1,270 newspapers and
    news pamphlets from the United Kingdom is part of the British Library
    Newspaper collection and the largest single archive of seventeenth-and-
    eighteenth-century United Kingdom news media available. Subscription is
    required outside the United Kingdom.

## Modern Scholarship

### E-books and Digitized Modern Printed Books

*ACLS Humanities E-book*
(www.humanitiesebook.org)
    This digital collection of over 3,300 full-text titles is offered by the Ameri-
    can Council of Learned Societies in collaboration with twenty learned
    societies, over a hundred contributing publishers, and librarians at the
    University of Michigan's Scholarly Publishing Office.

*Google Books*
(http://books.google.com/)
    Many of the scanned books in *Google*'s database are out of copyright. Mil-
    lions of texts are available, and the number is growing all the time, but the
    quality varies.

*Internet Archive*
(www.archive.org/details/texts)
    This free collection of online texts contains a wide range of fiction, popu-
    lar books, children's books, historical texts, and academic books.

*Project Gutenberg*
(www.gutenberg.org/)
   This first digital library contains 36,000 public domain e-books, primarily
   works of literature and mostly in English.

## Gateways

*Bibliography of the History of Art* (www.getty.edu/research/tools/bha/index
   .html)
   In this comprehensive bibliography of scholarly writing about the history of Western art, the database search includes both *BHA* (covering
   1990–2007) and *Répertoire de la Littérature de l'Art* (*RILA*), one of the
   predecessors of *BHA*, with records that cover 1975–89.

*ITER Bibliography*
(www.itergateway.org/resources)
   This database has over a million bibliographic references to scholarship on
   the European Middle Ages and Renaissance, 400–1700. Subscription is
   required.

*Voice of the Shuttle*
(http://vos.ucsb.edu)
   This gateway to online humanities research provides hundreds of briefly
   annotated links to humanities resources on the Web, emphasizing both
   primary and secondary materials.

# Notes on Contributors

**Jennifer Bowers** is associate professor and the social sciences reference librarian at the University of Denver Libraries. She is the author, with Peggy Keeran, of three volumes—on the British Renaissance and early modern period, on the British eighteenth century, and on the British Romantic era—in their coedited fifteen-volume series, Literary Research: Strategies and Sources.

**Heidi Brayman Hackel**, associate professor of English, University of California, Riverside, is the author of *Reading Material in Early Modern England: Print, Gender, and Literacy*, coeditor of *Reading Women: Literacy, Authorship, and Culture in the Atlantic World, 1500–1800*, and associate editor of the *Huntington Library Quarterly*. Her volume on *Midsummer Night's Dream* is forthcoming in the new Arden Shakespeare Language and Writing series.

**Sheila T. Cavanagh**, founding director of the *World Shakespeare Project*, is professor of English and Distinguished Teaching Scholar at Emory. The author of *Wanton Eyes and Chaste Desires: Female Sexuality in* The Faerie Queene and *Cherished Torment: The Emotional Geography of Lady Mary Wroth's* Urania, she has also published widely in pedagogy and Renaissance literature. She is active in the electronic realm as well, directing the *Emory Women Writers Resource Project* and having served for many years as editor of the online *Spenser Review*.

**Simone Chess** is assistant professor of English at Wayne State University. Her research interests are in early modern literary and cultural studies, with an emphasis on gender and sexuality. She has published articles and book chapters on the topics of bathroom activism, ballads and Shakespeare, early modern representations of blindness, and the role of oath making in "murderous wife" ballads. She is completing a book project entitled, "'Where's Your Man's Heart Now': Male to Female Crossdressing in Early Modern English Literature."

**Angelica Duran** is associate professor at Purdue University, where she teaches courses in English, comparative literature, and religious studies and has served as director of religious studies. She is the author of *The Age of Milton and the Scientific Revolution* and a number of scholarly essays, the editor of *A Concise Companion to Milton*, and the coeditor of *Mo Yan in Context: Nobel Laureate and Global Storyteller* and *The King James Bible across Borders and Centuries*.

**Joshua Eckhardt** is associate professor of English at Virginia Commonwealth University, the author of *Manuscript Verse Collectors*, and a coeditor of *Manuscript Miscellanies in Early Modern England*. He cofounded *British Virginia*, an open-access digital publisher of colonial documents. He also serves as a contributing textual editor for *The Variorum Edition of the Poetry of John Donne*.

**Jeremy Ehrlich** is director of education for the *Internet Shakespeare Editions* and former head of education at the Folger Shakespeare Library. He has taught Shakespeare at all levels and published widely on issues of Shakespeare pedagogy.

**Patrick M. Erben** teaches early American literature and culture at the University of West Georgia. His monograph, *A Harmony of the Spirits: Translation and the Language of Community in Early Pennsylvania*, posits multilingualism and translation as assets for the construction of spiritual coherence in early America. He is currently working on an edition of the writings of the polyglot early American author Francis Daniel Pastorius.

**Patricia Fumerton** is professor of English at the University of California, Santa Barbara, and director of its award-wining *English Broadside Ballad Archive (EBBA)*. In addition to numerous articles, she is the author of *Unsettled: The Culture of Mobility and the Working Poor in Early Modern England* and *Cultural Aesthetics: Renaissance Literature and the Practice of Social Ornament*. She is also editor of *Broadside Ballads from the Pepys Collection: A Selection of Texts, Approaches, and Recordings* as well as coeditor of *Ballads and Broadsides in Britain, 1500–1800* and *Renaissance Culture and the Everyday*. She is working on a new book, "Moving Media, Tactical Publics: English Broadside Ballads in the Early Modern Period."

**Tassie Gniady** has a PhD in early modern literature and is working toward a degree in information science. She was the first project manager for the award-wining *English Broadside Ballad Archive (EBBA)* and is now the graduate assistant for Science on a Sphere for the Advanced Information Visualization Laboratory at Indiana University.

**Peter C. Herman**'s most recent books are *The New Milton Criticism*, edited with Elizabeth Sauer; *A Short History of Early Modern England*; and *Royal Poetrie: Monarchic Verse and the Political Imaginary of Early Modern England* (*Choice* Outstanding Academic Title). He has also edited the Approaches to Teaching volumes for Milton's shorter poetry and prose and *Paradise Lost* (second ed.). He is working on a contextual edition of Thomas Deloney's *Jack of Newbury* as well as a book on the literature of terrorism. He teaches at San Diego State University.

**W. Scott Howard** is associate professor of English at the University of Denver. He is the founding editor of *Appositions: Studies in Renaissance / Early*

*Modern Literature and Culture* and editor, with Sara van den Berg, of *The Divorce Tracts of John Milton: Texts and Contexts* and of *An Collins and the Historical Imagination.* His work has received support from the MLA, the PEW Charitable Trusts, and the NEH.

**Janelle Jenstad** is associate professor of English at the University of Victoria, director of *The Map of Early Modern London,* and assistant coordinating editor of the *Internet Shakespeare Editions.* She is editing *The Merchant of Venice* for the ISE and *2 If You Know Not Me You Know Nobody* for Digital Renaissance Editions. With Jennifer Roberts-Smith, she is editor of *Shakespeare's Language in Digital Media: Old Words, New Tools.* Her essays have appeared in the *Journal of Medieval and Early Modern Studies, Early Modern Literary Studies, Elizabethan Theatre, Shakespeare Bulletin,* and various collections.

**Peggy Keeran** is professor and the arts and humanities reference librarian at the University of Denver. With Jennifer Bowers, she is the editor of the Literary Research: Strategies and Sources series published by Scarecrow Press and coauthor of three of the volumes in the series (on the British Renaissance and early modern period, on the British eighteenth century, and on the British Romantic era).

**Erin E. Kelly** is assistant professor in the Department of English at the University of Victoria. She has published essays on Foxe's *Acts and Monuments,* Cary's *Tragedy of Mariam,* Woodes's *Conflict of Conscience,* and Munday's *Sir Thomas More.* Her work in progress includes a monograph on representations of religious conversion in sixteenth-century English drama and an edition of *Taming of the Shrew* for the *Internet Shakespeare Editions.* She is an associate editor for the journal *Early Theatre.*

**Rebecca Laroche** is professor of English at the University of Colorado, Colorado Springs. She has published on Shakespeare, early modern women's writing, medical history, and ecofeminism. She is the author of *Medical Authority and Englishwomen's Herbal Texts, 1550–1650,* the guest curator of the exhibition *Beyond Home Remedy: Women, Medicine, and Science* at the Folger Shakespeare Library, and editor (with Jennifer Munroe) of *Ecofeminist Approaches to Early Modernity.* She is currently considering the importance of the collective experiential knowledge of plants in Shakespeare's oeuvre.

**Zachary Lesser** is associate professor of English at the University of Pennsylvania. He is the author of *Renaissance Drama and the Politics of Publication: Readings in the English Book Trade* (winner of the Elizabeth Dietz Prize for best book of the year in Renaissance Studies) and the forthcoming "Hamlet after Q1: An Uncanny History of the Shakespearean Text." The general editor of the forthcoming "Blackwell Introduction to the History of the Book in Britain," he has published numerous essays on early modern drama, Shakespeare, and book history in *Shakespeare Quarterly, ELH,* and elsewhere.

**Shawn Martin** is Scholarly Communication Librarian at the Van Pelt Library of the University of Pennsylvania. He has worked at the *Digital Library Project,* at the Colonial Williamsburg Foundation; the *Ohio Memory Project,* at the Ohio Historical Society; and the *Text Creation Partnership,* at the University of Michigan. He also serves as the executive director of the American Association for History and Computing.

**Kris McAbee** is assistant professor of English at the University of Arkansas, Little Rock, where she also directs the annual Shakespeare Scene Festival. She has published on the printing practices and archiving of broadside ballads, as well as on the sonnet sequences of Michael Drayton. She is a coeditor of *New Technologies and Renaissance Studies II.* Her current work explores the formation of the sonneteer as character type in early modern texts outside sonnet sequences. She heads UALR's partnership in the *English Broadside Ballad Archive* and is cofounder of UALR's Digital Humanities Collective.

**Laura McGrane** is associate professor of American and British literature and Koshland Director of the Hurford Center for the Arts and Humanities at Haverford College. She writes on eighteenth-century print and popular culture and the role of technology in liberal arts education. She is one of the founding members of the Trico Digital Humanities Initiative at Haverford, Bryn Mawr, and Swarthmore Colleges and has coorganized workshops on humanities labs and digital archivalism in conjunction with the Mellon-supported Alliance for the Advancement of Liberal Arts Colleges.

**Irene Middleton** teaches at Manchester Metropolitan University. She has published in *Cahiers Elisabéthains* and is completing a monograph on the cognitive effects of live performances of Shakespeare on post–World War II audiences. Her critical editions of early modern romances *The Mirrour of Princely Deedes and Knighthood* and *Ibrahim; or, The Illustrious Bassa* are forthcoming from the *Emory Women Writers Resource Project.*

**Ian Frederick Moulton,** professor of English in the School of Letters and Sciences at Arizona State University, is a cultural historian and literary scholar who has published widely on the representation of gender and sexuality in early modern European literature. He is the author of *Before Pornography: Erotic Writing in Early Modern England* and *Love in Print in the Sixteenth Century: The Popularization of Romance* and editor and translator of Antonio Vignali's *La cazzaria.*

**Joseph M. Ortiz** is associate professor of English at the University of Texas, El Paso. His research interests include English Renaissance literature, Italian Renaissance poetry, classical Latin literature, translation studies, and the relation between music and language. He is the author of *Broken Harmony: Shakespeare and the Politics of Music* and essays on Milton, Shakespeare, Aphra Behn, and Gordon Merrick, and he is the editor of *Shakespeare and the Culture of Romanticism*. He is currently working on a study of the relation between form and translation in Renaissance literature.

**Katherine Rowe** is provost and dean of the college at Smith College. The coauthor of *New Wave Shakespeare on Screen*, she served on the board of *Shakespeare Quarterly* and is associate editor of *Cambridge World Shakespeare Online*. She has received grants from the NEH, the Andrew W. Mellon Foundation, and the Pennsylvania Department of Education and is cocreator of the Folger Luminary Shakespeare apps.

**Marjorie Rubright** is associate professor of English at the University of Toronto. She is the author of *Doppelgänger Dilemmas: Anglo-Dutch Relations in Early Modern English Literature and Culture*. She holds the Francis Bacon Foundation Fellowship in Renaissance England at the Huntington Library, where she is writing her second book, "A World of Words: Language, Globalization, and the English Renaissance," which pursues how ideas about the cultural history of language and linguistic community shaped conflicting visions of globalization in the English Renaissance.

**Arnold Sanders** is associate professor of English literature at Goucher College and cofounder of the Brooke and Carol Peirce Center for Undergraduate Research in Special Collections. He has published on Malory, Spenser, Chaucer, Kempe, Renaissance Chaucer editions, and medieval manuscript compilations. His current research involves the manuscript of the Middle English poem *Pearl* and the growth of bookseller networks promoting rare-book collecting in seventeenth-century London.

**Gitanjali Shahani** is associate professor of English at San Francisco State University. She edited *Emissaries in Early Modern Literature and Culture: Mediation, Transmission, Traffic, 1550–1700* with Brinda Charry. Her work has appeared in journals such as *Shakespeare* and the *Journal for Early Modern Cultural Studies* and in edited volumes such as *Global Traffic: Discourses and Practices of Trade in English Literature and Culture, 1550–1700* and *Bollywood Shakespeares*. She is guest editing a special issue of *Shakespeare Studies* on diet and identity and in completing a book manuscript, tentatively titled "The Spicèd Indian Air in Shakespeare's England: Consumption, Culinaryism, and Colonialism."

**Evelyn Tribble** is Donald Collie Professor of English at the University of Otago, Dunedin, New Zealand. She is the author of *Cognition in the Globe: Attention and Memory in Shakespeare's Theatre*, *Margins and Marginality: The Printed Page in Early Modern England*, and (with Nicholas Keene) *Cognitive Ecologies and the History of Remembering: Religion, Education, and*

*Memory in Early Modern England.* She has also written essays on Shakespeare and Marlowe, early modern print culture, and Shakespeare and film. Her current project is "Early Modern Actors in Shakespeare's Theatre: Thinking with the Body."

**Phillip John Usher** is assistant professor at Barnard College. He is the author of *Errance et cohérence: Essai sur la littérature transfrontalière à la Renaissance* and of *Epic Arts in Renaissance France.* He is also the author of an annotated translation of Ronsard's *Franciade* and a coeditor of *Virgilian Identities in the French Renaissance.*

**Sarah Werner** is digital media strategist at the Folger Shakespeare Library. In her previous role as the Folger's undergraduate program director, she designed the library's first regular undergraduate course offerings and taught book history seminars. She is the author of *Shakespeare and Feminist Performance* and the editor of *New Directions in Renaissance Drama and Performance Studies* and is currently working on "A Handbook for Studying Early Printed Books, 1470–1800," an undergraduate textbook designed to introduce the workings of the handpress and the study of physical bibliography.

**Heather Wolfe** is curator of manuscripts at the Folger Shakespeare Library. She teaches English paleography and has published widely on the intersections and overlaps between manuscript and print in early modern England.

**Georgianna Ziegler** is Louis B. Thalheimer Associate Librarian Head of Reference at the Folger Shakespeare Library, where she fields reference queries from inside and outside the Folger and has curated exhibitions, including *Elizabeth I, Then and Now* (with catalog) and *Women Writers, 1500–1700.* She has published on early modern women, including Elizabeth of Bohemia, and on Shakespeare's heroines in the nineteenth century.

# Index

## Modern Language Association of America
## Options for Teaching

*Teaching Early Modern English Literature from the Archives.* Ed. Heidi Brayman Hackel and Ian Frederick Moulton. 2015.

*Teaching Anglophone Caribbean Literature.* Ed. Supriya M. Nair. 2012.

*Teaching Film.* Ed. Lucy Fischer and Patrice Petro. 2012.

*Teaching Seventeenth- and Eighteenth-Century French Women Writers.* Ed. Faith E. Beasley. 2011.

*Teaching French Women Writers of the Renaissance and Reformation.* Ed. Colette H. Winn. 2011.

*Teaching Law and Literature.* Ed. Austin Sarat, Cathrine O. Frank, and Matthew Anderson. 2011.

*Teaching British Women Playwrights of the Restoration and Eighteenth Century.* Ed. Bonnie Nelson and Catherine Burroughs. 2010.

*Teaching Narrative Theory.* Ed. David Herman, Brian McHale, and James Phelan. 2010.

*Teaching Early Modern English Prose.* Ed. Susannah Brietz Monta and Margaret W. Ferguson. 2010.

*Teaching Italian American Literature, Film, and Popular Culture.* Ed. Edvige Giunta and Kathleen Zamboni McCormick. 2010.

*Teaching the Graphic Novel.* Ed. Stephen E. Tabachnick. 2009.

*Teaching Literature and Language Online.* Ed. Ian Lancashire. 2009.

*Teaching the African Novel.* Ed. Gaurav Desai. 2009.

*Teaching World Literature.* Ed. David Damrosch. 2009.

*Teaching North American Environmental Literature.* Ed. Laird Christensen, Mark C. Long, and Fred Waage. 2008.

*Teaching Life Writing Texts.* Ed. Miriam Fuchs and Craig Howes. 2007.

*Teaching Nineteenth-Century American Poetry.* Ed. Paula Bernat Bennett, Karen L. Kilcup, and Philipp Schweighauser. 2007.

*Teaching Representations of the Spanish Civil War.* Ed. Noël Valis. 2006.

*Teaching the Representation of the Holocaust.* Ed. Marianne Hirsch and Irene Kacandes. 2004.

*Teaching Tudor and Stuart Women Writers.* Ed. Susanne Woods and Margaret P. Hannay. 2000.

*Teaching Literature and Medicine.* Ed. Anne Hunsaker Hawkins and Marilyn Chandler McEntyre. 1999.

*Teaching the Literatures of Early America.* Ed. Carla Mulford. 1999.

*Teaching Shakespeare through Performance.* Ed. Milla C. Riggio. 1999.

*Teaching Oral Traditions.* Ed. John Miles Foley. 1998.

*Teaching Contemporary Theory to Undergraduates.* Ed. Dianne F. Sadoff and William E. Cain. 1994.

*Teaching Children's Literature: Issues, Pedagogy, Resources.* Ed. Glenn Edward Sadler. 1992.

*Teaching Literature and Other Arts.* Ed. Jean-Pierre Barricelli, Joseph Gibaldi, and Estella Lauter. 1990.

*New Methods in College Writing Programs: Theories in Practice.* Ed. Paul Connolly and Teresa Vilardi. 1986.

*School-College Collaborative Programs in English.* Ed. Ron Fortune. 1986.

*Teaching Environmental Literature: Materials, Methods, Resources.* Ed. Frederick O. Waage. 1985.

*Part-Time Academic Employment in the Humanities: A Sourcebook for Just Policy.* Ed. Elizabeth M. Wallace. 1984.

*Film Study in the Undergraduate Curriculum.* Ed. Barry K. Grant. 1983.

*The Teaching Apprentice Program in Language and Literature.* Ed. Joseph Gibaldi and James V. Mirollo. 1981.

*Options for Undergraduate Foreign Language Programs: Four-Year and Two-Year Colleges.* Ed. Renate A. Schulz. 1979.

*Options for the Teaching of English: Freshman Composition.* Ed. Jasper P. Neel. 1978.

*Options for the Teaching of English: The Undergraduate Curriculum.* Ed. Elizabeth Wooten Cowan. 1975.